Clinical Legal E

Active Learning in your Law School

Clinical Legal Education:

Active Learning in your Law School

Hugh Brayne

Solicitor, Professor and Associate Director,
Sunderland Business School

Nigel Duncan

Principal Lecturer, Inns of Court School of Law

Richard Grimes

Solicitor, Senior Lecturer, Sheffield Hallam University

with

Roger Burridge, Adrian Evans, Laura Lundy and Nina Tarr

BLACKSTONE
PRESS LIMITED

First published in Great Britain 1998 by Blackstone Press Limited, Aldine Place, London W12 8AA. Telephone 0181-740 2277

© H. Brayne, N. Duncan, R. Grimes 1998

ISBN: 1 85431 831 4

British Library Cataloguing in Publication Data
A CIP catalogue record for this book is available from the British Library.

Typeset by Style Photosetting, Mayfield, East Sussex
Printed by Bell & Bain Limited, Glasgow

Contents

Setting the scene — Development of clinical education — Developments in the UK — A comparative picture — The clinic in practice — The in-house real-client clinic — The out-house clinic — Simulation clinic — Tensions and dilemmas in clinical education — Finding and securing resources — Providing training or education? — Serving the student or the client? — Making assessment part of learning — Equality of opportunity — The way forward

Why study law? — Studying law to become a lawyer — Studying law out of curiosity — Asking questions not swallowing answers — Can a clinical approach do any better? — Learning theory and the clinic — Integrating the academic and the practical — Clinical legal education fits the way people learn best — The importance of learning and the unimportance of teaching — Surface and deep learning as an outcome — Different processes of learning: the learning cycle — Learning styles — Ownership — Assessment issues — Validity — Reliability — Method — A final word

A reminder of our objectives — Why might the objectives not be met? In-house solicitor clinics — Three clinical case studies — The injured cyclist — Taking instructions: professional issues — Taking instructions: professional skills issues — Checking the facts — Preparing a claim — Preparing for the judge — Moving house: some lessons to learn, or the nightmare scenario — The facts — The clinic system, the investigation and the learning process — Some reflections on the case so far — Ethics in practice — Happy endings — The last will and testament — The facts — Learning from scratch — Matters ethical — Assessment in the in-house clinic — Can we assess fairly and reliably? — What do we seek to reward? — Some final pitfalls and anecdotes from an in-house clinic — Conclusion — Appendix: model standards in clinical legal education (CLEO 1995) — Purpose — Educational objectives and learning outcomes — Professional requirements — Operational practice

Introduction — External placements as a course on an LLB degree — Introduction to the Queen's programme — Casework on placement: an illustration — Making the most of an external placement — Conclusion — Longer-term placements — Supervision — Student activity — Working with other agencies to study legislation and the legislative process — Working with the Free Representation Unit on a vocational course — Advantages for the collaborating institutions — Conclusion

Some general observations on make-believe learning experiences — The place for simulation in undergraduate legal education — An example of simulation as part of a substantive law course (reliving *Donoghue* v *Stevenson*) — Description of simulated exercise — Objectives of the simulated exercise — Learning from experience: the educational basis for simulated casework — Using simulated cases as the basis for a clinical programme — An example of simulated casework — Aims and aspirations — Course structure — Skills analysis and exercise — Simulated cases — The university disciplinary hearing — Contextual studies — How are students assessed? — Testing skills, competencies and knowledge — The student perspective — Some conclusions

What do we mean by legal ethics? — Ethics and the law — Ethics and professional conduct — When should legal ethics be dealt with in the curriculum? — Role of clinical legal education — Use of real-client clinics — A perspective on ethics — Professional ethics — Use of simulations — The corporate lawyer — The public defender — The divorce attorneys — Students' reactions — Conclusion

Introduction — Genesis of clinical education — Types of cases — Replicating private practice — Skills training — Economics of clinical education — Externships — Marginalisation — Marginalisation from the students' perspective — Marginalisation of the faculty — Clinical teachers' work — Appendix: recommendations of the MacCrate Commission — Fundamental lawyering skills — Fundamental values of the profession

Richard Grimes: a perspective of optimism — Learning and empowerment — Learning and integration — Assessment — Resourcing the clinic — Staff development — Hugh Brayne: getting past the academic/vocational minefield— Adrian Evans: an Australian perspective — Introduction — Balanced legal education — Student and client empowerment — The essential issue of clinic control — Ethics in the clinical chain — Endnote

Preface

This book was conceived as one written jointly by the three authors, and has developed into one which incorporates significant contributions from other colleagues. Four of these require particular mention as they have written substantial chunks of text: Roger Burridge of the University of Warwick, Adrian Evans of Monash University, Laura Lundy of Queen's University of Belfast, Nina Tarr of the University of Illinois.

Reflecting the concern of clinical methods with learning from experience, we have tried to leave exposed the processes which have led to this finished product and any disagreements between us. Therefore we seek to distinguish between expressions of opinion which are the view of us all and those where one author is seeking to present a personal view. Thus 'I' normally relates to the personal view of the author of the chapter concerned. Whilst we individually have taken the prime responsibility for writing (or, where appropriate, coordinating) a particular chapter, all three primary authors have worked together in reviewing and editing the entire book.

The contributions to the book look something like this:

The Introduction was written by Nigel Duncan.
Chapter 1 was written by Richard Grimes.
Chapter 2 was written by Hugh Brayne.

Chapter 3 was written jointly by Hugh Brayne and Richard Grimes.
Chapter 4 was written jointly by Laura Lundy and Nigel Duncan.
Chapter 5 was written by Roger Burridge with some input from Nigel
Duncan.
Chapter 6 was written by Nigel Duncan.
Chapter 7 was written by Nina Tarr.
Chapter 8 was written by Richard Grimes, Hugh Brayne and Adrian Evans.

In addition, we would like to thank the following for their help: Andrew
Boon and Peter Hodgkinson at the University of Westminster, for information about their death row clinic; Jim Corke and Ruth Soetendorp of
Bournemouth University, for information about their sandwich scheme;
Sarah Cracknell of Sheffield Hallam University Law Clinic, for permission
to use comments from her Annual Report; Derek French, for an excellent job
of editing; Jeff Giddings of Griffith University, for insights and suggestions
which have helped us in a number of areas, in particular the state of play of
clinical legal education in Australia; Ole Hansen and Neil Kibble for their
advice on the legislation clinic course offered at South Bank University;
Professor Bob Hepple of Clare College, Cambridge, for introducing Nigel to
the Columbia University practice of law course; Professor Carol Liebman of
Columbia University, New York, for permission to reproduce materials from
the practice of law course and from the student feedback; Steven Wheatley
of the University of Central Lancashire, for details of their placement
scheme; and our students, whose work informed our own learning and whose
comments pepper this text. Where we refer to actual students and cases we
have changed the names.

The help of these colleagues is much appreciated. The responsibility for any
errors remains with us.

Hugh Brayne
Nigel Duncan
Richard Grimes

December 1997

Introduction

We are trying to do something unusual in this book. It is a book about legal education that is addressed both to the teacher (the one who has the power to change the course) and the student (the one who must follow the course and the assessments dictated by the teacher). Indeed, this power relationship, which is not altogether healthy, is one of the issues addressed by the methods we propose.

Perhaps we might start with an anecdote to explain why we want students to read about issues of curriculum and course design as well as teachers. The start of the Clinical Legal Education Organisation (CLEO), a small but growing body that brings law teachers who are interested in a clinical approach together in the UK, was actually triggered by student demand. Students at Sheffield Hallam University had read in *Legal Action* a short report about clinical programmes in Northumbria's Law School. They found out who was most likely to be sympathetic to the idea of doing something similar at Sheffield and organised a fact-finding visit. From there came a number of developments: the close links between Sheffield Hallam and Northumbria, and between two of the authors; a series of conferences which led to the involvement of all three authors; the launch of CLEO and now this book. One thing that unites us as well as our interest in clinical legal education is our commitment to the empowering of the student. In education this fashionable concept, more talked about than practised, means trying to get students to feel that they are not just the recipients, but in some way the owners of the learning process they go through. We want students to be the stakeholders, to use another fashionable term, in learning.

Writing this book has been a learning process in itself and we hope that the book reflects this fact. One of the characteristics of clinical methods is that learning comes more from the *process* of undertaking an activity than from the product of that activity. You will find in this book different perspectives presented in a debate which is ongoing (e.g., in terms of the advantages of simulated rather than real client work; or how best to assess). As authors we took the decision to include contributions from others involved in clinical legal education both in the UK and in jurisdictions where it is more developed. We present our differing perspectives, warts and all, in the hope of reflecting the clinical approach we advocate and in recognition that this is a more revealing insight into the advantages and problems inherent in adopting a clinical methodology.

What will different readers get out of this book?

Students: as well as an understanding of clinical legal education, its role in learning law and its practical aspects, you will get some picture of how decisions are made in the legal education world, how things are changing, how you can perhaps play a part in those developments and in your own clinical programmes.

Lecturers: you will get a different and, we hope, refreshing perspective on legal education as a whole, and the role clinical programmes could play. You will, if you are so inspired, come away with some ideas for your own programmes, ideas which we hope you will share with others and the results of those ideas we hope you will share with us in due course. We hope that you will, in the spirit of the previous paragraph addressed to our student readers, do your utmost to involve the consumers of the process in the design and delivery of your own clinical programmes.

The time is now ripe for a development of clinical approaches in UK legal education. It is currently going through major changes. The Lord Chancellor's Advisory Committee on Legal Education and Conduct is conducting a review which is challenging existing assumptions about what should be learnt on law degrees, vocational courses and elsewhere, and why. Their First Report, published in 1996, proposes more active learning by law students and makes specific reference to clinical techniques. These techniques provide the essence of active learning. Both branches of the legal profession and, indeed, employers generally, recognise that they need graduates with an ability to reflect and analyse and to become self-reliant. There is a growing recognition that knowledge of the law is best understood in the context within which it operates in our complex society. Most degree courses contain some contextual elements which can have a variety of benefits. They may put students in a better position to look critically at the law they study and how it affects the people to whom it is applied. This provides them with a foundation from which they can develop intellectually at the same time as acquiring knowledge and understanding of the law itself. Universities, the professions and other employers recognise that the purpose of undergraduate study is to help in this broader development, rather than simply to take in a body of knowledge. Most recently, the Dearing Report has emphasised the importance of acquiring usable skills as well as knowledge. (The National Committee of Inquiry into Higher Education, July 1997; this costs over £300 but is available free on the Web. See http://www.leeds.ac.uk/educol/nciche. See summary, para. 38.) Educational theory clearly suggests that learning is most effective when it involves students actively. Clinical techniques provide a powerful way of achieving all these goals. This book is designed to help students to make the most effective use of these techniques, where they are offered, to get more out of legal studies. The book will give law teachers ideas to reject, adopt or develop. It will also warn of many of the pitfalls which have affected clinical courses in the past, and prepare teachers better to develop courses to meet their own objectives.

What is clinical legal education and why should you experience it? There are two commonly used definitions: one broad, the other narrower.

The broad definition is learning by doing the types of things that lawyers do, which we expand on in chapter 1. It can take the form of simulated cases, including role-playing, which is an effective way of getting to understand the subtleties of how the law is actually applied. In its fullest form clinical legal education enables students to take on real clients' problems and work with them. That is what most of this book will be about.

The narrower definition takes as its focus the reason for using the method. Its premise is that through clinical techniques students are capable of learning far more than skills, and can develop critical and contextual understanding of the law as it affects people in society. Thus clinical education is defined as that which aims to achieve these intellectual and educational goals. The use of similar techniques with nothing other than skill development in mind would be seen as practical training, but not clinical in its true sense. We would endorse this underlying motive. It should be clear from the context where this narrower definition of the term is being used.

The distinction has significance for the stage of legal education at which clinical methods are used. Those observing the technique of clinic without considering the reasons for adopting it often voice the objection that this is all very well for vocational courses, where you are actually training to become a lawyer (both the Bar Vocational Course and Legal Practice Courses contain significant clinical elements, in the broad sense), but that it is unnecessary or inappropriate for undergraduate legal education. We would agree that if the purpose of clinical techniques was purely to develop technical abilities to become a lawyer it would not be an appropriate part of a law degree. Indeed it would be narrow and impoverished. Instead, we consider that the clinical approach can make a significant contribution to a number of the fundamental aims of undergraduate legal education:

(a)   It can provide experience of the most important context of all: how the law actually impacts on the lives of real people.

(b)   It can encourage students to reflect critically on what their lecturers tell them.

(c)   It can challenge the inherent elitism of a course of study based on appellate cases and under the complete control of lecturers by introducing cases at the stage at which they affect ordinary people and providing an outlet for different experience and different perspectives.

(d)   It can bring into focus the ethical dilemmas which underlie legal decision-making at all levels.

(e)   It can develop the research, analytical and communication skills which are essential for an effective education.

(f)   It can help people both to work more effectively with others and to develop independence and self-reliance.

What is more, our students consistently tell us that their clinical courses are the most motivating and involving aspects of their study. We think students will enjoy clinical legal education as well as benefiting from it.

Our general approach in this book is to illustrate the arguments we are making with examples of the courses with which we are ourselves familiar and, wherever possible, with student comment to give a real flavour of the experience of clinical work.

Chapter 1 introduces the concept of clinical legal education. It presents how and why it has developed in the USA and elsewhere and applies that experience to the situation in the United Kingdom with a brief presentation of the different models of clinic which may be found. The competing demands which inform the way in which clinical approaches actually work are explained and some suggestions as to the best way forward proposed.

In chapter 2, we explain the way in which the clinic can provide the most valuable opportunity for student-centred learning. This can be achieved not only to develop the vocational goals of the professional courses, but as a powerful tool for meeting the educational goals of undergraduate courses. In particular it will help universities to respond to the proposals of the First Report of the Advisory Committee on Legal Education and Conduct. We support these claims with an analysis of how clinical methods meet current understanding of how people learn.

Chapter 3 illustrates the ways in which these aims can be achieved in practice by delving into the experience of one approach to clinical methods: the student law clinic. This uses the experience of two such clinics, at Northumbria and Sheffield Hallam, to provide examples of what staff and students get up to. This gives us an opportunity to examine the extent to which we manage to achieve our educational objectives (we have shortcomings!) and to show how things work in practice. We explore both the learning and the assessment processes and show how the clinical approach actually brings the two together.

Chapter 4, recognising the difficulties of establishing a full real-client clinic within every law faculty in the country, explores the various ways in which live experience may be gained through work with other agencies. A major contribution to this chapter comes from Laura Lundy, whose clinical course at Queen's University, Belfast provides a model for working with a number of advice centres. The chapter also explores other ways of working with other organisations and other models, such as sandwich courses or vacation placements with employers. These include the opportunity for some students to work with clients on death row in the USA or Jamaica. Finally it considers the one current example of real-client clinical work on a vocational law course in the United Kingdom.

Chapter 5 looks at the use of simulations. Largely written by Roger Burridge it uses the experience of Warwick University to show how simulated clinical techniques may be used within subjects to enhance the learning of specific areas of substantive law as well as in a separate module to enable a critical evaluation of the legal system itself and the processes which take place within it. The experience of students on the Warwick courses is used to illustrate the way in which clinical methods assist in the integration of knowledge and understanding on the degree as a whole, as well as addressing the development of the skills applied on the course.

Chapter 6 considers the way in which clinical methods may support the learning of ethics in the legal context. This is illustrated with references to courses to which you will have already been introduced as well as Columbia University's 'profession of law' course, which uses simulated clinical methods to develop a critical approach to professional ethics. It explains why the study of ethics is less well-developed in the United Kingdom and suggests ways of integrating clinical and other learning methods to improve the quality of learning ethics on undergraduate and professional courses.

Chapter 7 places the earlier material in the context of a jurisdiction where clinical approaches are more developed. Nina Tarr presents the American experience as a source of information which is invaluable to those of us who seek to avoid repeating the mistakes made by others. In doing so, she also casts a critical eye on the developments in the United Kingdom and the approaches suggested in this book.

Chapter 8 acts as a conclusion in a variety of ways. It presents a summary of our arguments and a personal contribution from one of the authors which draws attention to the way in which the clinical approach permeates our own developing experiences as well as our approach to learning. In addition, Adrian Evans, writing from an Australian perspective, casts a critical eye over what we have written about clinic in the United Kingdom. This will draw attention to the limitations of what we have written as well as any merits. We believe it is only by entering into a debate which recognises our shortcomings that we will generate the new ideas which will improve the courses we offer and ultimately overcome the difficulties we all face.

We hope that this book will convince our student readers that the value of clinical work does not only lie in the development of your skills. It can play a major role in helping to develop your understanding of the law you learn, and your critical faculty. Its function is therefore educational as well as providing a basis for a career in the legal profession or elsewhere. It was for these reasons that the Pearce Committee in Australia recommended that 'a modern and properly funded law school should be able to develop clinical legal education as a significant dimension of its undergraduate legal education'. This book will help you and your tutors to be involved in this exciting new development.

We finish with two quotes from students who have experienced real-client clinical courses in the UK. The first was experience on an LLB degree, the second on a vocational course. The comments give some indication of the way clinical techniques can be used to provide very different learning experiences:

I feel that my placement has given me an invaluable insight into the differences between law in theory and law in practice: the welfare system that I had envisaged in welfare law was miles removed from that which I encountered weekly.

The best part of the course by far. With most course work, not a lot of motivation to get involved with it except for assessed work. After three to four years' studying it's wonderful to do something useful and practical. Learned more from FRU [Free Representation Unit] than the rest of the course, great help in developing skills and confidence — especially for advocacy.

1

Introducing the clinic

Setting the scene

The common thread in this book is our belief that the direct experience of doing law, as compared with listening to, reading or discussing others' views on practice and theory, represents a significant departure from, and an exciting addition to, the traditional means of legal education.

Simply put, clinical legal education requires students to take an active part in the learning process. They assume a degree of control over their own education and they see law in its real-life context. Learning by doing exposes students to real or realistic settings in which both basic concepts and substantive rules can be studied. At the same time, students may address the practical, policy and ethical issues surrounding a given problem. The clinic will almost certainly provide a vehicle for the introduction to and enhancement of skills relevant to the study and practice of law. Students taking clinical courses are encouraged, as an explicit educational objective, to reflect critically on the content of the experience and to redefine their needs and strategies in consequence.

But the clinic is more than that. As we try to demonstrate throughout this book, clinical legal education is designed to complement the rest of the students' learning experience. To do this with any success, however, we have to design law courses which integrate the clinical and other areas of study. The intellectual and pedagogic worth of clinical education lies in the part it has to play in the overall programme of study. It is not an end in itself but rather a means by which the law and the legal process can be understood. Understanding through both doing and reflecting is at the centre of the clinical ethos. This sometimes stands in stark contrast to the intensive content and assessment-led models prevalent in undergraduate and vocational legal education in the United Kingdom and other parts of the common law world.

The use of the clinic as a vehicle for study throws up very particular challenges, difficulties and rewards which will be explored in this and following chapters. For those who are involved with clinical programmes, it sometimes seems that all aspects of educating lawyers are under the microscope. We have to look at, and try to justify, our general objectives; what we teach and how; how students are assessed; and we have to keep re-evaluating what we are doing.

We are, as you may already realise, personally convinced that clinical legal education really works. This is based on years of doing it. It works because it is supported by educational theory. In this book we will attempt to set the clinical experience in this theoretical framework and we will identify the nature of the learning process and the specific outcomes that are being pursued. We will also look at the problems resulting from the clinical approach to learning, including resource implications. This chapter in particular and the book in general conclude with a prediction. Clinical approaches to legal education will become increasingly important in both the undergraduate and vocational stages and are likely to become a significant part of the law school curriculum.[1]

The purpose of this book is to aid this development by setting out in a clear and where possible concrete manner the issues surrounding the theory and

---

[1] This prediction is supported by the experience of a significant and growing number of legal educators in both the UK and other common law jurisdictions, notably Australia, Canada, India, South Africa and the USA. The importance of a hands-on approach to learning law has also been noted in recent professional and governmental reports (see Arthurs Report, *Law and Learning: Report to the Social Sciences and Humanities Research Council of Canada* (Ottawa: Consultative Group on Research and Education in Law, 1983); Pearce Report, Pearce, Campbell and Harding, *Australian Law Schools: A Discipline Assessment for the Commonwealth Tertiary Education Commission* (Canberra: Australian Government Publishing Service, 1987); MacCrate Report, *Legal Education and Professional Development — An Educational Continuum: Narrowing the Gap* (Chicago: American Bar Association, 1992); ACLEC (Lord Chancellor's Advisory Committee on Legal Education and Conduct), *First Report on Legal Education and Training* (London: ACLEC, 1996)).

practice of the clinic. We also want to offer help to academic and support staff as well as students in the establishment and running of clinical programmes.

Development of clinical education

Educating students through experiential learning and by using a hands-on approach is nothing new. Neither is it the particular preserve of lawyers — in fact, far from it.

Clinical methods have long been used in the education and training of a range of students from doctors and nurses to engineers, linguists, teachers and computer programmers. At a practical level, who would want to consult a medic who had not yet met a patient or did not have practical experience to complement his or her theoretical knowledge? Whilst the study of law may not necessarily lead students into the legal profession, the ability to apply the substance of the law clearly demonstrates the extent of students' understanding. As we hope we will show, it is also an effective means by which understanding of concepts, rules and ethics can be learned. The clinic also appears to motivate students in a way rarely found elsewhere in the curriculum.

Learning law through direct experience has until recently, and with very few exceptions, been limited to the end of the vocational stage of legal education. Trainee barristers and solicitors have to undergo a form of apprenticeship before becoming fully qualified and entitled to practise as such. This requirement has existed for many years, although its continuance and form have been the subject of the Lord Chancellor's Advisory Committee on Legal Education and Conduct's review of legal education.[2]

Pupillage and training contracts concentrate understandably on the education of would-be practitioners. But this does not mean that hands-on clinical experience is only relevant at the vocational stage of training. We argue that it is also highly relevant to those undertaking undergraduate study — as a focus for educating people in order to enable them to take responsibility for their learning both as students and in their future careers, whether as lawyers or otherwise.

---

[2] The Lord Chancellor's Advisory Committee on Legal Education and Conduct (ACLEC) issued a consultation paper on the initial stage (i.e., 'academic' or prevocational) of legal education in June 1994, on the vocational stage in June 1995 and on continuing professional development in July 1996. The *First Report*, op. cit. (note 1) was followed by a Second Report, *Continuing Professional Development for Solicitors and Barristers* in July 1997.

So, what of the role of the hands-on model in a degree programme? The study of law, largely through the traditional approach of analysing appeal case law, predominates in traditional law teaching across common law jurisdictions. The concentration on legal doctrine extracted from a study of leading cases was pioneered, if not started, by Christopher Langdell and others at Harvard Law School in the last quarter of the nineteenth century. This approach stood in stark contrast to the apprenticeship system (so far as it was a system) that had, up until then, been the only form of legal education and training.[3] Under the Langdellian method students concentrate on appellate decisions, analysing them and identifying principles upon which they were made. The result was and is fundamentally limiting as students are largely passive recipients of knowledge, relying on an account of the law by an 'expert' in that field supplemented by periodic involvement through the production of assignments and tutorial discussion. Without denigrating the quality of content of the lecture or competence of the lecturer nor dismissing the (pressured) interaction brought about by the Socratic question and answer approach, we suggest that the learning experience has only a limited focus. Even when it works well it largely develops skills of case law analysis and knowledge of legal doctrine. What more could the student be learning?

It must be acknowledged that the work of the Harvard school brought, for the first time, a method to legal study. The detailed analysis of case law is of course central to understanding law in the common law world. It might be worth noting that whatever value the Langdellian approach has may have been lost in any event with the modern tendency, in UK law schools, to concentrate on pre-digests of the raw material of law and to focus heavily on course content and the assessment of it. Pigs don't get fat by being weighed!

This imparting of knowledge in the late twentieth-century law school is now, more often than not, delivered to a large group of students who have little or no interaction with the lecturer. Students are normally expected to prepare for (relatively) smaller group work on topics set by staff on the issues deemed relevant to the subject being studied. Seminar or tutorial work frequently follows lectures. Able, confident or active students may dominate these group meetings, with others contributing little or nothing to the discussion.

This is not to suggest that the clinic was the first or only movement to react to what Langdell and subsequent law school teaching methods represent. Far

---

[3] For a more detailed discussion see M. Spiegel (1987) 34 UCLA L Rev 577.

from it. The legal realists,[4] the critical legal studies advocates,[5] feminist jurists[6] and those supporting a law in context approach have all found the narrow doctrinal system lacking. It does not take into account the realities of law in practice, the economic and political context in which law is made and operates, or issues of class, race and gender.

The clinic, however, does provide an opportunity of addressing both *what* is taught in law school and, most importantly, *how* to achieve many of the teaching and learning goals implicit in educating lawyers.

It was dissatisfaction with the form of instruction (coupled with other factors, including an awareness of the need to provide legal services in areas of unmet need) that led the first law schools to develop clinical approaches. We look first at our own UK experience and then compare this with the position in other jurisdictions, notably the USA, where the idea started.

Developments in the UK

The first overt clinical programmes started in the UK in the 1970s. These developments were not mere clones of US clinical practice; they were pioneering in that undergraduate law students on non-vocational courses were exposed to real-client and/or simulated work. Problems were, however, encountered. The rise and fall of a high-profile clinic at the University of Kent makes for interesting reading.[7] The innate conservatism of the legal system and lawyers focused critical attention on these innovatory programmes.

Should universities be involved in the practice of law? Wasn't this training rather than education? What if things went wrong and clients complained or even sued? Don't those wanting to enter the legal profession get the chance later, at the vocational stage or in their apprenticeship, to practise law? Wasn't concentrating on 'poor law' very political? These and other questions led to the demise of some of the early clinics and certainly thwarted the

---

[4] See K. Llewelyn, 'Some realism about realism' (1931) 44 Harv L Rev 1222.

[5] See G. Peller, 'The metaphysics of American law' (1985) 73 Calif L Rev 1151.

[6] See A. Scales, 'The emergence of feminist jurisprudence: an essay' (1986) 95 Yale L Rev 1373.

[7] For an account of the operation of the Kent clinic see W. Rees, 'Clinical legal education: an analysis of the University of Kent model' (1975) 9 Law Teach 125. We are pleased to report that the clinic is now alive and well again. A recent article describing their work in a specialised community mental health law clinic is described in K. Diesfield, 'Clinical legal education and training' (1997) July Legal Action 7.

growth of clinics[8] (in contrast to the development of clinics elsewhere, notably in the USA).

Although some law schools retained a clinical input on their courses (in particular Warwick), the academic community's enthusiasm for the clinic was, at best, low-key.

The position is now very different. According to recent research, clinical activities now form an integral part of the curriculum in undergraduate programmes in a large majority of both new and old universities.[9] Real-client clinics feature in one quarter of courses. Simulated clinics are more regularly found. An umbrella organisation (the Clinical Legal Education Organisation) is now in its third year and aims to act as a representative body and support group to those running and developing experiential learning.[10] This organisation is closely allied with its American counterpart, the Clinical Legal Education Association.[11]

So what has prompted this major shift in development? It is difficult to pinpoint cause and effect. Several factors, however, would seem to be relevant:

(a)   The quality of work produced by students on clinical units is high. This may be due to the sense of professionalism encouraged, especially in real-client work. Clinic students do well and are seen to do so. The enthusiasm this generates is infectious. The experience of a small number of clinics has seemingly prompted the development of support mechanisms fostering the growth of other clinics. This may not explain the rise of the clinic but certainly addresses recent developments in clinical education.

(b)   There is a growing awareness in higher education of the need for quality in both teaching and research. Control through quality assessment also accords with present government policy.[12] Regardless of the rationale

---

[8] For an interesting account of the early experiences in UK clinical education see Rees, op. cit. (note 7).
[9] See R. Grimes, J. Klaff and C. Smith, 'Legal skills and clinical legal education — a survey of law school practice' (1996) 30 Law Teach 44.
[10] CLEO can be contacted through: Sarah Cracknell, Sheffield Hallam University Student Law Clinic, Dyson House, Pond Street, Sheffield; tel 0114 2533703; e-mail s.a.cracknell@shu.ac.uk.
[11] CLEA can be contacted through: Mark Heyrman, University of Chicago Law School, 6020 South University Avenue, Chicago, Illinois 60637, USA.
[12] Quality control and review arises throughout the educational spectrum. ACLEC, *First Report on Legal Education and Training* (1996), sect. 5, pp. 19–23, recognises this as an important feature of the future of legal education. A statutory framework under the Further and Higher Education Act 1992, s. 70, also exists for this purpose.

behind this, the concentration on the quality of the students' learning experience is to be welcomed. This focus is directly addressed by clinical methods. The resource implications, however, are of crucial importance and are explored later.[13]

(c) There is a discernible call from the government, from industry, from the profession, from legal educators and from the student body for the linking of academic study with skills. These skills centre on intellectual development (particularly analysis and research), on skills pertaining to the practice of law (including advocacy, negotiation, interviewing and drafting), and on skills that can be seen as more transferable in their nature (for example, communication, study skills and time management).[14]

(d) There is increasing recognition that law should be taught in a framework where ethical, political, economic, social and cultural values are understood.[15]

(e) The experience of a small number of real-client clinics has acted as a catalyst for others. The success of the clinical programme at the University of Northumbria at Newcastle, for example, was a direct force in the creation of an in-house solicitors' practice at Sheffield Hallam University.

Taken as a whole, the time is opportune for the growth of a clinical movement within the UK. From the relatively isolated position occupied by a few clinics in the early 1970s, followed by a lull during much of the 80s, there has been a major rejuvenation of the clinical approach during the 90s. Today the clinic represents many aspects of good learning and teaching practice and has a clear and increasingly proven role to play within the curriculum.

It is interesting to compare this with the position in other common law countries.

A comparative picture

The USA, as the home of clinical legal education, warrants detailed mention. Similar developments, however, have taken and are now taking place in Australia, Canada, India, Malaysia, South Africa and the South Pacific. In

---

[13] See pp. 242–5.
[14] The importance of skills is specifically examined in ACLEC, op. cit. (note 12), sect. 2, p. 8, and the Law Society/Council of Legal Education, *Announcement on Qualifying Law Degrees* (1995). For a more thorough analysis of skills education see J. MacFarlane, 'Look before you leap: knowledge and learning in legal skills education' (1992) 19 J Law Soc 293.
[15] See ACLEC, op. cit. (note 12), sect. 4, p. 11, and the Law Society/Council of Legal Education, op. cit. (note 14), pp. 2–3.

Canada, and more recently Australia, the value of clinical methods has been
recognised and praised in governmental reviews leading to the expansion of
such programmes in law schools.[16] Nina Tarr gives a fuller picture of the
issues from a US perspective in chapter 7.

Clinical education is a major feature in many law school programmes. In the
USA 90 per cent of law schools use some form of clinical approach, and the
clinic is firmly entrenched as one important vehicle through which instruction
is given in the theory and practice of law.[17] Sophisticated programmes exist
that offer both in-house real-client clinics, externships (placements) and
simulated units. Specialist real-client clinics now exist dealing with a wide
variety of topics including housing, immigration, women's rights, criminal
defence, welfare-based problems, and constitutional law. Capital punishment
clinics are becoming increasingly common with the regrettable and rapid
increase in numbers on America's death rows. Classes, for example, run at
Georgetown University (Washington DC) with students teaching street law
(legal literacy) to prisoners; in the City University of New York students do
public defender work in contested criminal cases; the University of South
Carolina has a specialist juvenile crime clinic; at Yale there is a planning law
clinic working with members of the local community; UCLA (Los Angeles)
offers a highly developed simulation clinic in mediation; the University of
Hawaii has a clinic specialising in legal problems of the indigenous population.

With substantial funding coming from 'hard' and 'soft' sources[18] the
importance of the clinical arm of legal education is well recognised and
established. Despite (or some may say because of) the success of this
development, problems abound. It is a common position to see a clear
division within US law schools between the 'regular faculty' and the
'clinicians'. This manifests itself in differences in salary, tenure and other
terms and conditions, including in some cases, a physical division, with the
clinic occupying separate and often inferior premises.[19] However viewed, the
clinic is frequently both seen and treated as the poor relation.

---

[16] MacCrate; Arthurs; and Pearce, op. cit. (note 1).

[17] For full details of clinical and other programmes offered by US law schools, see *Barron's
Guide to Law Schools* (annual publication).

[18] 'Hard' and 'soft' funding is used in this context to mean internal (i.e., to the university or
college provider) and external (i.e., bodies outside the university or college provider, for
example, funding from central or local government or from a charitable foundation) respective-
ly. Some of the implications of this are examined by N. Tarr, 'Current issues in clinical legal
education' (1993) 37 Howard Law Journal 36.

[19] The Law Clinic at the University of Chicago, for example, operates from a basement (albeit
palatial by comparison with UK clinic accommodation), in stark contrast to the accommodation
afforded to the rest of the law department.

Many aspects of clinical work are not given academic credence. Until relatively recently those engaged principally in clinical education were not required (nor were they in a position) to engage in research and scholarly writing. Clinical teachers were more often than not seen as practitioners whose role was to teach practice. Time was not given to them to engage in research. This further compounded the view that the clinic was little more than a training workshop for the would-be practitioner.[20]

There are, however, significant differences in the context within which the clinic operates in the USA as compared with that in the UK. In America law is taken as a postgraduate course of study. Students are often mature (25 +) and self-funding. There is no obvious distinction between academic and vocational stages of legal education. Students who graduate in law frequently remain at their law schools to take a short crammer course before sitting the state bar exams (six weeks or so after graduation). They can enter practice on successful completion of the bar exams with no requirement of apprenticeship in legal practice or practical experience in law.

The need, therefore, for practical experience and skills training for American law students is both real and obvious. Indeed the American Bar Association standards suggest that a clinical programme should be run in all accredited law schools. Without experience of clinics, students would enter the workplace with little appreciation of the practice of law. It is understandable, therefore, why law clinics are widespread and why they are so popular. The majority of US law students do go on to legal practice. By contrast, it is presently estimated that only one half of UK law students take the practice route.[21] Around one half of all American law students have the chance of some clinical experience and in some schools this is compulsory.[22]

In its influential report in the autumn of 1992, the MacCrate Commission listed the skills and values that it saw as central to the study and later the practice of law. These are summarised in the appendix to chapter 7. The report recognised the role of the clinic in achieving these ends. At present

---

[20] A call for the need for clinical scholarship is made by P. Hoffman, 'Clinical scholarship and skills training' (1994) 1 Clinical Law Review 93 and also in the contributions to the *New York Law School Law Review*, vol. 35, No. 1 (1990).

[21] See ACLEC, op. cit., paras 3.2 and 3.5 and app. F.

[22] At the time of writing real-client clinics are compulsory at: City University of New York, University of Montana, Washington DC School of Law, University of New Mexico. Simulation clinics are compulsory at: University of Vermont, University of Hawaii, Thomas Cooley School of Law. Information from responses to a survey conducted over the internet 1994/5. To subscribe contact 'listserv@acc.wuacc.edu' followed by 'subscribe law clinic(name)'.

US law schools are considering how to incorporate the MacCrate recommendations, which are likely to form part of the American Bar Association's
(ABA) validation criteria for law school courses. (The ABA accredits law
schools which meet certain minimum standards. A person's qualification
from such a school is a prerequisite to taking the bar exam.)

Although American clinical teaching, dating effectively from the 1960s (but
debated at a much earlier stage in the 1930s[23]), seems to be targeted towards
the requirements of legal practice, there are still parallels that can be drawn
that aid our understanding of developments in the UK.

We suggest that the study of law is of limited value unless it is directed at
understanding the law which is practised; the law that affects the lives of real
people. This is the hard evidence from which legal theory can be constructed
and hypotheses tested. To study the theory without the evidence is in that
sense unscientific. An understanding of law and an ability to apply that
understanding requires the study of law in its operational context. In our view
this applies equally to those students who wish to practise law *and* to those
who do not. Law studied out of the context of practice is an artificial concept.
The law clinic is a vehicle through which this educational process can be
advanced in a way to which students readily relate and by which they are
stimulated.

You only have to turn to the pages of the American academic journals or the
agendas of conferences and meetings on clinical issues to see the common
ground in the UK and US clinical debates. The contents of these discussions
are strikingly similar to the issues being raised (albeit only in the last few
years) within the academic community in the United Kingdom.[24] Learning
outcomes and objectives, standards, assessment and teaching methods are all
widely discussed, as is scholarship and resourcing.

The taking-off point for the US clinical movement was the anti-poverty and
civil rights campaigns of the early 1960s. The growth since then, principally

---

[23] The origin of the clinical approach to law teaching is often attributed to Jerome Frank and
in particular his article, 'Why not a clinical lawyer-school?' (1933) 81 U Pa L Rev 907, and is
discussed in S. Ellmann, I. Gunning, and R. Hertz, 'Why not a clinical lawyer-journal?' (1994)
1 Clinical Law Review 1.
[24] Contemporary debates in the US clinical movement centre on the objectives, form and
content of clinical programmes. Resourcing, assessment, ethics and standards also feature.
Numbers 1–3 of vol. 1 of the *Clinical Law Review* contain articles and essays on these issues.
Subscriptions to the review can be made to: Randy Hertz, New York University School of Law,
249 Sullivan Street, New York 10012, USA.

as a result of a heavy injection of charitable moneys and federal funds (e.g., Ford Foundation and more latterly Title IX money[25]), has been steady and marked. This has brought another set of major difficulties which have not, as yet, featured in the UK movement.[26] Many US clinics have taken up a welfare brief serving the needs of the local minority groups and the indigent population. Such clinics are often driven at least in part by the clients' needs. Funding has been linked to this service provision.

Although it is both understandable and commendable to have as an aim the service to the community, the educational purpose behind the law clinic should not be lost. This point is debated in more detail later in this chapter and in chapter 2. Of course any real client must be given, for professional and ethical reasons, a quality of service at least equal to that provided by a competent practitioner. We believe that it is the view of UK clinical teachers that, subject to this caveat of professionalism, it is the function of the clinic to provide primarily for the students and not to meet the demands of each and every potential client, however compelling the client's needs may be. Every effort should of course be made to refer the client to an adviser who can help. The issues surface frequently in this book — see chapters 3, on the in-house clinic, 7, on the American perspective, and 8, where there is an Australian commentary.

With this historical and comparative perspective in mind, we turn our attention to the different models of clinical education and the use and the implications raised by each in terms of their own operation and the curriculum in general.

The clinic in practice

Clinical legal education may be simply described as learning law through application, practice and reflection. But the way in which the concept is turned into a programme of educational experience varies.

Clinical legal education is, we suggest throughout this book, quite different from traditional legal education. The lecture–seminar method so common in

---

[25] See Tarr, op. cit. (note 18), pp. 37–8. Title IX funds are federal grant moneys made available under the Higher Education Act 20 USC, s. 1134(U) 1988. They have now been abolished leaving a funding gap.
[26] The rise of fee-generating clinics features in commentaries in 1 Clinical Law Review 677 and 685. The pressure on UK real-client clinics to become self-financing in whole or part may well follow, especially in the light of the restructuring of legal aid (for a brief summary of the implications generally of this development see R. Smith, 'Essential reading' (1995) 92 (20) Gazette 16).

the education of law students is, on one level, capable of satisfying the learning-by-doing definition, providing the form of delivery actively involves the student. The reality is, however, that lectures are predominantly content and assessment led; they consist too often of students being given information. It is unusual for lectures to meet many, if any, of the clinical demands. They rarely involve students in the real or realistic experience of the law in practice. A well-structured lecture and seminar programme, using perhaps group work, presentations and case studies, and achieving a high level of student interaction and participation, is of course of value as a learning experience. However, unless it goes beyond the passive involvement of students, a learning opportunity has been missed. In our view the lecture as a means of conveying information and concepts is a very limited teaching and learning mechanism. Its value may increase if it is used in an integrated sense with other more student-centred approaches.[27]

We suggest that there are three types of clinic that provide the environment in which high levels of experiential learning occur. These are:

(a)   in-house real-client clinics,
(b)   out-house real-client ('real-world') clinics,
(c)   simulation clinics.

The aims and objectives of each are in principle the same — the exposure of students to law in a practice setting and to the analysis, management and process of the problems arising. The way in which each is structured to achieve this differs. But the need to reflect on the experience and the process and results of that reflection are central to all clinical programmes.

The three generic types of clinic described above are examined in detail in chapters 3, 4, and 5, but the principal characteristics are set out below.

The in-house real-client clinic

In this model the clinic is based in the law school (hence 'in-house') and the unit is offered, monitored and controlled in-house too. The clients are real,

---

[27] For a study of the potential clinical approaches which may be applied to more conventional forms of classes see J. MacFarlane, *An Evaluation of the Role and Practice of Clinical Legal Education with Particular Reference to Undergraduate Legal Education in the UK*, PhD thesis, South Bank Polytechnic, 1988. M. Le Brun and R. Johnstone also explore teaching methods which promote student learning in *The Quiet (R)evolution* (Law Book Co., 1994), ch. 6.

with problems requiring actual solutions (hence 'real-client'[28]). The client base may be selected from the general public at large or from a section of the public, for example, staff or students at that institution or through specific referral from another agency (for example, law centre, Citizens' Advice Bureaux (CAB) or local solicitors).

The service might be advice only or advice and assistance. Clients may be interviewed, advised orally and/or in writing, and helped with the preparation of their cases. The word 'case' should not be assumed to mean disputes. Clients may, for example, want to draft a will or discuss a new partnership. This help may take the form of the clinic corresponding with opponents, third parties, their lawyers, insurance companies and the courts. The clinic may offer representation either in a specialist area (for example, before industrial tribunals and social security appeal tribunals) or more generally. In the UK, restrictive rules on rights of audience impose constraints on student advocates. But tribunal and arbitration hearings (e.g., under the county court small claims procedure) offer students direct advocacy opportunities. The clinic may operate as a paralegal service (which means that there are no solicitors involved and hence no need to adhere to the Law Society's codes) or a fully fledged solicitors' practice.

Clearly some of the consequences of real-client work will depend on the extent of the service offered but there are principles which apply equally across all real-client work.

Once a case is taken on, and subject to professional practice rules, the client's best interests are of paramount importance. The service must be realistic about what it can offer and must be able to deliver what it says it can. We suggest that the only acceptable standard of work is that of the competent legal adviser or representative. Students must be aware of this exacting requirement and must be supervised and supported sufficiently for that to be secured and maintained. The clinic must be able to operate in a way that preserves client confidentiality.

The Clinical Legal Education Organisation (CLEO) adopted a set of model standards in 1995 for real-client work, that deals comprehensively with these

---

[28] We have used the term 'real-client' in preference to the widely used term 'live-client', but you will come across both terms in the literature on clinical legal education. We did think that while many students encounter the opposite of the real client, through simulation, none encounter the opposite of live clients — but someone did suggest at a conference that they had represented a dead client in their clinic. It must have been hard to get instructions, let alone comply with professional practice rules.

and other related issues. Those standards appear as an appendix to chapter 3.[29] As explored in chapter 3, the implications of real-client clinics are considerable. Indemnity insurance cover, supervision, assessment, continuity of service (especially during vacations), resourcing generally and the high standards expected of professionals are issues that are ever-present.

The out-house clinic

An attractive alternative or addition to the in-house real-client clinic is a clinic that involves students in existing legal work outside the college or university. Those responsible for running such units effectively tap into existing services. These may be found in private legal practice, local and national government, private and nationalised industries, and the voluntary sector. Again the format is varied. The clinic is 'real-client' in the sense that it involves real individual clients and their problems. The 'client' could be seen, for example, through the offices of the local CAB or community law centre. The client may be the State in the case of a clinic run in conjunction with, say, the Crown Prosecution Service or Benefits Agency. Where a student works in the housing department of the local district council the client is the council. It is the real-world input, coupled with clearly worked-out learning objectives, that can turn this into a meaningful learning experience. As with the in-house clinic, care must be taken to establish educational criteria, for otherwise the opportunity for a clinical experience becomes little more than an unstructured observation of someone else's practice.

The clinic may operate on the basis of advice giving only, or it may offer representation as well. Students can, for example, take an option to work with a free representation unit. Such agencies are run by trade union councils and other non-statutory bodies. The clinic might also take the form of a placement, short or long term, in, say, a solicitors' office or barristers' chambers. Students may shadow others in practice or industry. The position may also be remunerated (for example, on a degree sandwich course). The term 'clinic' is used in the widest sense, presupposing that the use of the out-house service is part of the student's actual and formal learning experience.

The principal difficulty in this approach lies in the supervision and monitoring of the clinic. All supervision in clinical work is time-consuming and

---

[29] Model Standards in Clinical Legal Education adopted at the Plymouth Conference CLEO, June 1995. This document uses the term 'live client' not 'real client' (see note 28). The document has been slightly amended to provide up-to-date references.

challenging. In the out-house clinic it is physically removed from some, if not most, of the day-to-day activity of the law school and therefore potentially more difficult to integrate and control the student's learning experience.

Chapter 4 examines in detail examples of out-house clinics.

Simulation clinic

As the title implies, this clinic recreates selected elements of the problems, practice and procedures otherwise found in a variety of real-client work. This may be done in a number of ways. Cases can be acted out in their entirety, from the taking of initial instructions to a negotiated settlement or court hearing. Such sessions can be run as intensive courses (where the concentrated effort tends to make the exercise increasingly real in the students' minds[30]), or spread through all or part of the academic year in weekly slots. Parts of a case might be examined in greater detail than others, for example, making a bail application in criminal proceedings or drafting pleadings in a civil action. Particular skills can be concentrated on (for example, legal research, interviewing or advocacy), using staff, students or professional actors to enable role-play to take place.

The attractions of this type of clinical education are several. The risks and unpredictability of real-client work are removed. The process can be regulated to suit the purpose. The same materials can be run and rerun. The cost of offering a simulation clinic may be substantially less than the real-client variety in terms of the intensity of supervision and the need for clerical support. There is not the same requirement in terms of premises and equipment. The staff and students do not carry the same degree of professional responsibility. Students can be allowed to make mistakes. Simulation can work well in conjunction with a real-client clinic using the real cases as material for reproduction (subject to the rules on client confidentiality).

The rub is that students regularly report that simulation has less of the cutting-edge feel found in the real-client experience. It is also hard to craft

---

[30] This approach was taken at Sheffield Hallam University on the compulsory legal skills module (2nd year LLB) 1994/5. The unit was delivered in one week with student attendance required 9 a.m. to 5 p.m. on each day. A simulated case study was conducted as a 'real case' from the initial taking of instructions to the final court hearing. Each student had the opportunity to conduct part of the case as a member of a group who took overall responsibility for the case. The cases were recorded in the form of a case file akin to one that would be used in a solicitors' office or Crown Prosecution Service.

exercises and administer the simulation, for example, finding witnesses or expert opinions. However, simulation remains a very important aspect of clinical work, both in the UK and abroad, and it is examined in more detail in chapter 5.

Tensions and dilemmas in clinical education

It will become apparent to those not familiar with clinical programmes (and will already be known by those who are), that both the theory and practice of the clinic are beset with challenges. Some of these result in real tensions and dilemmas for both staff and students.

The following chapters will explore some of the problems arising in more detail, but for present purposes these can be identified by setting out the competing elements.

Finding and securing resources

Any discussion of clinical education would be incomplete without a consideration of the resourcing implications. First impressions might suggest that clinics, whether simulated or real-client, are resource intensive. The resources here include the human, the financial and the physical. Clearly this creates a tension in so far as the clinic's often considerable needs are concerned, especially in the context of pressure on, and cutbacks in, funding for higher education. Even if adequate resources are secured for a clinic, this may have a knock-on effect on other parts of the curriculum and funding of the law school generally.

Those advocating the development of clinics must be prepared to address the issue of funding head-on. A starting point might be to try to identify sources of funding. 'Hard' money (i.e., mainstream university or college funds) and 'soft' money (external funding, including sponsorships, grants, legal aid) can both be targeted. There are, however, difficulties, notably the over-reliance on soft money and the vulnerability that this can produce (that is, the law school does not take financial responsibility for the clinic, which then rises or falls at the whim of the external funder).

Resourcing, especially for real-client clinics, must be adequate in order that professional standards as well as principles of good practice are upheld. This can be a strongly persuasive tool in the sense that without proper funding a programme cannot be offered. The inherent but unavoidable danger in insisting on proper professional standards is, of course, the loss of the clinic if the funder is looking for savings or is otherwise unwilling to resource it fully.

This discussion has little meaning unless it is clearly understood what the resources devoted to the clinic are buying. If the virtues of the clinic are as claimed — an enhanced student-centred learning experience which complements study on the rest of the course — the resources given to the clinic must be weighed in terms of this overall educational outcome. In other words, the clinic may cost more than other units on a programme, but may well produce more in terms of the quality and even quantity of education that results.[31]

Providing training or education?

What is it that the clinic offers and how does the clinic fit into the curriculum of the law school?

It is a premise of this book that the clinic is not about equipping students to become practitioners. The aims of a clinical programme, at least in the context of legal education in the UK, are to provide students with a very particular learning experience. This experience enables students to question, research, analyse and apply both the facts and the law in an attempt to resolve problems taken from a real or realistic setting. In the process of addressing such problems, the student is required to consider the practical, ethical, social and moral considerations surrounding law and the legal process.

This necessarily involves the use of lawyering skills as tools for problem solving.

The fact that students develop skills relevant to them beyond the scope of the syllabus of the clinic is welcomed. That many students intend to enter the profession is acknowledged. But the clinic, at least at undergraduate degree level, is not primarily concerned with vocational training and skills induction. It is about promoting learning and the understanding of concepts, rules, techniques and ethics and is designed to enhance overall intellectual development. It is also about producing students who can constructively criticise the operation of law.

---

[31] Unpublished analysis at Sheffield Hallam University supports the assertion that students do better in other parts of their studies after working in the clinic compared to equivalent students who took a conventional option. The results of a five-year study are expected in March 1998.

If this is understood the clinic ceases to be an adjunct to, and starts to be seen as a complementary feature of, the overall educational process. The principle of integration is developed in chapter 2.

Those interested in the law clinic as a pedagogic model might wish to look at the US clinical experience, where the legal academy has suffered severe and lasting schisms based on an 'us versus them' perception. To have a significant effect on legal education, the clinic must be seen to be as much a part of the study of law as lectures in land law or seminars in contract. To be effective the clinic must, therefore, be about education and integration. Its many side benefits include a thorough grounding in skills and an experience suitable for those who wish to train for industry or the profession.

Serving the student or the client?

A further tension, again particularly prevalent in the USA, but also a notable feature in UK real-client clinics, arises in the competing demands of the students and the clients. Whilst not diametrically opposed, the needs of both can cause conflict.

Funding in the early years of the real-client movement in the USA was closely tied to the delivery of a 'poor law' service. The legacy of this has had a lasting impact.[32]

In our view the goal of service provision only has a place in either degree or vocational level study if it also serves the educational aims set for the clinic.

Having said this we believe that learning about the inter-relationship between law and social deprivation, and having the experience of helping people who cannot afford or find legal help, makes for a good fit between education and service. Provided that the legal services which address the clients' problems do serve this educational objective at the time, there is no difficulty in meeting both sets of needs. But the clinic must monitor and regulate the flow of cases to ensure that the learning experience is prioritised.

None of this is to suggest that a selective service is a poor-quality one nor that the clients are in some way laboratory guinea pigs. Once a real-client case is taken on there is only one acceptable standard of work — that of

---

[32] See Tarr, op. cit. (note 18), pp. 32–5).

professional competence and ethical practice. Careful selection of cases coupled with effective supervision play a part in the attempt to guarantee that standards are maintained and that the clinic does not become service driven. Put another way, the organisation and design of the clinic coupled with the selection of cases must meet the predetermined educational goals. Once cases are taken on, it is the clients' best interests that are paramount. In serving those interests, the educational objectives are also pursued. The willingness of staff and students to serve the client or the insistence of the funders that such a service be provided can compromise the educational purpose.

Making assessment part of learning

One measure of the educational worth of any unit or course is the setting and achieving of realistic and useful assessment criteria. 'Realistic' and 'useful' in this context mean an assessment regime that achieves its teaching and learning objectives, matching student progress with the projected outcomes of the course.

The clinic, by its very nature and structure, lends itself to *formative* feedback and assessment. By this we mean a process where the student learns from the assessment and is not simply graded by it. It is user-friendly and readily encourages self and peer assessment. Group work is often used as a base for learning and this can be reflected in the assessment methodology.

The limits imposed by unseen examinations are unsuitable for and unacceptable to many clinical units. The traditional unseen three-hour exam, where the student may have little idea of what will be examined, is in our view of limited use as a method of assessing learning (it may be justifiable as a competency test). The question must also be asked, 'What is being assessed?' An examination can only present pre-packaged simplified information to the student, who has little time or information for analysis. Intellectual skills are likely to take second place to reproduction of material and memory testing.

In posing alternatives, however, the challenges are many. Assessment in a form other than examination or essay assignment can be labour-intensive. It is sometimes difficult to ensure that all students, especially in real-client work, are exposed to the same quality of material on which they are to be assessed. Assessors are open to the challenge that they are likely to favour those students they have enjoyed working with. How does the assessor avoid unconscious discrimination?

The assessment of a student who does not receive detailed feedback on a regular basis is educationally problematic. Clinic gives the opportunity for regular and detailed feedback. Students often achieve high grades in clinical work, and this often ruffles feathers in the more traditional camp on grounds of supposed loss of academic rigour. The traditionalists may argue that such levels of support are bound to produce high marks. But whoever said that setting and marking an exam script are objective or that assessment should be used as a means of marking students down? The important issues are: do we know what we are assessing and do the students learn from the assessment process?

What the clinic does provide is an opportunity to break with historically accepted assessment conventions. It gives the students a chance to make assessment a part of the learning experience. It provides students with an environment within which they can, through their efforts and motivation, reap just rewards.

Equality of opportunity

Institutions, within academia and outside it, are rightly and increasingly concerned with issues of equal opportunity. The clinic gives rise to particular considerations in this context. First, how are students selected? (Clinical programmes are normally very popular and often oversubscribed.) Secondly, if the clinic is so good, why should some students get the chance of it and not others? If it is made compulsory, is this fair on those who don't want to learn experientially? Thirdly, how does a real-client clinical programme ensure that all students have the same equally rated experience from which they can learn and can be assessed? Finally, when students do well, particularly on clinical options, are they effectively given preferential treatment because they are able to secure higher grades than students not taking such courses?

The way forward

The introduction to this book and this chapter have attempted to locate clinical legal education within current debates on the future, form and content of legal education as a whole in the UK.

Drawing from the lessons learnt in other jurisdictions, notably the USA, we suggest that the clinic is not only here to stay but has an important role to fill in the education of lawyers. Different approaches to how we educate our lawyers are now clearly on the professional and political agendas.

The Lord Chancellor's Advisory Committee has recognised this, as have the Law Society and the Bar. Academics are increasingly giving a clinical approach more credence. The establishment of CLEO has been an important step towards the acceptance of clinical methods. A forum for discussion has been created coupled with a base for conferences and the planned establishment of a scholarly journal.

The clinical movement in the UK has a sound basis in both theory and practice. The rest of this book looks at both in more detail.

2

Student-centred learning and the clinic

> In the first year they scare you to death. In the second year they work you to death. In the third year they bore you to death. (Anonymous law student).[1]

Does this quote ring any bells for you? Has your study of law so far turned out to be an unexciting slog? You are told you will have to work really hard, there is a shortage of jobs at the end, there's a lot to get through, and the exams are really tough. Then you find you are on a treadmill of more cases, more statutes, more essays, more exams. . . . And finally you conclude that studying law is a bit boring. Thank goodness you can leave university behind and get on with something more interesting: perhaps the practice of law, or the end of law altogether.

Relax: perhaps you are not alone. The Lord Chancellor's Advisory Committee on Legal Education, reporting in 1996, found that 'legal education . . . has a reputation as a highly instrumental, even anti-intellectual discipline'.[2]

---

[1] Quoted in R. Rains, *The Eighteenth-century Jurist, Twentieth-century Legal Education and Preparation for the Twenty-first Century,* paper to the 3rd International Conference on Lawyers and Lawyering, Windermere, 1994.
[2] The Lord Chancellor's Advisory Committee on Legal Education and Conduct, *First Report on Legal Education and Training* (1996), at p. 58.

OK, the committee is only describing a reputation, but is this a case of 'no smoke without some fire'?

So what learning experience do we want to create on a law degree? What, indeed, is the point of studying law at all? I'll try to answer that question, as without an understanding of goals and learning outcomes, the discussion of how to design a learning experience is pointless. Then I want to consider, with the help of some educational theory, how it could perhaps be different.

But first, it may help me — and in due course you, the readers — if I say a little about my personal approach in this chapter.

First, if I say I am a firm, occasionally evangelical, believer in clinical legal education, you will know where I am coming from. My personal interest and experience has been with real-client work, but I hope what I say is also relevant to those who are interested in simulations.[3]

Secondly, I believe that in conveying opinion there is little point in dressing it up in apparently neutral language. Hence I prefer to say 'I find that . . .' rather than 'it is submitted that . . .' or 'the better approach seems to be . . .'.[4]

Thirdly, I want to be explicit about who I am addressing this chapter to: I am chiefly concerned in getting the flavour across to the law student, while making links for both lecturers and students between what is known about learning theory generally and the opportunities provided in clinical legal education. So from now on 'you' means the student, and 'we' means lecturers.

Fourthly, I consider that a university environment should be empowering for all its stakeholders (sorry if that sounds like jargon). The educational experience belongs as much to the students as it does to the lecturers; there should be no secrets in course design. Staff should share their ideas freely with each other, with other universities, and above all with their students. No

---

[3] Actually I think most writing about education is based on value judgments about what is good for a student, what the essence of law is etc.; if I admit that I start out with prejudices, you, the reader, can more quickly uncover the areas where you disagree or where my argument has logical flaws or untested premises. Also I hope you will be encouraged to admit your own prejudices.

[4] My co-authors made a brave attempt to get me at least to pay lip-service to academic writing conventions. I seem to have reacted the other way. But if you understand what I say then they will probably forgive me. I particularly want this chapter to be accessible to students and teachers to whom this debate may not all be familiar.

one should feel that they do not know why things happen the way they do, or find that all discussions take place behind closed doors. Universities are places for ideas. The ideas in this chapter happen to be mine. I want them to stimulate debate and demand amongst students as well as lecturers (customers as well as suppliers of education). I do not apologise for the attempt at direct and, if I can achieve it, unpretentious language. I am aware of, but not put off, by the kind of criticism contained in the following excerpt from a book review:

> . . . many writers seem unable to write on skills without resorting to a wholly different style which seems to believe that the reader's age has dropped by 10 years and which might be caricatured as 'now boys and girls, today we're going to . . .'.[5]

Why study law?

This part of the chapter looks at, and rejects, the argument that legal education at degree level is about studying the theory of law and not the practice of law; it looks at the way the vocational aspirations of students influence the content of the course and the attitude of both students and staff; and it looks critically at the conventional approach to teaching and assessing law. Because each strand of the discussion is connected to the other strands I have given up the attempt to deal with each in a separate section. The discussion in this part of the chapter is intended to prepare you for the later discussion of educational theory and clinical method.

Your studies are taking three or more years during the prime of your life, no doubt precious and expensive years. Is the experience stretching you, intellectually, emotionally and morally? Is it just a means to an end: entry to the legal profession, or a qualification leading to some other career?

Why study law at degree level?

Brownsword catches something of the flavour of what we might aim for when he says that a law school should be 'making steam come out of their students' ears'.[6] That sounds to me like the kind of place to be.

Unfortunately for the clinical or skills law teacher there is — and here I paraphrase Brownsword's argument — only one kind of steam that matters at degree level. Theoretical steam is good; practical steam is bad; vocational

---

[5] G. Broadbent (1995) 29 Law Teach 110.
[6] R. Brownsword, 'Where are all the law schools going?' (1996) 30 Law Teach at p. 17.

steam is utterly awful.[7] Hence the only justification for introducing law through the realistic context of the clinic, and thereby diluting the pure study of legal docrine, would be because the students are going to go into legal practice. There is no need for those who do not intend to practise to know about law in its practical context. 'Real' universities do not get involved in vocational things during their degrees.

This premise is untested and to my mind absurd. The practical context of law is, surely, the equivalent of the field trip in geography, the laboratory experiment in science, the hospital wards in medicine, or speaking when studying French. Or is law like theology, where there is no earthly context in which to study it, merely statements of faith to be picked to pieces, just like appellate court decisions?

In the discussion later in this chapter of learning theories, which looks at the difference, for example, between surface learning and deep learning, and the idea of a learning cycle, I will set out what I consider to be a respectable body of opinion that rejects this traditional approach to what matters in higher education in favour of a more active hands-on approach.

Would it be unfair to sum up the traditional approach with the refrain: we don't want to get our hands dirty? Getting involved in the practice of law and serving vocational needs distracts the student's attention from real learning. If that is a valid objection, would you be entitled to expect 'clean hands' law teaching to be a hothouse of educational innovation? If law teaching need not relate to the needs of practice no one law degree need even resemble any other. What do we find on the ground, however? We find large parts of current and conventional law degree teaching suffers from the vocational requirements apparently laid down by the professions for those intending to practise. The dreaded contamination of student experience with some experience of the practice of law may indeed be postponed until the vocational stage, but the professions dictate and the law schools acquiesce. We design our degrees around the profession's tramlines.

What are these tramlines? They are the syllabuses of the 'core/foundation' subjects.[8] The legal professions insist that those who want to get on to a vocational course after their degree must have passed seven foundation

---

[7] It has been suggested, for example, by a speaker at a conference to discuss the Lord Chancellor's Advisory Committee report at the Institute of Advanced Legal Studies in July 1996, that 18–21-year-olds are not capable of understanding both legal theory and its practical context. The student's ability to understand both in chapters 3–5 suggests this is untested and erroneous opinion. Yet no one contradicted the speaker (not even me, but I was there!).

[8] The word 'core' is commonly used instead of 'foundation', which demonstrates the hold the professions' requirements have. Strictly the seven foundations do not need to be studied as discrete subjects, so long as the elements are covered somewhere.

subjects.[9] Law students would rightly complain if their schools did not offer these seven pillars of wisdom. (Indeed most degrees are structured so that the student gets all or most of these core subjects whatever their career intentions.) Is this not already vocationally orientated? Like it or lump it, as law teachers and law students we are not free to design a degree that is free of professional requirements — all we can do is carry out what we think matters in legal education within that framework.

I believe that a clinical approach offers an exciting way through and beyond the ultimately sterile debate about 'learning for legal practice or learning for life'. But, I guess, we'd better run through that debate before leaving it behind.

Studying law to become a lawyer

Using the study of law simply as a means towards becoming qualified as a lawyer is what the word 'instrumental' (with its implicit criticism), used by the Lord Chancellor's Advisory Committee, means.

No one actually claims to be running a purely instrumental law degree.[10] In 1993 and 1994 the Higher Education Funding Councils for England and for Wales required all law schools to self-assess their own teaching quality. None claimed to be running a law degree purely to train lawyers:

> All the LLB courses, whether 'black letter', contextual or practice-orientated, sought to provide qualifying professional degrees allowing graduates to proceed to the Legal Practice Course or Bar Finals, *as well as* providing an undergraduate education in law.[11]

And yet the debate goes on, and while it does clinical legal education can become sidelined as a result of the accusation that it's only relevant to those intending to practise (and therefore not relevant to law degrees which have wider aims). Later on in this chapter I hope to show that a clinical style helps

---

[9] These requirements are set out by the Bar and Law Society in their 1995 'Announcement on full-time qualifying law degrees'. Although detailed control of course content is much relaxed, this still lays down that 7/18ths of a law degree must be taken up with the study of the seven foundation subjects.

[10] Twining, in *Blackstone's Tower: The English Law School* (London: Stevens & Sons, 1994) discusses at pp. 64–85 the fictitious University of Rutland where the students and lecturers are quite clear that what students actually want is to get qualified. The stated aims of the degree are broader.

[11] Higher Education Funding Council, *Law Subject Overview Report* (1994), emphasis added.

learning. If you agree that it does, then — at its worst — does it really matter that it is also of some vocational relevance? Vocational skills are often transferable. You don't have to become a lawyer to have benefited. Even if the skills were of no value to anyone outside the practice of law — which would suggest that lawyers are a very strange professional group best avoided — would it matter so long as acquiring them did not interfere with learning the legal doctrine?

Studying law out of curiosity

The root of the word 'education' is Latin and means 'leading out'. If the etymology is of any help to us, it means that what the student knows, wants, and can do is at the centre of the learning process. It implies what is now termed 'student-centred education'. I start from a preference for the student actively finding learning rather than the teacher putting the learning into the passive student. Teaching then becomes the means and is not an end in itself (a point perhaps to remember when giving or receiving a lecture). Contrast this with what Woods calls 'teacher-based' learning:

> In 'teacher-based' learning the teacher selects the knowledge, creates the learning environment, develops and uses the evaluation materials, presents the knowledge and the problems, and provides a personal image of the professional. The students are locked into the pacing and sequencing used by the teacher. They have little control over the situation.[12]

What drives student-centred learning? By definition it cannot be solely the teacher who drives it. What makes a person want to know about the concepts and contents of law? I would suggest a desire to know, to understand, to explore, and that this can be distilled into the concept of curiosity. Sometimes it seems that curiosity is drummed out of our undergraduates rather than cherished. Which lecturer has not had or overheard the conversation in the staff common room regretting that third-year law students just don't seem to ask questions or have opinions?[13]

---

[12] D. Woods, 'Problem-based learning and problem solving', in D. Boud (ed.) *Problem-based learning in education for the professions* (Sydney: Higher Education Research and Development Society of Australasia, 1985) quoted in D. Cruickshank, 'Problem-based learning in legal education' in J. Webb and C. Maughan (eds), *Teaching Lawyers' Skills* (London: Butterworth, 1996).

[13] J. Webb describes this problem in 'Why theory matters', in J. Webb and C. Maughan (eds), *Teaching Lawyers' Skills* (London: Butterworth, 1996): '[P]assivity may be developed or reinforced by the experience of higher education, particularly where teaching methods emphasise the passive acquisition of propositional (content-based) knowledge'.

The signs of curiosity in a young child, who is programmed to learn as part of his or her genetic inheritance, are the constant repetition of the question words: Why? What? When? How? Where? Who?

Which of these questions do we emphasise in legal education? During the academic stage you gain knowledge (answers to the question 'What?'). What are the elements of an offence, for example? To a lesser extent the 'When?' questions are answered. When was this case decided, that Act passed? But if you look at the 'How?' questions they are often how to answer an exam question in the 'right' manner.[14]

Then when you are preparing for practice on the vocational course the questions focus on 'How?', 'When?' and 'Where?' How is the affidavit drafted? Where and when is it filed?

I believe students should be exposed to all of the questions during every stage of their education, and I believe this for at least three reasons:

(a)   The most important force driving intellectual curiosity is the desire to understand why. Education that starts from wanting to know why the world is like it is (in this case the world of law) goes with the flow of human curiosity. It's not enough to teach students how legal concepts and arguments fit together; they should be encouraged to question why. There is a much discredited metaphor about the young learner being a *tabula rasa* (Latin for empty slate) waiting to be filled up. That is a teacher-centred model. A metaphor I would prefer is the vacuum cleaner: a learner is preconditioned to suck up knowledge. (Both metaphors, however, are so simplistic as to be not much more than a way of, I hope, reviving your attention. The vacuum cleaner does not capture the intelligent absorption and selection, critical appraisal and assimilation of new information, the testing and rejection of hypotheses, that actually accompanies the thirst for learning.)

(b)   Law is about the way society regulates itself. Society is made up of people. What effect does a particular decision have on real people? In other words, who does this law affect? Ignoring the 'Who?' is a long-standing

---

[14] How to carry out legal research might be claimed for the degree stage, and certainly all law schools have an introductory programme in legal research. My experience is that students quickly learn that this is not necessary to pass assessments. Enquiries of graduates on to the LPC at Northumbria in 1995 (reported in H. Brayne and P. Breakey, 'Research on the LPC' (1995) 3 Web Journal of Current Legal Issues) confirms this. Students lacked basic skills in legal research, had never used tools such as *Halsbury's Laws*, and C. Little, P. Leighton and T. Mortimer (1997) 31 Law Teach 208 find students depressingly reluctant to use primary sources or undertake legal research.

tradition during the law degree. People are reduced to caricatures, often given ridiculous names and unreal circumstances, and the effect of legal doctrine on their lives is of no interest. Look at a standard batch of legal problems you are asked to solve. You learn to manipulate criminal doctrine by having one-dimensional people slaughtered and attacked in page after page of hypothetical problems; we teach you family law by having people from fictitious faraway lands contracting polygamous marriages in highly dubious circumstances and then having peculiar sexual problems; we teach contract by having people shouting bargains across rivers and rushing around like headless chickens trying to retract offers they have just dropped into the postbox. These people have no lives; they are not even portrayed as if they are people; they only have legal problems. The justification is that we are teaching you to think like a lawyer. But which lawyers think like this? More importantly, which lawyers should think like this? You are being taught to detach law from its context, to become aloof from the effect law has on people.

(c) It seems bizarre and artificial to separate the questions from each other: what is the intrinsic merit — unless purely to gain a vocational qualification — of learning the elements of, say, assault occasioning actual bodily harm while failing to consider how such an offence is proved, where and when it is tried, who makes the decisions to prosecute, and whether the defendant can afford a representative anyway. I am not suggesting that all aspects of all law can be usefully digested and learned together; there is a case for bite-sized chunks, but if we stick to a food metaphor, there should be a wholesome diet throughout, not just refined foods. Stretching the metaphor, would the following describe the sequence of academic and vocational education with any accuracy?: three years on fish fingers, corn-flakes and white bread; a further year on pavlova, rice pudding and After Eights; then with a stomach that has never tried anything else, troughfuls of unrecognised raw foods with few cooking instructions.

Asking questions not swallowing answers

Much of current legal education sends out the message to students that questions inevitably have answers. Indeed there are such things as right answers. This encourages convergent thinking, where success is measured if everyone ends up thinking the same way. (Then we award first-class degrees to those tiny numbers who, despite our focus on right answers, maintain an independence of spirit and produce answers that go beyond and deeper than what we expected. We still value non-convergent thinking, but do not know how to teach or foster it. The success of the radical thinker comes up again later when we look at learning styles.)

How has this arisen? It is actually quite simple. We assume that we have to teach a syllabus, because of the history of servitude to the professional bodies, and therefore develop the idea that there is a definable amount of knowledge you need. (And through our teaching and assessment strategies we are the gatekeepers to this holy grail.) So we ask questions which can be solved by possession of that knowledge, not questions which fall outside it; we ask questions which are about tort, not land, not crime, because it is a tort tutorial. If we haven't taught it (the teacher-centred model) then you can't know it. We, being experts within our years of experience teaching to a syllabus, ask you questions which we derive from our own knowledge of these areas, and to which we — not wanting to lose control or appear ignorant — already know the answers. (And it is very hard to dream up questions to which we do not know the answer, because we probably don't know till we come across the answer that there was a question. To the lecturer: when was the last time you set a question to which you did not know the possible answers?)

I am not saying that this is how legal education is everywhere, all the time. I do not have the personal experience to say that.[15] But if any of these criticisms ring true at all — you do not have to swallow them in their entirety — I want to ask you if clinical legal education is a promising vehicle to do a better job.

Can a clinical approach do any better?

A quotation I never tire of repeating is one I picked up from Graham Gibbs,[16] who describes education as what is left when the facts are forgotten. What you actually know matters little. How you find, use and assimilate knowledge is important. How what you learn changes you as a person is even more important.

In clinical legal education, as you will already have gathered if you have read the previous chapter, we are used to the criticism that 'What you are doing

---

[15] Perhaps you need to know what my experience is in order to judge. I have at the time of writing lectured for 12 years, including one as a head of a law school. I served as a subject specialist assessor for the Higher Education Funding Council, as well as making monitoring visits to Legal Practice Course institutions for the Law Society. I have trained and worked as a schoolteacher, been a law student and also taken a degree in psychology. None of this gives me empirical data. All of what I say is therefore a combination of impressions, acknowledgment of my own shortcomings as a teacher and manager in legal education, and internalisation of the aspirations and successes of those who have made progress in bringing about change in legal education. Systematic research data about how law is taught are not, to my knowledge, available.

[16] G. Gibbs, *Twenty Terrible Reasons for Lecturing* (Oxford Centre for Staff Development).

is all very well for professional training; but it's not legal education'. Roger Brownsword (remember the steam coming out of the students' ears which I quoted with approval) dismisses clinical legal education as being outside the remit of a law school's 'mission'.[17] For Brownsword the mission is 'scholarship, the pursuit of knowledge, the free circulation of ideas, and the like, all for their own sake'. I agree wholeheartedly. How do we get there, not just for lecturers and a handful of successful students, but every year for every student? This is an age of mass higher education. Students are still exceptionally bright (law schools are typically getting applicants with 'A' levels at or above C grade, a level of attainment apparently beyond the reach of most of the population, including many other university students). But it cannot be assumed that they will by themselves acquire the habits of and disposition to the laudable aims of a good law school mission. Weigh them down with lectures, tutorials and assessments and the enthusiasm they start with may not last anyway. Surrounded by an elite of enquiring scholarly teachers with their excellent research records they are themselves left to plod through the syllabuses I discussed earlier, perhaps catching tantalising glimpses of this higher mission.

A vital point of departure for me and all who have contributed to this book is that life at law school is shared. If the mission of intellectual enquiry does not permeate the learning of every student, we fail. A school of brilliant staff thinkers who throw scraps of enthusiasm towards students, but otherwise just prepare them for predictable knowledge-based assessment is, I suggest, not achieving that mission.

Let's go back to the criticism that all we are doing in the clinic is professional training. Who is making this criticism? Is it those students who have taken part in clinical legal education? Not to my knowledge.[18] Is it coming from the people whose job it is to monitor quality in legal education, the Higher Education Funding Council? Clearly not: in their 1994 report on inspections of law schools they spoke warmly of experiments in this area, and recognised that the clinical component of Northumbria's degree was a vital factor in that law school's rating as 'excellent'.

Is the criticism of a clinical approach coming from the profession? Those practitioners who gain direct experience of clinic tend to say to us: 'If only

---

[17] See note 6.
[18] See chapter 3 for some glimpses of student feedback. See also R. Grimes, 'Reflections on clinical legal education' (1995) 29 Law Teach 169. I make the same point in H. Brayne, 'Law students as practitioners', in J. Webb and C. Maughan (eds), *Teaching Lawyers' Skills* (London: Butterworths, 1996).

we had had it in our day', or 'Just tell your students to do clinical work if they want to get an edge over their colleagues'. The MacCrate report in the US was all about education for the profession. (See chapters 1 and 7 for more about this highly influential report which, amazingly, has had approximately zero impact in this country.) It was eloquent in its praises for clinical method.

It is a criticism coming from within the legal academic community, that same community described by ACLEC as having a reputation for delivering anti-intellectual courses. The criticism is essentially that clinical learning (like skills learning) lacks intellectual rigour. Academic rigour requires students to concentrate on the essence of the subject, which they cannot do if there is a practical context. Here are some statements expressing the criticism of hands-on law in a real life context:

> There is a clear and vital distinction between studying legal processes for the purpose of developing the mind by seeking to understand them, and being trained to operate effectively as a professional lawyer.[19]

> University law schools concern themselves with the study of law not lawyers.[20]

Toddington, a severe critic of the legal skills movement, claims that students have to get a theoretical framework at the start of their learning: 'We cannot avoid a critical conception of law and the legal *ab initio*'.[21] He writes that what the legal professions do (which he denigrates as clerical or managerial activities) is not an important area of study. We say: Why not? Perhaps we should remind ourselves that learning law, or any subject, is not an end in itself. It is a means to an end. Which end? There is the controversy that matters. Starting, as do some critics of clinic, with the presumption that learning law is valuable in itself, and at that a particular type of law with a particular set of legal skills attached, allows them to define everything outside that approach as a heresy. If we are going to pluck ends out of the air, I prefer the end that studying should be enormously enjoyable. And guess what: clinical method fits that end (of course, because I invented it as the aim in order to justify the way I like to teach law).

I do not share the belief that students get a clearer vision of law if they have to see it *without* its human creators at work. Nothing I have read or

---

[19] S. Greer, 'What are law degrees for?' (1994) SPTL Reporter.
[20] A. Bradney, 'Raising the drawbridge: defending university law schools' (1995) 1 Web JCLI.
[21] S. Toddington, *The Emperor's New Skills: The Academy, the Profession and the Idea of Legal Education* (Studies in Law) (University of Hull, 1995).

experienced satisfies me that an avoidance of the practical helps students. A partial picture is less illuminating than a full picture.

I can, however, see the opportunities freedom from vocational needs can create. There could be almost unlimited scope for educational innovation and diversity. I and the academic world of law teachers can probably unite around one thing: the recommendation by the Lord Chancellor's Advisory Committee[22] that the professions should leave the law schools free to design their courses rather than dictating syllabuses that we are only theoretically free to ignore.

There is a historical legacy of subservience to the professions. For years the Law Society and the Council of Legal Education carried on stuffing more and more content into the syllabuses. In fact they are now beginning to relax this approach,[23] and we legal academics could begin to take off the yoke — now more perceived than real — of syllabus coverage. There is room, without offending the Law Society or the Bar, for more critical analysis, study of law in context, and the relationship of theory to legal practice. Room can be created by abandoning our addiction, which we peddle to the students, to legal knowledge.

Happily the Lord Chancellor's Committee recommend doing this, and go further than the professions' relaxation of syllabus coverage. They conclude that a law degree should not be about subject coverage at all. In their aims for a law degree they do not talk of any foundations which are based on subject knowledge. For ACLEC the degree should develop in the student certain personal qualities as well as basic knowledge:

(a)   Intellectual integrity and independence of mind. This requires a high degree of self-motivation, an ability to think critically for oneself beyond conventional attitudes and understanding and to undertake self-directed learning; to be 'reflective', in the sense of being self-aware and self-critical; to be committed to truthfulness, to be open to other viewpoints, to be able to formulate and evaluate alternative possibilities, and to give comprehensible reasons for what one is doing or saying.

(b)   Core knowledge. This means a proper knowledge of the general principles, nature and development of law and of the analytical and conceptual skills required by lawyers.

---

[22] ACLEC, op. cit. (note 2), paras 4.11–4.19.

[23] The joint announcement by the two professional bodies in 1995 makes quite plain that there is 'no attempt to lay down a detailed syllabus. . . . It is not necessary for the foundations to be taught under any particular title or in a single course. Indeed there is value in encouraging students to work across traditional subject boundaries.'

(c) Contextual knowledge. This involves an appreciation of the law's social, economic, political, philosophical, moral and cultural contexts. This appreciation may be acquired in part by the study of legal subjects in a law degree in their relevant contexts, or by taking a non-law or mixed degree which provides these perspectives.

(d) Legal values. This means a commitment to the rule of law, to justice, fairness and high ethical standards, to acquiring and improving professional skills, to representing clients without fear or favour, to promoting equality of opportunity, and to ensuring that adequate legal services are provided to those who cannot afford to pay for them. These values are acquired not only throughout the legal educational process but also over time through social-isation within the legal profession.

It's not, ACLEC guides us, just about getting enough subjects to be able to progress to professional training; nor is it a study of law as if it did not impact on people, and was founded on abstract concepts. It is a proper combination of *how* — the instrumental bit of learning to tackle legal problems and get satisfactory outcomes — and *why* — standing back, with the leisure of being a student in an enquiring community, and saying why is the law operating in this way and not that way? And it is about the personal development of the student, not just what you know but what you are and what you might become. If I allow myself to read between the lines, I suggest that ACLEC implies that the knowledge of law is the means to intellectual and personal development, and that the stated aim of acquiring core knowledge is actually only a means to that end on the degree, while a necessary aim in its own right only for those who will practise law.

If my interpretation is right ACLEC stands the conventional wisdom on its head. You only need to acquire knowledge of law if you intend to practise it. Otherwise your goal is the development (through legal knowledge, of course) of your skills and qualities. Those who advocate skills development can turn to those who favour a knowledge-based approach and say: 'Yes, I suppose knowledge is necessary if you're only interested in the later practice of law'. I look forward to the day.

In any event these statements of what a law degree should be about are highly relevant to the law clinic. Clinical education can and, I think, should play a part in meeting these educational objectives. Why?

(a) It integrates the academic and practical.[24]
(b) It conforms to the way people actually learn best.

---

[24] Which the ACLEC report also recommends.

Learning theory and the clinic

Much of what I say about legal education and learning theory goes over ground that has been well trodden in education. Law lecturers can get an excellent overview in the early chapters of Webb and Maughan's *Teaching Lawyers' Skills*.[25]

Integrating the academic and the practical

Legal educators talk a lot nowadays about the 'swamp'. As jargon goes, this one is easier to grasp than some. Here is an American student at Columbus School of Law[26] taking part in clinical work reporting from the swamp. (I'll explain the concept itself after you've visited the swamp with her for a minute.)

'I know when he gets out . . . he will kill me,' my client stated, as matter-of-factly as if she had just told me the sky was blue. From across the conference room table I could feel her terror under my own skin. Panicked by her fatalism, I quickly tried to steer the conversation to something I thought I could actually fix — making it more difficult for him to find her by strategising a plan for her to relocate. She reluctantly followed my new direction, but I could tell she was unsatisfied with my response. This woman suffered with much more complex problems than I, with just my 24 years of life experience and one and one half years of legal education, was equipped to handle. . . . I realised there was nothing I could do, ultimately, to save her.

This is an account by an American law student. This student is deep in the swamp. This is not a bad thing. It is where she can get some real learning. Compare her experience with a typical problem set for a tutorial in this area of law:

Jane lives with John; John, following an argument, slashes Jane's face with a knife and is arrested. Pending his trial for assault causing actual bodily harm John is released on bail. Jane is worried about him committing further violence against her. Advise Jane.

---

[25] (London: Butterworths, 1996). Chapters 5 and 6 of the collection are about clinical legal education.

[26] J. Howard, 'Learning to "think like a lawyer" through experience' (1995) 2 Clinical Law Review 167.

Jane and John do not inhabit the swamp; the student and teaching staff are on the safe 'high ground' and Jane and John are one-dimensional concepts with whom there is no relationship. Everything is certain and manipulable, probably based on lectures the students have been to, and the student expects that at the end of the class the teacher will provide an answer.

The terminology of swamp and high ground was coined by Professor Donald Schön, who was not a lawyer but an educationalist of influence in professional training circles. What follows is based on his article 'Educating the reflective legal practitioner'.[27] Schön writes:

> Imagine a high cliff overlooking a swamp. On the high cliff you can continue to work on your doctoral thesis. You can run microeconomic models of the economy. You can carry out to the nth decimal place the linear algebra applied to inventory control. You can be rigorous in a way that you can describe very well. The trouble is that you begin to suspect that the problems you are working on are relatively less important. . . . [People] feel acutely that in the swamp below their high cliff there are extremely messy social/technological/economic/political problems that are actually of great importance. But the trouble is that in working on these problems professionals don't know how to be rigorous in any way that they have been trained to recognise. And so they — we — face a dilemma: whether to remain on the high hard ground working in a rigorous describable way on relatively trivial problems or to leap into the swamp and work on the problems we see as critically important, but in ways that don't fit any of the images of rigour that we have learned.

Life is so difficult, so complex, Schön is saying, that educators prefer not to tackle it in its reality and unpredictability in their teaching. According to Schön — and I think it will help for a moment to digress from the swamp into a little academic history — universities were traditionally concerned with 'the pure production of knowledge', that is, knowledge for its own sake and not knowledge for the sake of developing professional or any other skills. There was no room for practical subjects. The only way subjects like medicine, business or law could get alongside Latin or theology was to

---

[27] 2 Clinical Law Review 231. Law teachers are also recommended to read J. Webb, 'Where the action is: developing artistry in legal education' (1995) 2 International Journal of the Legal Profession 187 for an account of Schön's thinking in the context of clinical teaching at the University of the West of England. A readable account taking the debate forward is also given in G. Laser, 'Educating for professional competence in the twenty-first century' (1992) 68 Chi-Kent L Rev 243.

pretend that they were not practical. They therefore focused on doctrine and theory.[28]

But what you learned on the high ground was never enough to equip you for the real world of practice:

> And yet the people who live in the practicum [Schön's word for the world of learning through practical experience] — those who teach the physicians on the wards, for example, or teach the engineers in the labs — often confront a strange predicament, which is that the knowledge that seems relevant to the problems they address is often not the knowledge that is taught in the classroom, although it's supposed to be.

There is a risk here of re-entering the debate about whether degrees are about preparing for practice. Let's leave it that given the existing obedience of law schools to the perceived dictates of the professions, there is a precedent for at least preparing the students for the real world. But even if students do not intend to practise, what are they learning law for? To be able to manipulate legal doctrine? Only those lucky enough to become law teachers can make that into a career. To be able to think, analyse, communicate and critique? If the latter, then they are better off learning to do so in a fashion relevant to the uncertainties of the real world, which is a swamp.

Clinical legal education, in particular real-client work, is by definition unpredictable. The client does not come with a legal problem. There are no facts. What the student finds is a tangled web of issues from which a legal problem may or may not be distilled — in the case cited above it was perhaps a domestic violence problem. Let's consider again the American clinical student in the interview petrified for the personal safety of her client. Here are some of the skills that the student needs to develop:

(a)   Fact management skills.

---

[28] A superb account of the development of the English law degree is contained in Professor Bob Hepple's inaugural lecture to the Faculty of Law, University of Cambridge, May 1996 ('The rebirth of the liberal law degree' [1996] CLJ 470). It is highly readable. He cites Blackstone's inaugural lecture in 1758 at Oxford, in which Blackstone advocated the integration of learning theory and practice: 'A competent knowledge of the laws of that society in which we live is the proper accomplishment of every gentleman and scholar; and highly useful, I had almost said essential, part of liberal and polite education'. Blackstone also thought an understanding of legal principles as well as legal practice essential to the lawyer, otherwise 'the interpretation and enforcement of the laws . . . fall wholly into the hands of obscure and illiterate men'. Despite Blackstone's influence, according to Hepple, academic lawyers embraced legal doctrine and rejected the study of law in its practical context.

(b)   Psychological understanding and counselling skills: how to listen to this distressed client, establish her wishes and empower her with useable information.

(c)   Problem-solving skills: using non-legal as well as legal information, such as whether there is a refuge available, whether she can change the locks, leave the area or call on the services of a relative to protect her.

(d)   Communication skills: explaining in spoken and written words; drafting any necessary documents; advocating for the client with other agencies (the DSS or homeless persons unit, for example) and perhaps the court.

(e)   Legal research skills: not only what is the law in this area or areas (domestic violence? homelessness? social security? property ownership? criminal assault? evidence?) but also what is the procedure for applying it usefully (getting legal aid, calling the police, drafting an originating application and affidavit etc.).

(f)   Work and time management skills: the work may need to be done now, not the night before the assignment is due in; excuses for not getting on with the job will let the team and the client down.

(g)   Teamwork skills: the student cannot 'solve' the problem alone; other students, the client and the supervisor become the team, working as equally respected partners. No one, except perhaps the client, has any superiority of rank in this team or knows the right answer.

(h)   Attitudes of professional responsibility: this client has a need for a real service, not a third-class performance, just enough to pass the assignment. We either do our best or we don't take the case on. And of course all the rules of professional conduct must be obeyed: confidentiality, proper service standards, avoiding conflicts of interest and so on. (How do we reconcile an urgent assignment due in tomorrow, to be handed to a tutor who does not acknowledge the relevance of clinical practice, and a duty to get on with the client's case? What about that night out with the mates?)

(i)   A sense of justice: the student cannot begin to handle the real problem presented without an emotional response. How can people treat each other like this? Why has she nowhere to turn to? Why can't the police just take the man away? Why does she have no money to get housing? What use is an injunction in the face of a violent person? These can be channelled in due course into intellectual outlets of enquiry — studying housing policy, research on domestic violence, the history of the law and recommendations for improvements and so on.

(j)   Wisdom: hardly anyone talks about this as a learning outcome. A brilliant law student may be totally lacking in judgment. Making decisions that actually matter beyond assessment is unnecessary in most law degrees.

Our clinical student needs to mature quite fast, and with it (particularly with the support of a wise role model) can develop rudimentary wisdom. Wisdom comes from experience, including making mistakes and learning from them. The wider and deeper the experience the greater the opportunities to acquire it. It is unlikely that wisdom can ever be inserted from outside; it matures inside. When the student has a problem to solve and the supervisor does not have the answer, the student must and generally does rise to the occasion.

This is holistic study of law. Bits are not parcelled up and labelled 'family law', 'litigation', 'jurisprudence', 'legal practice' or whatever. I am not suggesting that the 'high ground' of legal doctrine and theory is abandoned. But what is so wonderful to observe with clinical students is the illumination of what they have learned on the high ground with the understanding that comes of encountering the same material in the swamp — and indeed finding that it is something of a life-raft (or whatever saves lives in swamps). The satisfaction to student and learner alike of the 'aha' experience — the moment, for example, when a student who had studied tort and contract on the high ground was drafting a pleading and spontaneously blurted out: 'I think I know what a cause of action is'. Yippee!

We did not know beforehand we were going to tackle this problem, or what it would consist of.[29] We cannot predict that today we will learn about causes of action.[30] The problem gives us the motivation and the material for learning about a number of issues. Once we undertake it, we have to tackle the whole of the problem, not just a part of it. 'We' here means the supervisor and the student; the learning is aimed at the student, who must make use of and develop knowledge and skills extending over a wide range of cognitive, emotional and behavioural contexts. Is the legal learning — the precious coverage of syllabus doctrine — impoverished as a result of this holistic experience? I hope what follows will persuade you that that is unlikely to be

---

[29] We could have devised it as a simulation, although simulations — even those that are based on real cases — are structured by the lecturer and are therefore never entirely unpredictable and swamp like. That is not a criticism. It is the student who needs to be in the swamp, and that can be an artificial swamp. The lecturer, who scripted the problem, does not have to be in the swamp at this time. An advantage of live-client work is that the lecturer also spends time in the swamp and is forced to keep learning alongside the student, and like the student is aware of the alligators (such as allegations of making a mess of the case made by the client to the Office for the Supervision of Solicitors).

[30] When I teach a conventional class the best I can predict is that I will talk about causes of action, not that students will learn about them. If they had the opportunity to hear me talk about the subject and still didn't get it, I can blame them for the failure — so I don't have to face up to the fact that I am not teaching effectively. When I teach clinical style I never need to blame the students for not grasping something; they themselves know they need to know it and they use me and other resources until they have succeeded.

the case, given the huge body of experience on the learning process now available to higher education teachers, all pointing one way.

I have to admit that I have no knowledge of research outcomes directly on this point of how much actual legal knowledge the students gain in the process. But I would add: Who cares? For in the end: 'Knowledge does not keep any better than fish'.[31]

Clinical legal education fits the way people learn best

The remaining bit of the chapter is about educational theory. There is so much researched and written in this area that, having started to dig a little, I have reached two conclusions:

   (a)   Along with Webb I am appalled that the legal academic community has shown so little real interest in learning theory up to now.[32]
   (b)   It is time for both research and staff training into how the theory actually relates to the teaching of law.

However, there is little point in wringing our hands and complaining: there's so much to learn that I can't get started. (Or the defensive reaction: there's so much to learn that the only way to cope with it is to dismiss it as a load of social science rubbish.) I have been a law teacher and a clinical proponent for many years. Although I learned all this type of theory when I did my teacher training, I made little sense of it then (there is an important point even in that — good material without practical understanding is as useless to me as to anyone else). I have been teaching law, designing courses and running a clinic, without deep understanding of learning theory. When I came to investigate learning theory for the purpose of writing this chapter I was pleased to discover that it fits what I am doing in clinical work, and humbled to realise how much better I could do my job if I could incorporate the lessons already understood by others into my own work.

From my perspective all the material I have read leads to similar conclusions. Different theorists emphasise different points, but to me the differences matter little. Here is what I have found.

---

[31] A. Whitehead, *The Aims of Education* (1932), quoted in N. Entwistle, *Styles of Learning and Teaching* (David Fulton Publishers, 1988).
[32] J. Webb, 'Why theory matters' in J. Webb and C. Maughan, *Teaching Legal Skills* (London: Butterworth, 1996). Webb notes with concern that in a recent book devoted to legal education there are only two contributions which refer to the work of non-lawyers on how people learn. Would that we were already so wise!

The importance of learning and the unimportance of teaching

Is this you or a student you recognise?

> I play the examination game. The examiners play it, so we play it too.
> . . . The technique involves knowing what's going to be in the exam and
> how it's going to be marked. You can acquire these techniques from sitting
> in a lecturer's class, getting ideas from his point of view, the form of his
> notes, and the books he has written — and this is separate to picking up
> the actual work content.[33]

Your lecturers are keepers of vital information: what's on the syllabus, what
has been taught (and can therefore be examined). You cannot ignore them.
But what about learning? If you take your lecturers as your role model, it
might be interesting to ask where they learned the material they are now
teaching you. Unless they are teaching Roman law you can assume that little
of what is now on the syllabus was taught to them by their tutors. They have
learned it independently for the purpose of teaching you. They did not need
to be taught. Take law practitioners as your role model instead. How many
of those who have found niches in areas like intellectual property or medical
negligence were taught anything of their subject at law school? Very few.
They have learned on the job.

Learning cannot be imposed, or inserted. You are not an empty receptacle.
Learning is a process of making sense of new material in the light of existing
knowledge attitudes and skills. The lecturer's lament: I don't know how they
could have misunderstood my lecture, I told them clearly enough (followed
by hoots of superior derision as an exam howler is read out in the staff
common room), assumes that knowledge is transmitted without any alteration
from teacher to learner. Think of something you do well: play an instrument?
a game? drive a car? make people laugh? juggle? Did anyone tell you how
to do it? Yes, when you were ready to learn, and willing to extract and use
the guidance they gave you. But in none of these situations did your teacher
simply tell you what to do and hey presto you were competent. You worked
at it, using your teacher and other materials as your guide.

'Treating students as co-seekers of knowledge and wisdom and having an
empathic understanding of their problems and potential' is how Beswick and

---

[33] This quote comes from C. Miller and M. Parlett, who are cited in N. Entwistle 'The
teaching-learning process', in J. Richardson et al., *Student Learning Research in Education and
Cognitive Psychology* (Open University Press, 1987).

Ramsden describe the ideal relationship.[34] The same authors write further: 'Above all the structure of the curriculum, the learning methods and the assessment, should be such as to permit students to find personally congenial and even idiosyncratic paths through the subject matter'. Live-client work, and lifelike simulations, bring about entirely different learning situations for each student. While each problem or case study may take the student through comparable experiences, no element is the same as the other student's experience. The student is working at a given moment on his or her own agenda and pace, or that agreed with peers, client and tutor in relation to the problem at hand. Each next step is negotiated with the team.

I can think of a recent example, where I did not know the 'right' answer, and the team had to debate and construct a pathway. The clients had been injured in a fire. Their instructions were that they had no idea of how it was caused. We wanted to find out, in order to explore whether the landlord may have been in breach of a duty. Apart from the obvious need to conduct legal research into what legal duties might exist, we had the problem of the evidence. A particular problem was how to ensure that the evidence, that is, the property in its burnt and unrestored state, remained available for a forensic expert to look at. Here is the dilemma. If we asked the landlord to preserve the property in its burnt state, that was an obvious tip-off to destroy any evidence. If we did not ask him, we were potentially negligent. We didn't yet have legal aid to pay for an immediate expert investigation. So should we do something before legal aid was available to instruct a forensic expert, or should we wait and hope?

There was no point in teaching the team the right answer. I did not know it. (I still don't, for that matter. Except with hindsight we could not know how the landlord would react.) Together we had to find a path through the psychological issues of predicting how our behaviour would affect what the landlord did, and procedural issues of working out what choices in relation to pre-action discovery our professional responsibilities required us to make.[35] We had to cover our own backs and protect the clients' interests. What we learned — yes, clinical work is a learning process for lecturers as

---

[34] D. Beswick and P. Ramsden, *How to Promote Learning with Understanding* (Research Working Paper 87.1), (Centre for the Study of Higher Education, University of Melbourne, 1987).

[35] For those readers not yet familiar with the concept of pre-action discovery or alternatively inspection it is a mechanism for enabling someone to ask for the opportunity to inspect property or documents, in order to decide whether to commence proceedings. If information or inspection is not forthcoming an application can be made for the court to order it — but there is no guarantee of success, and there is a risk of having to pay legal costs to the other side.

much as students — was procedural (orders for the preservation of evidence and legal aid), forensic (how fires are investigated) and legal (the law relating to houses in multiple occupation and landlords' duties). We developed a collective judgment of what was the best course of action in the clients' interest. Whether or not this was 'right' we wrote to the landlord and said please let our experts inspect, and please do not tamper with the property without letting us have advance warning. And, finally, we recognised the limits of our own competence.[36] Having got the case started we collectively decided that we did not have the time and resources to comply with our professional obligations, and referred the case, with the legal aid we had obtained for the client, to private practice.[37]

The students found this problem difficult. But this did not put them off. I too found it difficult. These were part-time students coming in to do their case work in the evening, and absenteeism, normally a genuine problem with part-timers, was virtually nil (and never unexplained). The students were not working for the teacher. They were working for the client and for their own desire to learn. Each, even though working closely and learning with the members of the team in problem-solving and reflection, was creating his or her own 'idiosyncratic pathway through the material'; each equally valid as a learning pathway since no pathway had been predetermined.

I contrast the experience of working alongside this group of students with a description by Wittenberger of why lecturers behave defensively.[38] She describes the way learners get anxious when they are not understanding or identifying with the lecture material or delivery. The teacher picks this anxiety up:

[H]e [the lecturer] becomes the one who feels inadequate, frightened, stupid, helpless, confused, and he in turn may try to escape from this in a number of ways. He may meet fear of his ignorance with a dazzling

---

[36] Perhaps learning that you cannot handle something is one of the most important lessons. A student in the clinic who says 'I don't know' is often better able to learn than one who says 'I can handle that'. (Unless he or she really can.) Contrast this cautious approach to competence with the normal essay where students are expected to know the answers and advise with apparent confidence.

[37] My co-author, Richard Grimes, thinks a case as complex as this was bound to be beyond our capacity. We agree, however, that that was not a reason for not getting it started so long as our service remained as good and as fast as a solicitor in private practice. Is there a tendency in clinical programmes to be reluctant to refer difficult cases?

[38] Isca Saltzburger Wittenberger, *Emotional Aspects of Learning* (unfortunately I cannot say where this piece was published: I obtained it from a photocopy held by the Educational Development Service, University of Northumbria).

display of theoretical knowledge, fear of impotence by exerting power, fear of chaos by a rigid approach to his subject and a rigid control of his pupils, fear of inadequacy and humiliation by claiming superiority and making his students feel small.

I guess you didn't know your lecturers felt insecure like this, although you've suffered in your time from the outcomes. Our fear of our inadequacy as teachers and lawyers may make us bad lecturers, not wanting to take risks. So we take it out on you. This is less likely to happen in clinical work. The relationship between 'teacher' learner and subject matter is more democratic. The teacher is facilitator and has no need to show off. I find as supervisor of clinical work that it positively helps to display as little knowledge as possible (while using it if I happen to have it to guide student enquiries gently and to check the accuracy of their legal research or the desirability of their proposed actions).

Surface and deep learning as an outcome

This is a concept that cannot be overstressed. Let us take two student interviews reported by Gibbs.[39] As it happens they are geography students:

> Interviewer: When you use the word learning in relation to this course, what do you mean?

> Student: Getting enough facts that you can write something relevant in the exam. You've got enough information so you can write an essay on it. What I normally do is learn certain headings. I'll write a question down, about four, five different headings, which in an exam I can go: 'Introduction' and I'll look at the next heading and I know what I've got to write about without really thinking about it. I go to the next heading and regurgitate.

This student is using the same technique I used at university. There is a lot of learning, and an effective strategy for passing exams. But we are looking at 'superficial' learning. Contrast the second quote, a student describing how she reads a text:

> Well, I read it, I read it very slowly, trying to concentrate on what it means, what the actual passage means. Obviously I've read the quotations

---

[39] G. Gibbs, in S. Brown (ed.), *Students at the Centre of Learning* (Standing Conference on Educational Development Paper 66) (1991).

a few times and I've got it in my mind, what they really mean. . . . You mustn't regurgitate what [the teacher] is saying because that's not the object of the exercise.

The student is trying to understand the meaning of the material. This is a 'deep' approach to learning.

Here is how Gibbs, in the same paper, describes the range of learning, starting with superficial learning:

1.   Learning as an exercise in knowledge. The student will often see learning as something done to them by teachers rather than as something they do to, or for, themselves.
2.   Learning as memorising: the student has an active role in memorising, but the information being memorised is not transformed.
3.   Learning as acquiring facts or procedures which are to be used. What you learn is seen to include skills, algorithms, formulae which you apply etc. which you will need in order to do things at a later date, but there is still no transformation of what is learned by the learner.
4.   Learning as making sense. The student makes active attempts to abstract meaning in the process of learning.
5.   Learning as understanding reality. Learning enables you to perceive the world differently. This has been termed 'personally meaningful learning'.

The film *Educating Rita*, if ever you get a chance to see it, is a good display of the student moving through the surface to deep. The student (a mature working-class Liverpudlian) is desperate for knowledge and demands to be 'taught' (level 1). Soon she is quoting literary texts and opinion with skill (level 2). She clamours for the techniques of literary criticism and essay writing (level 3), but towards the end integrates her learning into a picture that is her own view of literature that makes sense for her (level 4). All the time she has been moving towards level 5. Her learning gives her a different view of life. And, incidentally, the film provides a very good example of the role of the teacher. Michael Caine plays the drunken disillusioned lecturer who constructs a learning pathway totally and idiosyncratically concocted for Rita. He is an important resource, and an essential catalyst, but the learning is student-driven.

Using the more familiar world of legal concepts, at level 1 we have the student writing down the teacher's words of wisdom, such as 'Lord Atkin said that you owe a duty of care to your neighbour'. I have, while toying with the ideas of Gibbs, taught my three children (then aged 2, 8 and 10) to repeat these words back to me. They all managed something resembling the correct words. In a sense they now have some knowledge of tort. Level 2 I would not inflict on them, but do expect of my students, that they memorise these kinds of things. At level 3 I would expect my students to know that they must, when drafting particulars of claim in negligence, be able to describe the breach of the duty. They could use precedents and repeat stock phrases ('The defendant was negligent in that she failed to accord precedence to the plaintiff etc.'). At level 4 the students are becoming independent of me. I can tell them about the difference between fault-based liability for injury and no-fault or insurance-based compensation, but they must themselves get to the point of saying 'Aha, that's why *Donoghue* v *Stevenson* was such a landmark case, but I prefer the no-fault system in New Zealand or the presumption of fault in France'. At level 5 the student is changing as a person. This is hard to describe, harder still to assess. It might involve a new outlook on life, a change in political direction, a reordering of personal priorities, an increase in judgment and wisdom, or a confirmation of existing views with an underpinning of new confidence.

You need to learn at all levels. The superficial learning of fact, of information that has not yet been assimilated, can be one of the foundations for the deeper learning. (Strictly, something superficial is not a foundation — but do you get what I am trying to say?) Knowing some law is the basis for forming independent judgments about it. But perhaps each level of learning is a foundation for every other level. Increased judgment makes understanding of new knowledge easier.

If you agree that deep learning is desirable then one of the ways to encourage it is to create opportunities for the student to feel a need to make sense of the world. Learning theorists describe a process sometimes called cognitive dissonance, where fact A jars in some way with fact B. The student, like all humans, preferring order and predictability, senses a need to resolve the discrepancy, to fit the concepts into a sensible relationship. If we are faced with information that doesn't fit into our preconceptions of how the world works we have to work hard to make it fit or adjust our preconceptions. Teachers create dissonance to motivate students. Give them two conflicting judgments and ask them to find common threads.

Clinical experiences have a built-in dissonance. When a new problem, or new information about an existing problem, is brought in, little is predictable, and many elements of the problem do not yet make sense. With simulations it can be engineered for the students to feel this need to make sense of many disparate elements of incoming information. With real clients this goes for me as supervisor as well as the students. We inevitably need to know more to be able to understand the issues and move towards any advice or action. Levels 1 and 2 are simply not available: the knowledge and the answers are simply not on offer. Level 3 is only of marginal temptation: I might want to give the students a formula to apply to the problem, but I would rarely have one available. A checklist for an interview, a precedent for a drafting exercise, could not be applied mechanically because it would not match the needs of the situation. The student has to make sense of the situation by investigation, research, analysis, discussion, testing hypotheses and listening. The learning tends to start at level 4. Change at level 5 is up to the student; but the more experiences he or she has in which his or her sense of reality is tested, the more likely it is that, at some point, personal growth will occur. This may be personal growth in an ethical sense, and as chapter 6 will try to show, that is essential as ethics cannot be 'taught' — it is intrinsically an internal development rather than a conformity to external rules and sanctions.

Different processes of learning: the learning cycle

Just as the outcomes of learning could be described as ranging from surface to deep — knowledge, skills, attitudes — it is helpful to recognise that learning can take place in many ways. The theorists often quote Kolb, who devised a cycle to describe the different ways in which the same learning can be tackled. I have already suggested that simply telling someone a bit of new information is at best surface learning. The essence of Kolb's findings is that 'Learning occurs not in the doing but in the reflection and conceptualisation that takes place during and after the event'.[40] What the student does to that information can make it go deeper. If the student does nothing with it, it is likely to be lost both in meaning and memory. We all know that students should go over their lecture notes afterwards or risk forgetting what little they wrote down. Educationalists encourage teachers to stop lecturing every 20 minutes so that students can discuss the things that have been covered in 'buzz groups'. (See, e.g., D. Bligh, *What's the Use of Lectures?*[41].) This can alleviate boredom and tiredness, but it serves a deeper function. It gets the student on to another part of Kolb's cycle.

Let's first look at the cycle (figure 2.1), and then apply it in law teaching.

---

[40] D. Kolb, *Experiential Learning* (Prentice-Hall, 1984).
[41] Published by D.A. and B. Bligh, 1971.

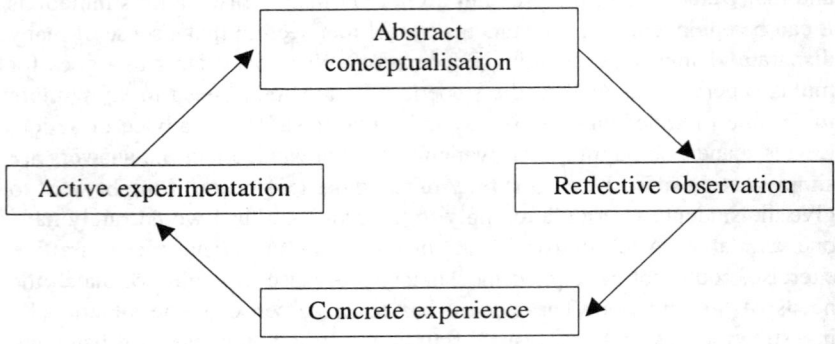

Figure 2.1   Kolb's learning cycle

Figure 2.1 represents a process which goes clockwise. Take the Lord Atkin
concept I tested out on my children. 'Lord Atkin said you owe your
neighbour a duty of care.' Even before repeating this back to me, they
wanted to know what it meant and why I was asking them to do it. I asked
them to repeat it before I would answer their question. The 'concrete
experience' was this new bit of information. It meant nothing much. So they
naturally reflected on it (quarter past on our clock diagram). We then talked
about it — the linking process between the concrete experience and the next
two stages. I did not torture them any further, but let's take how it works
with you the law student. With or without help, you are asking questions like:
What do you mean by neighbour? What is a duty of care? Why do I owe it?
Always? When do I not owe it? As you get answers, partially through
dipping into your own previous knowledge and partially through obtaining
further concrete experience (information from lecturer, colleagues, textbooks) you move to half past and perhaps see the concept. It's all about
situations where people can be held responsible for causing harm that they
ought to have foreseen. A curious student, with or without lecturer stimula-
tion, wants to know, as does my eight-year-old son, does that mean if I leave
my bike out on the street and someone trips over it I have to pay them? The
student experiments with new ideas, but needs concrete information or
experience to be able to obtain the data to feed the ideas. The cycle is never
completed: it goes round and round, within each learning experience, and for
life. And so it should.

Much of the criticism of syllabus-based teaching can now be seen to be its
emphasis on the concrete experience, with too little requirement for the

student to keep going round the loop. Getting your notes and memorising them does not take you very deep. I would like to think of Kolb's cycle as a lifelong corkscrew: keep on going round and round and it takes you deeper and deeper.

In clinical experience it is more likely that the student will be turning the corkscrew quite fast. My student, Lawrence, saw a woman whom I will call Christine. Christine brought Lawrence a range of 'concrete' experiences: information such as 'My husband's parents are trying to get an increase in their share of the farm my husband jointly owns with them'; exposure to Christine's emotions (very upset) and recognition of his own personal reactions to this ('I felt uncomfortable; I didn't know whether to just let her cry or what'). Lawrence, even before seeking guidance, is starting to reflect: What are her rights? Is it important that her name isn't on the title deeds? Does she have any rights as a wife? Is the problem about the relationship with her husband, or the relationship between the husband and the parents? Why isn't the husband here too? And so on. With his colleagues and supervisor we actively assist in the reflection after the interview (and after reviewing the tape of the interview). Sometimes with our help, and sometimes on his own, Lawrence begins to form the concepts that will help him tackle the legal dimensions of this problem: working out what duty he owes to Christine as adviser, what his relationship is to Christine's husband (who has not come to Lawrence for the consultation), what are a wife's rights to ownership and occupation, what questions need answering about the relationships. Does it matter that the property is a farm as well as a house? Are there any children? The experimentation follows as he tests out hypotheses in the law library: class F land charge?[42] Breach of contract? But he needs concrete information, by going back to sources of law and fact? What is the presenting problem? How are relationships with the parents? Who drew up the original agreement?

If Kolb's theory is valid, then this example of a clinical problem suggests that a student cannot avoid going round the cycle. Perhaps students don't know or don't need to know that that is what they are doing.[43] But even students reputed to be weak, and whose academic results so far do not inspire, start turning the screw when they get their teeth into a real case. I

---

[42] A way of protecting the occupation rights of a spouse against sale or mortgage of the property.
[43] I am convinced that the more students are informed about the reasons a course is designed a particular way the better. We are trying out introducing first-year law students to learning theory at Kingston.

think of Bill, who started off so badly that he was hardly ever present at a firm meeting, was getting his coursework in late more often than not, and suffering from a serious and depressive motivation problem. Bill seemed to be the exception to the rule that clinical work motivates automatically. Cases had to be passed to other students because he was letting them drift. Bill eventually met and struck up a mutually respecting relationship with two clients who wanted to run a minicab company. They needed to know if they could form a partnership, would Bill draft it, and would he advise them in relation to taxi licences? So here is the concrete experience. The interview on tape looks concrete, in fact, or even wooden. Bill sits there as information is given to him by the clients. He barely reacts, and I am inclined to judge this a very poor interview. But I am not seeing a complete picture. What I see is not what is going on either in terms of Bill's processing of the information or of his relationship with the clients. Bill comes out of the interview already reflecting on the areas of law involved, the priorities for his clients, whether they need to get their assets valued, where he needs to find information about taxi licensing. And he reflects on these problems, works out the key issues, checks the law, gets more information, and ends up with some excellent problem-solving. The learning is totally student-centred: I cannot teach in this area of law; all I can do is check the process by which he has obtained the information and unravelled the problem. Bill's clients think the world of him, even though he ends up advising them that their plans of running the business legally without a taxi licence are ill-founded.

Perhaps it was a poor interview, judged on its own. Without doubt it was a springboard into further learning, or a way to start into a learning cycle around this area of law.

Learning styles

Not all tasks are the same, and not all students are the same. A variety of learning experiences are more effective than one style. Honey and Mumford,[44] a team of educationalists, have suggested that Kolb's four phases of learning correspond to an extent to individual preferences in learning.

Activists: like new experiences; excitement; a high profile. They like role-play, chairing meetings, brainstorming, but tend to learn less from passive situations like receiving lectures, poring over mounds of data, getting too theoretical.

---

[44] P. Honey and A. Mumford, *Using your Learning Styles* (Peter Honey, 1986).

Reflectors: like having time to work out their ideas and reach decisions; they want to get to the bottom of things. They learn less when pitched in at the deep end or are not given time to complete a task.

Theorists: want to fit everything together and proceed methodically. They perform least well with unresolved ambiguity and, according to the authors, where the situation is emotionally charged.

The pragmatists, finally: like what they are learning to be relevant and like to be given the tools to do the job with. They do not want too much theory.

The fact that we find different preferences and aptitudes in learning, however, is not always a reason to pander to them. The pragmatist needs a bit of theoretical understanding; the activist can learn to reflect. Learning situations that develop all four styles cater to all strengths and address weaknesses. Variety in learning opportunities are important. And here I ask you, if working in real-client clinical programmes, to beware of the danger hinted at when you get to chapter 3. Some clinicians may be attracted to this work — I know I am — because they are pragmatists not theoreticians. There is a risk of solving practical problems and being chuffed at getting a satisfied client, while overlooking the opportunity to develop new concepts or, for example, to recognise the relationship between legal problems and social or ethical issues. I would recommend sharing with students the concepts just discussed so that they can, I hope, begin to recognise their own strengths and weaknesses and preferences, and which parts of the learning programme may benefit them most. Honey and Mumford's booklet offers a simple question-naire test which students can take (and lecturers too) to see if they have a particular style.

Let's stick with learning styles for the moment. It is a common refrain to dismiss students as being to blame for their poor learning performance. 'We just don't get the calibre of students we used to.' That is sad and perhaps the complainant needs a career change. Bligh's research[45] suggests that within the narrow range of intelligence found in the student community such differences as there are in IQ have no relationship to performance. Good performance is more likely to stem, he suggests, from motivation. Moti-vation, he finds, is provided by relevance of subject matter, interaction with others, curiosity, high self-esteem and positive feedback. All these factors can be injected into the learning situation. They are likely to be found in the

---

[45] D. Bligh, *What's the Use of Lectures?* (D. A. and B. Bligh, 1971).

practical context of clinical work. Student feedback at Northumbria University over the years certainly confirms to me that each of the requirements for motivation is met in clinical work.

This is the first time I have mentioned interaction with others as part of the learning theory. It is implicit in much that has gone before, in the need for a variety of activities, the need for discussion with tutor and peers. But it is in itself a motivational factor.[46] There are rewards from interaction with clients (including the reward a role-playing client can give). Bill, who advised the would-be taxi drivers above, needed the impetus of the relationship with the client. There is a close relationship with the tutor (on a more democratic and informal footing than the usual teacher–student power relationship); and there is an opportunity which I would strongly recommend to have students work with each other, not individually, on tasks.

Before leaving the topic of differences in learning styles between students, I would like to relay a finding reported by Entwistle.[47] He did the sensible thing, and tried to find out what he could about the characteristics of those students who do best at university. If we know what approaches lead to the best result, we can either select that kind of student, or teach that way, or both. However, Entwistle's results are not that straightforward. He did not find one type: he found three clusters of characteristics associated with success.

Predictably there is the group who are conscientious, able and motivated — the teacher's ideal. They do well. But in equal numbers there are two other clusters: first, students driven by self-doubt and fear of failure who work long hours and do everything they are told (but do not stray too far from the path). And secondly, students who take a radical approach to the subject and are interested in the aesthetics of the subject — that is, the relationships between its parts, its concepts.

Much of learning theory, it now seems, connects. The student driven by an aesthetic appreciation of the whole subject is likely to take a deep approach to learning. At the other extreme the ones driven by fear to work ever harder are giving themselves a hard time — succeeding on assessments, if what they

---

[46] When I took my Part 2 Law Society course at a polytechnic in 1975 everyone sat in the same place in the lecture theatre for six months and there was no small-group activity. I hated every minute of it. Yes I passed, but I learned little of interest or practical use to me.

[47] N. Entwistle, 'A model of the teaching-learning process', in J. Richardson et al. (eds) *Student Learning: Research in Education and Cognitive Psychology* (Milton Keynes: Open University Press, 1987).

measure is superficial — and are taking a more superficial approach. Perhaps with our obsession with rigorous assessments we are forcing too many students into the neurotic, surface approach to success. Entwistle confirms in the same piece that students spend the most time carrying out the tasks they perceive will be rewarded by assessment. So there is, in the clinical context, little gain in learning to handle a difficult interview or solve a complex legal problem if the task in the assessment is a surface one, such as: 'Write how you would conduct an interview with a client whose baby cries throughout'; or the classic 'Advise John or Janet' problem. Indeed assessment of clinical work should require and reflect deep learning.

Ownership

Perhaps you will agree with the following assertion, that all learning is ultimately learner centred. We have looked at motivation, about making meaning out of your experiences, about playing to your strengths. All of this suggests that you are at the centre of the learning process. You are not a blank slate on to which learning can be inscribed. So we as teachers could usefully spend time trying to get you to identify with the process, to own it. Here are some ways, whether we are talking clinical or not.

Students can set their own objectives, or at least discuss them, at the beginning of the course. That way the students can explore their expectations and measure the extent to which they are being met. This can be helped by a learning journal and a learning contract, as described in chapter 4. Tasks to be carried out can be negotiated. Feedback on a student's own performance can start from that student, and move to his or her peers, before (if ever) the teacher's feedback is called for. Constant reflection on the student's progress and strengths, and ways of addressing perceived weaknesses, allows the student to construct a meaningful personal learning programme. A clinical programme needs to build this in. Seeing clients and tackling problems, even doing so successfully, is only one part of the learning, but students may be tempted to see it as the ultimate goal. It is important to use the huge range of learning opportunities that clinical work throws up by having the students review, in discussion and recorded in writing, how these experiences match their expectations and progress. Lecturers devising programmes are advised to consult their institution's teaching and learning advisers, as this advice is not unique to clinical work.

We are talking about developing self-confidence and the ability to go on learning. This is what ownership of the learning process is about, and once started there is no reason to stop just because the assessment is over or the student has graduated. The following quotes struck me as tying this together:

> It sounds so amazingly obvious, doesn't it? It is hardly worth saying. The final thing I have learned is that life does become more clear and more purposeful when I take responsibility for making up my rules for myself, and give up looking over my shoulder, waiting for someone to come up and clap me on the back and say 'That's right, here's a prize'.[48]

> The ultimate goal of all subject teachers . . . is to produce individuals who are not dependent on others for making judgments about a particular body of knowledge.[49]

It's all about freeing the student to get on with learning without our wisdom and guidance, while, we hope, always remembering the little we were able to do to help. Clinical legal education is the place where I personally feel most able to do this for the student.

Assessment issues

Assessment comes at the end of the chapter. There are many reasons. First, I put it off because it is a difficult topic. Secondly, my experience is that clinical work is more fun than clinical assessment. Thirdly, as a sage has previously said, you do not make pigs fatter simply by weighing them. Assessment matters less to me than learning. However, it does matter to students who want to be rewarded; and it matters to colleagues, who want to see that clinical work is subjected to the same academic processes. And it matters to the outside world, which often wants a quantitative rather than qualitative summary of a person's value to them.

There are perhaps two ways of ducking out of doing a piece of work in academic writing: to say that a topic is beyond the scope of this book or article, or to say that more research is needed. To say that the topic is confusing, painful and that I would prefer to sweep it under the carpet is perhaps more credible, but I will try to give an overview of issues and practice in assessing clinical work.

I have, in this chapter, made derogatory remarks about syllabus-orientated assessments that require repetition of knowledge. I have praised the kind of learning that results in development of personal and intellectual skills.

---

[48] J. Wylde, 'Coming to know: a personal experience in experiential learning', in S. W. Weil and I. McGill (eds), *Making Sense of Experiential Learning* (Open University Press, 1989).
[49] D. Boud, 'Some competing traditions in experiential learning', in S. W. Weil and I. McGill (eds), *Making Sense of Experiential Learning* (Open University Press, 1989).

Professor Jim Stark, then Director of the Civil Rights Clinic at the University of Connecticut, USA, told the conference on clinical methods held at Northumbria University in 1992 that after trying all other alternatives, the most satisfactory method was the one he used. Over the course of working with a student for a year he gave the student a grade at the end which was simply based on his professional judgment.

Of course there are criticisms of this methodology. It lacks rigour, it is not criterion referenced, it cannot be externally validated, and so on. But are these not also valid criticisms of other methods? All assessment which cannot be machine marked relies on judgment. (Even machine marking is only rigorous to the extent that the same answer gets the same mark, but it means the questions asked have to be reduced to right and wrong, which may not always be rigorous or valid.) Markers frequently find themselves in examination boards arguing that a particular candidate's mark does not reflect her true ability. On a good day and with a medical certificate a board may even bump up a borderline classification of a degree to what it thinks the candidate is truly worth. Why? Because, if allowed, we prefer to rely on the rigour of judgment that goes with working with a student over a long period rather than the hit-or-miss result of an examination performance.

An alternative approach is to produce detailed performance criteria and to assess the student's ability to match these. Those familiar with assessment on the Legal Practice Course know about these, and I have argued elsewhere[50] that there is a risk of students performing to a checklist rather than producing a quality holistic piece of work. This may be good enough to assess threshold competence (I have my doubts) but it is certainly not a particularly valuable way of conveying the message of what qualities matter when looking after a client's problems. Students with real clients intuitively avoid this approach to their work, as can be evidenced when comparing videotapes of simulated assessed interviews with real-client assessed interviews.

Judgment is a key component of any assessment. I admit to marking work (of all sorts, as an internal or as an external examiner) according to the predetermined criteria and then realising that the mark is 'wrong' in my opinion. It is possible to hit all the targets and still produce a piece of work lacking in depth, lacking in analysis, lacking in maturity. In such a case I adjust the marks downwards and then find reasons to justify such a mark

---

[50] H. Brayne, 'Assessment on the LPC, a year's experience' (1994) 28 Law Teach 227.

within the criteria. For students reading this in alarm, more often than not I do the reverse and push a mark up because hitting what the marking scheme decided should be the elements of a good performance failed to anticipate how this candidate would deal, intelligently and lucidly, with the task.

Assessment in the clinic is a matter for judgment. A number of questions arise for anyone planning how to assess (and I hope this will also be useful to the student who faces an assessment). We need to consider validity: are we rewarding something that is actually worth achieving? We need to consider, particularly in the context of the clinic, what we want to assess: the skill of performing, or the more complex skills such as analysis, research, reflection and critique. We need to consider reliability: are all candidates given as fair a chance as possible to prove themselves when undertaking comparable challenges? And we need to be aware of the variety of methods which might be used (as well as being able to invent new ones as our experience grows).

Validity

This is where assessment starts. What are the objectives of the clinical programme? Does the assessment actually set out to measure achievement of those objectives? The objectives of the programme with which I am most familiar, at Northumbria, were never clearly formulated until the development of the Exempting Degree. They were then defined in a practical, vocational way. They included the following:

Students will learn to understand and apply law and procedure in a clinical context.

This affords the student an oppportunity, in a practical context:

• to develop and enhance the skills of drafting, negotiating and research;
• to develop and demonstrate skills of interviewing and advocacy in real and simulated contexts;
• to apply in context the essential rules of professional practice for solicitors.

Students will work in groups and develop their skills in working together, and the management of time and resources.

As it happens, five years later, I would not choose these objectives. But given these objectives, I hope it is clear that assessment focusing on demonstration of competence in practical skills relevant to legal practice is appropriate. We did not ask for reflection, enhancement of understanding of legal doctrine or contextual analysis of the law and procedure the problems threw up. We were asking students to be competent, albeit supervised, legal practitioners, and we wanted evidence of competent interviewing, drafting etc.

Assessing vocational skills is not appropriate on non-vocational courses. Therefore the above objectives are not appropriate, and the methods of assessment applied at Northumbria are irrelevant, to academic clinical programmes. Here are some possible objectives relating to more academic outcomes and to more generic rather than vocational skills:

(a) enhancing skills of research, writing, oral communication;

(b) understanding principles of group and interpersonal dynamics, and developing abilities to lead, to work in a team, to conduct meetings, to listen empathically etc;

(c) developing an ability to make and justify ethical judgments;

(d) learning about access to justice, its limits and scope for improvement;

(e) learning about personal responsibility and obligations as a lawyer to clients, potential client groups and the disadvantaged;

(f) learning about the relationship between legal principles and legal procedures;

(g) learning about the relationship of legal doctrine to client expectations and outcomes, identifying weaknesses and scope for reform of procedure and law;

(h) developing an ability to solve problems and to identify strategies for doing so;

(i) exploring the relationships between law and other disciplines, such as philosophy, economics, or psychology.

If some of these are a programme's objectives, there is no point measuring only — or even principally — a student's ability to behave more and more like a competent solicitor. Measuring devices are needed to enable a student to show, through working on real or simulated legal problems, and through building beyond that work, an understanding or a competence that probably cannot be evidenced simply by looking at the work that was done for the client. A programme of activity, and following that of assessment, has to be built over and above the real-life legal work. That programme has to be given equal value, in timetabling for staff and students, and resourcing in terms of library facilities. With hindsight I now realise why in my experience at Northumbria I was always disappointed at the lack of critical evaluation and reflection from the students. (See chapter 3, which was written while I was there, whereas this chapter was written 18 months later.) We gave no time for it and we didn't ask students to prove they had done it. (But I notice that student feedback on the Warwick programme — see chapter 5 — seems to focus as much on vocational skills as on intellectual analysis, and as you will see in that chapter, that programme is far more explicitly non-vocational. It is easy, and perhaps acceptable, to include within the academic objectives and assessments a skill element. If you don't understand and handle the skill, how, in reality, can you comment on it or deconstruct it? Are we, in seeking to avoid measuring pure skills, tilting at windmills? What is wrong with skills plus analysis as explicit objectives? Alternatively, given the predominance in the student perception of vocational skills and objectives, should we stop trying to deny their importance and begin instead to stress their relationship to our other educational objectives?)

How to assess achievement of some of these objectives? I will throw out some suggestions after considering the vexed question of reliability.

Reliability

Student A takes on a live case which goes to a full hearing at the industrial tribunal. The supervisor gets excited and properly provides a great deal of one-to-one supervision. The student becomes very competent very quickly in several target areas, and is thus more capable of performing well on an assessment of vocational skills. She has a wealth of experience from which to develop evidence of achievement in understanding law in context issues, having experienced law in context in some depth. Looking things up in books — whether an employment law encylopaedia, a White Paper on reforming legal aid, or a text on the psychology of interviewing — student A has this experience against which to test and develop the findings. Asked to reflect, whether on the law or on her own performance, she has a firm basis to start from.

Student B's client did not turn up; his second client's problem settled; his third client gave confusing instructions and eventually the clinic and the client had to part company. The course was over. Student B has had less excitement, less one-to-one supervision, and now has less material on which to base an assessment.

Does it follow that student A gets a better mark than student B?

The answer, of course, is that if student A has achieved the objectives for the course to a higher standard, there is no other conclusion possible than to say that student A gets a better mark. So it is not a reliability issue so much as an organisational issue (aiming to introduce students to a comparable diet of experience — easier with simulations than real client work, easier with in-house clinics than placements, and of course easiest of all in a non-clinical environment of second-hand experience and controlled pre-set tasks).

The conclusion I draw at this point is that this is not an assessment issue but a fairness issue. But there is an assessment issue lurking in there too. The evidence of student A's competence may be inseparable from the input that the supervisor has had in that case. Student A must have achieved a high standard of competence in advocacy, pleading, client communication, because the supervisor's own practising certificate is at stake. Student A has done well and had no chance of failing unless — as I have required only a few times — removed from the case to protect the client and the supervisor.

Should the assessment have been of student A's final work, much improved by the supervisor, or the initial work, before supervisor input? The former is a waste of time: why should I assess my own work? The latter is daft — assessing the student before the learning has taken place.

If there is an answer it requires the assessor to be intimately aware of the case the student has worked on, since only the supervisor can disentangle the elements of input; it requires judgment by that supervisor (which can then be defended or justified in a process of moderation); but the real answer is perhaps to limit the weight placed on this work, in recognition that it is probably not performance of the skills of the lawyer that is a primary objective of the course. If the assessment task is to develop insights and competence as a result of the experience, two things follow: first, subject to whatever constraints exist in the clinic about sharing client material with other students, other students can use the experience of student A's tribunal triumph/defeat and reflect on it, the law, the procedure, the advocacy, the role of the parties, the balance of power between the parties, the need for law reform and so on; and secondly, we should not assess even student A on her performance as such. The motivation for performing well is contained not in its effect on assessment but in the excitement and satisfaction of doing the job. I know this because students have always risen to such challenges, long before they were assessed (at Northumbria) for the work. We should ask student A to describe what she did, lessons learnt, skills developed. If we are measuring vocational skills we can then compare this with the evidence. If

we are assessing other outcomes we can create assessment tasks. So let's turn
to method.

Method

It is probably accepted by the majority of clinical teachers that students
should keep some kind of journal during their experience of clinical work,
and that they should submit this frequently for formative assessment, as well
as using it in some way for eventual summative assessment.[51] How it is
assessed depends on what the objectives are, and its use is probably more to
enable the student to retain information on which to build than to provide the
primary evidence of achievement. A journal may be worth a small, but
noticeable (in terms of motivation) percentage of an overall grade. Its quality
in terms of accurately reflecting on what happened and what was learned
from the student's own and from shared experience should be expected to
improve over the course of the programme, and the assessment should reflect
the quality attained at the end.

But building on both the experience of handling client matters (or simulated
tasks) and the experience of meticulously recording this experience in the
journal, the opportunity for assessment is probably in tasks that the non-
clinical lecturer would recognise and perhaps even support. If what we want
to assess is ability to research, a proper research report drawing on a real
problem encountered can be marked and graded as if it was any other piece
of student assessment. If we are assessing understanding, say, of the
socio-legal context of an experience, we can assess the student by setting an
assignment which, instead of starting from a hypothetical problem invented
by the tutor, starts from the problem actually dealt with by the student. It
will still require wide reading, a bibliography, a structured argument, and all
the other things that can be internally and externally scrutinised.

If the objective is oral communication, as well as watching our student in the
tribunal (using, as I noted, material which I helped develop and therefore
which does not truly reflect a student's competence), I can create either
vocational exercises based on real experience (such as preparing and
conducting a cross-examination of the 'witness') or I can ask the student to
present to the class a paper based on, but going further than, the real
experience gained. For example, the talk from student A might be: 'Arguments for extending legal aid to industrial tribunals', in which knowledge of

---

[51] Formative is designed to help the student to learn; summative assessment provides a judgment
about what the student has achieved.

practice and law in the tribunals, readings about economics and law, and experience of conducting a case could all be combined (together with, I would hope in a good performance, material learned from shared work or class discussions on other cases the clinic is handling). The talk from student B might be: 'Access to justice, the difficulties of matching supply and demand', and this might be informed partially by the experience of clients not turning up, or cases settling quickly when taken on and prepared well. If what we are looking for is written communication ability, essays can be set on the same topics. In either situation each student has unique access to materials which can be used to provide a real underpinning to intellectual skills demonstrated in the piece of work.

If group work is an objective, three things can be done: observation by the tutor of the group at work; reflection by the individual on his or her interaction in the group, preferably supplemented by some evidence of reading and understanding a little psychology of group dynamics; and an element of peer evaluation. A fourth element can be evaluation of the quality of the peer evaluation — in other words the ability to evaluate the performance of others and to provide quality feedback (as well as to learn from the performance of others) becomes a skill and an objective in its own right.

We have at various points in this book used concepts of ownership of learning and democracy in management of learning. One of the things that can alienate the student is the lack of control and identification with the process of assessment. Exams may just be nasty things that have to be done, with surprises in the questions part of the rigour of the process. Stress survival is part of the test — as well as the good fortune to be in good health on the crunch day. Unseen exams create an 'us and them' situation. Everything I have said already about reflecting and building on the foundations of working on real-life problems could be carried over to assessment in examination. That would still be an examination, but it would be less stressful, since the student would know that the test would require some kind of building on work done and well understood by that student.

But I wonder at this stage how much scope there is to move forward into more democratic assessment. Having reached the limits of my own experience what now follows is speculative. We know that at Sheffield Hallam it is possible to ask the student to self-assess, and then to negotiate with the student to arrive at a final mark. We know from Northumbria that a student selects from work done those parts he or she wishes to present as evidence for assessment. (See chapter 3.) What we have not yet experienced is actually negotiating an assessment methodology with the student. (Which begs the question: should we be negotiating the objectives of the programme first?) Perhaps, given the close working relationships which develop in clinical work, this is the arena where such experimentation can take place. There is no reason why rigour is at risk, if (as is inevitable) the external examiner has to be satisfied that the assessment is appropriate.

Perhaps I have moved into daydreaming. It is time to conclude the chapter.

A final word

The arrival into the mainstream of law teaching of lawyering skills, of law in context, and all the other ideals of ACLEC which I also espouse may be worrying for reasons not to do with the aims of the programmes or the value of the skills. Lecturers without training or research experience in legal skills are suddenly able to teach students how to deal with situations ranging from a client in deep distress to the sociological and economic issues of the provision of services to the underprivileged. I have seen lecturers pass judgment on student performances of tasks which the lecturers themselves do not know how to conduct and have not even read about.

A little knowledge can be dangerous. The skills movement in law has turned people who have never thought about topics such as legal writing or negotiation, and perhaps never done any of these things in their professional lives, into people who profess to teach it. I have fallen into this trap myself. I was humbled after teaching legal interviewing for nearly 10 years, and even writing on it,[52] to take a one-year counselling course. The whole of this intensive course was about one thing — dealing with people face to face. I learned a little psychology, a little counselling theory, I conducted hours of role-play and even more actual client counselling, all of which was taped and played back by my supervisor.

What did I learn? Why is this relevant? Most of all I realised that as yet I know very little about interviewing. And so? I cannot actually teach interviewing, or much else.

What I like about clinic, especially with real clients, is that I do not have to pretend to teach and to have the key to the knowledge and the skills that

---

[52] H. Brayne and R. Grimes, *Professional Skills for Lawyers* (London: Butterworth, 1994), ch. 4).

students will be judged on. I can only be there to facilitate my students during their own learning. If — the big if — we accept the holistic approach and decide that there is more to learning law than doctrine, then a clinical approach to *learning* law may avoid the potential danger of *teaching* skills as yet another subject to add to the overloaded syllabus.

3

In-house real-client clinics

A reminder of our objectives

In chapter 1 we set out a number of educational objectives for the undergraduate (or indeed postgraduate professional trainee). A student who has really begun to 'think like a lawyer' should have begun:

(a) to understand the context in which law exists;
(b) to reflect critically on legal doctrine and the operation of law in practice;
(c) to understand and apply ethical principles;
(d) to solve problems through factual and legal analysis;
(e) to understand and begin to apply the professional legal skills;
(f) to direct his or her own learning.

This chapter takes the reader on a tour of some actual cases handled in real-client clinics. We examine the various events that occurred in the life of three student-managed cases, and occasionally stray from these three if interesting material can be illustrated by dipping briefly into another case. By examining real cases we try to see whether these objectives were met. We will illustrate our shortcomings as well as, more enjoyably, slapping ourselves and our students on the back.

Why might the objectives not be met?

Ambitious objectives are harder to meet than tame ones.[1] We cannot meet all the objectives all of the time. But even allowing for setting high targets, we need to be aware that our own enthusiasm for clinical work can get in the way. We, and our students, are keen to get on with cases. We enjoy being lawyers. We are running a real legal office, and as such we are servants to the imperatives of case handling, such as deadlines, and client demand. Sometimes managing our caseload shifts from being the means and becomes an end in itself. While all experience by students of well-managed, closely supervised, legal practice is, probably, of educational benefit, we can forget — or not yet know how — to take overt and planned steps to extract the full range of learning that is potentially available to the student in each real-client case. Students are strongly motivated to get on with real legal practice. Riding this energy is fun. Slowing the students down and counselling patience, while we stand back and unpick other issues, can seem like being a spoilsport. And slowing down is often impossible where professional standards of work require prompt action.

So you may wish to challenge us as you read this chapter: You are having fun, gaining experience, but what are you doing, what are the students getting, that they cannot get elsewhere on the degree or in later life?

What we maintain is the answer to these questions is that the clinical experience is a more powerful and motivating learning strategy. In particular:

    (a)   we are linking understanding of legal doctrine with practice and ethics;

---

[1] It is of course easier to meet objectives that are not ambitious, such as 'knowing a lot about the law of tort and solving hypothetical problems'. Teaching to such objectives is a bit like the old practice of coaching schoolchildren to pass the 11-plus, or more recently, distorting a year's education to take SATs (centrally-designed Standard Assessment Tasks) in schools. If a clinical programme fails to meet its objectives every time, should objectives be revised to match the activity, or the programme altered? In any event, all the law schools do not meet all their objectives all of the time. When the Higher Education Funding Council inspected law schools in 1993 and 94, it reported: '[E]xcellent courses were those whose objectives were clearly defined, were understood and accepted by all staff . . . and could be achieved. In nearly all cases, curricula were clearly defined and appropriate to stated objectives. However, where this was not so was usually because there was no agreement about the overall aims or because of a lack of clarity about the relationship between academic and practical/vocational matters within the curriculum. . . . [S]kills training was not always geared closely enough to the educational and practical needs of the students, leading to disenchantment and missed learning opportunities.' *Quality Assessment of Law 1993–94* (Higher Education Funding Council Report QO 1/94). The need is to avoid complacency and keep reminding ourselves that we don't just 'do' clinical legal education, we do it for a reason.

   (b)   we are taking time to handle cases properly and look things up;
   (c)   students are experiencing both teamwork and self-reliance;
   (d)   for those who may become lawyers, we are teaching good practice
while students are not under fee-earning pressure;
   (e)   students are enjoying and stretching themselves, learning about real
responsibility, and meeting real challenges;
   (f)   we are attempting to integrate the clinic into the wider curriculum.

In-house solicitor clinics[2]

You may be helped by knowing a little about the concept of the university
solicitor clinic. We have chosen two universities which, until recently, were
the only two places using this model[3] (and because we have been heavily
involved in running them).

The University of Northumbria at Newcastle has had a clinical advice
programme for 15 years. The fully fledged Student Law Office was launched
in 1991, taking advantage of a relaxation in the parts of the Solicitors' Practice
Rules restricting what employed solicitors could do. It can now offer a full
range of solicitor services. The in-house clinic at Sheffield Hallam followed
on in 1992. At Northumbria the clinical work is now part of the four-year
exempting programme, which enables a student to cover all elements of the
Legal Practice Course and the Bar Vocational Course while also obtaining the
LLB degree. The clinical work is therefore intended to address both academic
learning and legal practice skills. At Sheffield Hallam University the degree is
a three-year degree, with the clinical experience geared therefore to undergraduate academic objectives. Despite these apparent differences, both
universities have worked closely together in running their programmes,
cooperating at many levels — sharing of teaching and assessment materials,
participating in each other's induction courses and advisory panel meetings,
and holding meetings of staff and, occasionally, students. A detailed history of
the Northumbria programme, and an account of the clinical methodology at
Sheffield Hallam, is set out in chs 6 and 7 of *Teaching Lawyers' Skills.*[4]

There are, of course, other ways of running a real-client clinical programme.
The absence of a practising solicitor is not a bar to clinical work — see

---

[2] The section describing the student law office at the University of Northumbria was written
when Hugh Brayne was at that university. It does not purport to describe recent developments.
[3] The University of Kent at Canterbury now also has a clinical programme run by in-house
solicitors. We do not know of any others at present. Kingston Law School is starting a small
solicitor-run scheme around the date of publication.
[4] J. Webb and C. Maughan (eds) (London: Butterworth, 1996).

chapters 4 and 5, for example. Much of what we do could equally successfully be carried out in an in-house non-solicitor clinic, so this chapter is of relevance even if you haven't got a willing solicitor to run your clinic. There are actually very few monopolies in terms of legal work:[5] anyone can give advice of a legal nature. If you do not go on the court record or represent clients in open court, and do not draft conveyancing documents or apply for probate, the rest of the work can be done by law students and lecturers. Agencies such as many Citizens' Advice Bureaux have worked happily without solicitors for years. At the University of Plymouth, for example, students take part in extensive tribunal representation work, and have taken a lead in cases involving sex discrimination in the armed forces. There is no suggestion that solicitor clinics offer a superior experience: however, we have chosen the solicitor route because it suits our own and our universities' needs. We are both solicitors: why not?

Whether or not you have solicitors, you can be sued if your advice is negligent, so generous insurance cover is recommended before any advice is ever given to anyone.[6] Students have been known to set up their own advice sessions without staff involvement.[7] Not only can this affect the reputation of the law school if things go wrong, it is very risky if there is no insurance. We also doubt whether an unsupervised trial-and-error learning experience is effective.

By running a solicitor clinic we subject ourselves to Law Society supervision. We must buy expensive practising certificates, abide by the rules of professional conduct (see further chapter 4), and be prepared, if the worst should happen, to appear before the Solicitors' Complaints Bureau. Why have we submitted voluntarily to this bureaucratic, expensive and time-consuming burden? Many universities run excellent programmes without using solicitors as supervisors.

Here are some of the advantages, as we see them:

(a)   Academic staff are continuing to experience law in the real world.

---

[5] Under the Solicitors Act 1974 as amended by the Courts and Legal Services Act 1990, and the Legal Aid Act 1988, the monopolies enjoyed by solicitors with practising certificates include: appearing on the court record (but anyone can advise a litigant in person); representing in open court (but again advising the litigant and appearing in tribunals and small claims is possible); instructing counsel; obtaining legal aid and recovering legal costs in successful cases; conveyancing (a monopoly shared with licensed conveyancers) and obtaining probate.
[6] This is not necessarily a big obstacle: at Northumbria, Sheffield Hallam and Kingston the universities' insurers agreed to cover staff and students for negligent advice without any increase in the premium. So far no claims have occurred.
[7] I have even seen it run without staff knowledge at an institution which I will not name.

(b) We expose students to real legal practice — applying for legal aid;[8] costing files; going on the record;[9] instructing counsel;[10] and submitting to the Law Society's code of conduct.[11]

(c) We can, if to do so has educational value, take cases to their conclusion, even where a right of audience is required (although this means staff or — subject to resources, such as legal aid — counsel, not students, representing in open court[12]).

(d) Clients perceive that the work is supervised by solicitors,[13] and may have greater confidence in using the service.

(e) Student confidence is increased in the same way.

(f) Clients on legal aid can be somewhat protected from adverse costs orders,[14] and can use legal aid to pay for things like expert opinions.

(g) Sticking to professional standards keeps us all on our toes.

(h) Many of our students want to be solicitors themselves[15] and are learning relevant information and skills.

Clinical programmes in other jurisdictions (the USA, Australia and South Africa, for example) all tend to use qualified staff.

Three clinical case studies

Three cases studies are selected, out of the more than 1,000 cases dealt with in our universities' clinical histories. Each brings different learning experiences to the students and staff involved. Occasionally we stray into material

---

[8] The Legal Aid Act 1988 does not specify that work must be done by solicitors. However, Regulations under the Act require this, such as the Civil Legal Aid (General) Regulations, reg. 12. Regulation 65 permits delegation: 'Nothing in paragraph (1) [which prevents solicitors passing work to non-solicitors] shall prevent a solicitor from entrusting the conduct of any part of the case to . . . a competent and responsible representative of his employed in his office or otherwise under his immediate supervision'.

[9] Solicitors Act 1974, s. 20.

[10] Code of Conduct of the Bar of England and Wales, para. 210(a).

[11] All solicitors are bound by the Solicitors' Practice Rules 1990.

[12] See *Nicol* v *DPP* (1995) *The Times*, 22 November, [1996] Crim LR 318, an appeal by way of case stated against imprisonment following a refusal to accept a bindover — the Student Law Office's first reported case. The decision clarified the law but declared the bindover to be legal, and will be appealed by the Student Law Office to the European Court of Human Rights. See also P. Plowden and K. Kerrigan, 'Who benefits? Case management and clinical legal education' (1996) 30 Law Teach 315.

[13] But of course we have to guard against clients trying to bypass the student adviser and go straight to the solicitor. This is a reason for supervisors minimising personal contact with the client.

[14] Legal Aid Act 1988, s. 17.

[15] This is particularly relevant for students on the University of Northumbria's four-year exempting degree. This combines the academic and vocational stages of legal education, so that graduates can enter training contracts without going through a separate Legal Practice Course.

from other cases, to plug gaps or illustrate additional points of interest. To protect confidentiality client names are changed. Student names are also changed. Facts and documents are otherwise unaltered.

(a) The cycling accident. The case is simple in terms of the law and procedure, but it provided a good range of learning opportunities for two inexperienced students. We use it to illustrate learning opportunities particularly relating to professional conduct, litigation and the workings of a legal office.

(b) The breach of contract. This case illustrates professional practice issues, the ways in which what students know about law (or need to find out) can and must be used in conducting a client's case, and the excitement of working together on a case.

(c) Drafting a will. This case shows that important issues arise in a non-contentious case (one that is not defined by a dispute). Legal skills need to be exercised, including research and drafting. Once again the professional and ethical context of legal practice is opened to examination.

The injured cyclist

This case is from the University of Northumbria at Newcastle. We call the client Tony Wheeler.

It started in November, and was first handled by a student we call Derek. The following summer a student we call Carol took over, and took the case to its conclusion a year later (18 months after first instructions).

This is how the file ends:

Dear Hugh

Just a note to thank you and all the staff[16] at the Law Office for your incredible amount of patience involved in settling my case. I am exceptionally pleased that I followed your advice by pushing on to court. Carol performed admirably in the face of an awkward and determined opponent. I am also going to write to the county court to express my displeasure in their incompetence. Thanks again for all your help.

Yours sincerely

Anthony Wheeler

---

[16] Presumably Mr Wheeler was not so much ignoring the student input as according them staff status — an oblique but meaningful way to heap praise on them.

Carol had faced counsel in the small claims court. Counsel had been instructed by some very determined solicitors acting for an insurance company. And she won convincingly.

Here is Carol's own account from her end-of-year self-evaluation (leaving out extracts not related to this case). The full detail is reproduced because her perception as a student raises important issues which we hope arise from clinical practice. Hearing it from a student is perhaps more convincing than hearing it from us:

> At the beginning of the year I was assigned a personal injury case which had been ongoing for almost one year. Had I realised at that time I would be required to prepare for and conduct an arbitration hearing I may have thought twice about taking the case on due to my inexperience and lack of self-confidence. I am very grateful now that I did take the case as I have learned a great deal from the experience.
>
> The practical skills I have learned from my experience in the Law Office are vast. I began my year with no experience of practical legal work. . . . One of the first skills I acquired was the ability to write formal letters to a variety of people such as the defendant's solicitor and the court. This was not an easy task as first my supervisor required perfection before a letter was sent and the defendant's solicitors were not at all receptive to the idea of the Student Law Office. I felt pressured not to let the Office down with inadequate letters which would give the defendant's solicitors the opportunity to criticise.
>
> One of the most important skills I learned is that of legal research. Every question which became apparent during the case needed an answer and finding the correct answer was never an easy task. At first I was required to investigate components of a personal injury case. This was quite straightforward even though the tort of negligence remained a mystery to me until [halfway through the case]. The more specialised the research the more difficult it was to find the answer. Questions about the conduct of the arbitration, the detailed rules of a payment into court and the subject of quantum, interest and taxation all had to be addressed. With little help from my supervisor in the beginning I found it almost impossible to find the answer. As time progressed and with some hints my skills of legal research began to develop until I could even understand and use the Green and White Books[17] with a degree of competence.

---

[17] These are the practitioner reference books for county and High Court practice. The fact that a second-year student has heard of these books, let alone feels comfortable using them, is a good indicator of learning how the law really works.

Communication with my client was also good. Interviews were relaxed and friendly although my legal advice was always taken seriously and questions were always asked. Preparation for the interviews was necessary as the client had to be informed about various aspects of law including the benefits and negatives of a payment into court and a decision had to be made.

Throughout my experience I found myself applying the law in theory to the law in practice. I feel that through the practical experience of negligence the theory has become somewhat easier. My practical experience has also related to the theory of litigation. The preliminary investigation of a case, the documents necessary to begin an action and the preparation and conduct of the hearing were all aspects of the litigation course and were all practically carried out by myself.

The most rewarding experience of the Student Law Office was the arbitration hearing. The preparation for the hearing involved a lot of work.[18] Our firm met as a group to discuss the facts of the case and the questions that would have to be asked to extract the facts and the evidence. I was left to myself to write a series of questions to put to my client, the witness and the defendant.

Before the hearing I did not really know what to expect. We had a mock hearing a week before which was very useful and many adjustments were made to the presentation and content of the case. By the day of the hearing I felt fully prepared, which gave me confidence. I somehow managed to control my nerves and presented the best case I could on behalf of my client. I was reassured by the fact that my supervisor was at hand and was grateful that he communicated points to me that I had to pick up on during the course of the hearing. I was also relaxed by the informal nature of the hearing and the attitude of the judge to myself as a student was very helpful.

Judgment was given in our favour without myself having to give a closing argument,[19] which confused me at the time. A number of times during the hearing I felt rather like an amateur and out of my depth but these occasions were only brief as all my concentration was on the case and the events going on.

---

[18] This is a perceptive comment. Advocacy is the excitement, but Carol recognises that it is built on a foundation of preparation.
[19] Nevertheless the preparation of a closing argument was a valuable and necessary part of the case planning — see below.

The satisfaction I felt after winning the case and compensation for my client made all the worry and apprehension worthwhile. I learned a great deal from conducting the hearing including how to examine and cross-examine witnesses, how to take relevant notes and how to question on points raised that were not prepared for. By the end of the hearing I understood why it was impossible to totally prepare for any eventuality and that every lawyer must be able to think on their feet in some situations.

In conclusion I feel very lucky and proud that I successfully represented my first client and had the opportunity of developing my own skills. The Law Office was in general a very good experience and I feel the practical experience I have gained is invaluable. The Law Office did involve a lot of work and at times I felt it was necessary to spend less time and effort on my own work; however, the experience gained has undoubtedly contributed to my degree as a whole.

The student's own perceptions of what she learned and developed are extremely important. How many lecturers think they have taught a topic clearly but find the student still confused, or worse, blissfully ignorant of his or her misunderstandings? Carol's learning was put to the test and we have every reason to believe this self-appraisal. Here is a summary of Carol's learning:

    (a)   pride in outcome;
    (b)   getting a sense of what lawyers are for;
    (c)   enhanced self-confidence;
    (d)   writing;
    (e)   legal research;
    (f)   understanding of the law of negligence;
    (g)   working in a team;
    (h)   interviewing and advising;
    (i)   conducting litigation, including a hearing;
    (j)   relating theory to practice;
    (k)   thinking under pressure;
    (l)   prioritising work;
    (m) sense of being a professional.

So let's take a look at the case itself and examine some of the history and some of the learning opportunities. The office procedures described are those we use, currently, at Northumbria. During this first case study, 'I' refers to Hugh Brayne.

The headings for the discussion which follows are designed to collect together issues that arose during the life of the case, in the order in which they arose. Because a real case is not like a syllabus, the headings do not exactly match the learning objectives set out at the beginning of the chapter.

Taking instructions: professional issues

Interviews are conducted by the student(s) without the presence of a supervisor.[20] Generally this is in pairs — two learning opportunities for the price of one, as well as mutual support and reduced likelihood of anything nasty developing. The students are doing the work, yet I, the solicitor, not the student, put my head on the metaphorical block. My name, with the word 'solicitor', appears on every letter in any case I supervise, together with the name of the student(s).[21] This imposes on me personally a professional duty to the client to attain a 'proper standard of work'.[22] How does this responsibility square with students taking responsibility for a case, and being seen by the client to do so. Can I allow learning from mistakes, when that mistake may cost me a practising certificate?[23] The Law School insists students go over this possible conflict of priorities with clients before any retainer is established.[24] We try to make it clear that our priority is to educate the student, and that if a case does not lend itself to that educational process, then we are unable to assist the client. We explain both in the first meeting and in the leaflet which the client receives and, if happy, signs, that this may mean having to drop a case without completing it.[25]

---

[20] I used to sit in on interviews, but gradually came to realise that this put the client and the student into a difficult and embarrassing position. The client would not know what to make of my presence if I kept my mouth shut. If I spoke, more often than not the client would then address me not the student. I can supervise equally well, at far less personal cost, by being available for consultation during the interview, hence a protocol for students to consult their supervisor before the client leaves, so that any gaps and misunderstandings can be looked at.

[21] The notepaper has a space at the top for names. 'The solicitor handling this case is . . . and the student handling the case is . . .'.

[22] Solicitors' Practice Rules 1990, r. 1. See also the Law Society's *Guide to the Professional Conduct of Solicitors*, ch. 3, which states at 3.01 'A solicitor is responsible for exercising proper supervision over both admitted [i.e., qualified] and unadmitted staff'.

[23] Instructions should be declined where 'the solicitor is not competent to act, for example because he lacks expertise in the area of the client's instructions' (*Cordery on Solicitors*, 9th ed. (London: Butterworths, 1995) at E253). Therefore a solicitor cannot leave the case to the student in its entirety, and the standard of work must, eventually, be that of the solicitor and not the student.

[24] A retainer is the contractual relationship between the solicitor and the client. The duties of the solicitor are expressed in the contract and implied by the rules of professional conduct. A retainer implies duties on the solicitor as soon as it is established. For full details see *Cordery on Solicitors* (note 23) sect. E and F.

[25] A copy of the leaflet we are using at Kingston University is available if you send a stamped addressed envelope to Lance Robson at Kingston Law School, Kingston Hill, Kingston upon Thames KT2 7LB.

The first question after the initial interview, therefore, is whether to take on the case at all and, if so, how far to offer to go. While I, as supervisor, may have a fairly clear idea of the answer, the matter has to be debated by the student and his or her colleagues. The debate is minuted in the firm's weekly minute book.[26] The team has to look at professional practice issues such as:

(a)   Is there a conflict of interest with any existing client? Students must meticulously check the names of client and proposed opponent against the card index of former clients and opponents; they can at the same time be introduced to the professional conduct rules that explain conflict of interest issues.[27]

(b)   Is the case within our capacity? This question again raises the opportunity to address the rules of professional conduct.[28] Do we, as a team, have the time to do justice to the case? Do we have access to expertise from colleagues and time and facilities for research if the supervisor is in unfamiliar territory?

(c)   Does the student believe that the case is one which will interest him or her? Rarely do students decline work, and rarely does a case bore them once started, but in my experience it is good to probe their real interest in the potential subject matter of the case as early as possible, as interest in the subject matter may enhance learning. (This does not mean that a student must have studied the relevant area of law already — see case study three for an example of the interest generated by moving into trusts and property through a real case rather than a lecture.)

(d)   How long is the case likely to last? Is this the right time of year for the student to take on a big case? (The answer may be yes, of course, even if this year's student can only do a small proportion of the work. But ideally students should have a chance to understand the whole life history of a case.)

(e)   Is there any personal prejudice for or against this client or the opponent? For example, we have debated whether to act for a landlord attempting to evict a tenant. On educational grounds we went ahead. Is this

---

[26] At the time this case was taken on the firm's meetings were not minuted, and we merely reviewed the progress of each case one by one. Therefore the minutes of the discussion cannot be reproduced.

[27] Such issues actually arise very rarely. Once one of our students spotted in the early stages of the interview that she was related to the client's landlord, and immediately withdrew for a consultation with the supervisor. We do not take cases against staff or students of our university. A student adviser may well ask (and if not can be prompted to ask), Why not?, creating further opportunities for discussion.

[28] 'A solicitor must not act or continue to act in circumstances where the client cannot be represented with competence or diligence' (*Guide to the Professional Conduct of Solicitors* at 12.02).

the right allocation of resources for a service that is publicly funded? Are we obliged to help the weaker party? If we sue a solicitor for negligence, will the local profession see us as 'anti'? In Mr Wheeler's case I must declare my own interest: I am a cyclist and have spent a lot of time campaigning to improve the lot of cyclists. Therefore I am not neutral in the case. I can therefore discuss with the students whether my (or their) commitment would be equal (or should be equal) if acting for the motorist.[29] To what extent should or even can a lawyer be detached? This can lead to discussions on wider ethics, such as the question of acting for people the lawyer finds distasteful, such as an alleged child abuser.

(f)   What service can be offered to the client, and do the students and client understand the possible limitations of what a lawyer can do for the client?

Taking instructions: professional skills issues

If clients consent — and they almost always do — initial interviews are video recorded. Students are encouraged to review their videos in the light of criteria provided.[30] However, when this case started we were not doing this. I have therefore picked another student's review of his interview to illustrate the process. The example chosen is of a high-quality self-evaluation. Few students make the time available to reflect adequately on their performance.[31] They appear to be too keen to get on with the next task. Getting students to mark their own interviews — self-assessment — would increase motivation, although it is not the summative mark that matters, so much as the reflection and learning. Students cannot learn to do this on their own, but the amount of staff input required is enormous, even to teach each student how to critique without staff assistance. Doing this properly would

---

[29] Experience shows that it is hard to select cases on grounds of merit, whether that merit is based on increasing access to law or perceived educational value. Students generally want to take on work and become very attached to their clients and the cause, whatever the merits. This raises a very large question about whether we should be schooling the students in detachment (quelling this eagerness) or revelling in their unbridled enthusiasm (and accepting any disappointments that may then follow).

[30] These criteria were developed by Tessa Green and Hugh Brayne, initially on behalf of the Council for National Academic Awards. See T. Green and H. Brayne, 'Lawyering skills in a clinical context' in P. Jones (ed.), *Competences, Learning Outcomes and Legal Education* (Institute of Advanced Legal Studies, 1994). The criteria are discussed fully in H. Brayne and R. Grimes, *Professional Skills for Lawyers* (London: Butterworth, 1994).

[31] Perhaps because the technique is underdeveloped. We supervisors do not ourselves necessarily practise and examine our skills in the way we expect students to be able to do. I have taken to recording myself two or three times a year and critiquing my own performance to see if this will help me get students to do it.

be a course in itself,[32] and that is a question of deciding whether it is a priority in legal education, compared, say, to learning a new area of law.

Extract from a student's interview self-assessment[33]   This is quoted at length as a way of showing how a student's reflections on outcomes can be linked to the learning objectives, in this case those relating to the skill of interviewing.

ATTITUDE TO CLIENT

How well did I:

(a)   Introduce myself to the client?
I introduced myself and interviewing partner clearly and slowly on meeting the client. When [the supervising solicitor] entered the interview room I introduced her as my supervisor. On reflection, I should have possibly introduced her as my supervising solicitor to define her role and status properly.

(b)   Make the client feel at ease?
I did not begin by immediately asking the client the reason for her coming to the Student Law Office. A few minutes was spent asking the client whether she had problems finding the Student Law Office; whether she had problems parking etc. By using 'small talk' I believe that the client was reasonably at ease and comfortable by the time of the substantive stage of the interview. However, a problem of interviewing in the [particular room] is that there are no coat racks. Offering to take the client's coat to put them at ease is a relatively empty gesture when all that can be done is to fold it over the back of the chair, especially when there is not a spare chair.[34]

---

[32] At Northumbria we allocate a small number of marks to a student's end-of-year account of his or her performance. We have yet to clarify if we are rewarding good writing, good lawyering, or good self-awareness. My own view is that a greater reward for self-awareness, including negotiating with a student a part of his or her own grade, would pay long-term dividends for each student. It would increase self-awareness and understanding. It would make assessment more transparently geared to learning rather than labelling. But even if my view prevailed, I doubt that without extensive training lecturers, myself included, actually know how to teach the art of self-critiquing. Lecturers, like anyone else, find it easier to critique other people than themselves.

[33] The self-assessment shown here is an extract only, to give a flavour of what this student learned from reviewing his own performance. Where material is omitted, the subject heading has nevertheless been retained to give you some idea of the matters covered.

[34] Inexperienced students can become fixated on ice-breaking formalities. In role-play the danger is particularly acute, and I have seen students working through the checklists of weather, did you find us all right, parking etc. In real-life interviews students seem to be less clumsy and more aware of using a variety of ways of building rapport and breaking the ice.

(c)   Listen attentively?

My interviewing partner was given the task of recording the facts given by the client. This enabled me to listen without the distraction of taking notes. However, I did take down key points as a reminder and to help me concentrate on what the client was saying.

While I did listen and concentrate on what the client was saying, I do have a problem with sitting still. I tend to rock backward and forward while I am listening (and when I am talking) which may be distracting for a client. This is a problem that I am aware of and which I constantly attempt to rectify.

Questions such as 'And what happened next?' were asked to reassure the client that I was listening. Passive listening such as nodding was also evident throughout the interview.

(d)   Notice any problems of understanding?

While the client did not acknowledge that she had any problems with understanding anything I said, there were many occasions in which I was unsure whether or not the client did in fact understand. In such instances I reiterated the point to attempt to clarify the position and asked whether she had any queries. An example of such a situation involved an explanation of how the Student Law Office worked in relation to legal aid. This is not surprising considering some students also have the same problem. However, I did not try to overemphasise the point when I discovered that the client was above the eligibility level in any event.

(e)   Give the opportunity to ask questions?

[Response omitted.]

(f)   Explain clearly?

[Response omitted.]

(g)   Allow client to make decisions?

[Response omitted.]

EVIDENCE OF PREPARATION

How well did I:

(a)   Demonstrate that I had prepared a structured interview?

[Response omitted.]

(b)   Understand any documents produced?

[Response omitted.]

(c)   Show familiarity with law and procedure?

[Response omitted.]

OBTAINING INFORMATION

How well did I:

(a)   Allow client to explain problems in own way?
At first the client was allowed to express herself and explain in her own words the nature of her reasons for coming to the Student Law Office. However, the client was not coherent in giving the facts. She did not start from the beginning as asked and did not give the facts in chronological order; she jumped from month to month without any structure to her explanation. The client had to be stopped on more than one occasion to ask her to explain in chronological order and had to be guided and prevented from jumping from different points when explaining the facts.

(b)   Ask questions at the appropriate time which were:

(i)   Open? Open questions were asked at the appropriate time such as 'And what happened next?' and 'When did that happen?'[35]

(ii)   Focused? Focused questions such as 'What was the date on which that happened?' were asked.

(c)   Accurately obtain available details of:

(i)   The factual situation? [Response omitted.]

(ii)   The client's main concerns and wishes? [Response omitted.]

(d)   Obtain or ask for relevant documents?
[Response omitted.]

(e)   Identify where further information was needed and how to obtain it?
[Response omitted.]

(f)   Use time effectively?
[Response omitted.]

IMPARTING INFORMATION

How well did I:

(a)   Explain legal terms and procedures (where necessary)?
[Response omitted.]

---

[35] The student still has something to learn here as the second example of an open question is rather closed! It is still a proper question to ask the client. What matters is that the student is analysing his own performance.

(b)   Avoid giving premature advice?
[Response omitted.]
(c)   Explain next steps to be taken by solicitor and client?
[Response omitted.]

DOCUMENTING THE INTERVIEW

How well did I:

(a)   Summarise factual issues?
[Response omitted.]
(b)   Identify legal issues?
[Response omitted.]
(c)   Summarise accurately advice given and instructions received?
[Response omitted.]
(d)   Clearly identify next step for adviser and client (including dates)?
[Response omitted.]

The analysis shows reflection on strengths and weaknesses by a conscientious student. Opportunities for further learning are clearly presented. We could, in a tutorial or small group, explore in greater depth some of the student's statements. For example, I would challenge him in the choice of words 'the client was *allowed* to explain . . .'. This can lead into a useful discussion over who takes control in an interview, issues of empowerment and proper behaviour of a lawyer in an interview.[36] We could reflect on what is going on for the client in this situation: should she be expected to tell a clear story on demand?

Even where a student has not produced a written analysis, debriefing can touch on similar issues. The student can be asked questions such as: 'During the interview, who did most of the speaking? To start with? At the end? Who do you think should do most of the speaking?'

Checking the facts

We return to Mr Wheeler's case. After the interview a full client statement was needed. Why? During the interview Derek had consulted me, told me all the important facts, and again afterwards we had talked at length. Why do we insist on getting everything written down before going any further?

---

[36] See further Brayne and Grimes, *Professional Skills for Lawyers* (note 30), ch. 3, on the question of who takes charge and who needs to be empowered in a legal interview.

We do this to ensure that we do not start the file with an incomplete understanding of the facts. Facts are, surprisingly, not something law students learn much about. We traditionally give them a diet of pre-digested and unchallengeable information on which to sharpen and demonstrate their legal understanding. If this case became a traditional tort examination question, it could be reduced to something like: 'Biker, who is cycling northwards along High Street at 20 m.p.h., collides with a car driven by Driver, who is driving southwards along High Street and decides to turn across Biker's path into Side Street, which is to her right'. These are essentially the facts as alleged by Mr Wheeler. But a legal analysis premised on these facts would be brief (a quick reference to the duty of care of the motorist and the duty of the cyclist to avoid injury to himself) and easy. So we lecturers like to throw in a bit about Biker's lights not working, a dog running across the road, Biker having an eggshell-thin skull, being dropped by Medic on the way to the hospital which, at the time, is undergoing a power failure caused by Electro, who severed a cable. . . .

The point about writing out a statement is to get the student to set out not only what the client has said, and wants, but also to be as clear as possible where each bit of the information comes from. There are no 'facts' until a court declares what they were. In fact the judge has no personal knowledge either, and is merely declaring his or her opinion. We have after the interview only Derek's notes and Derek's memory of what a client has said, and usually a tape to go back to if necessary. I want it all written down in a coherent statement, where the events can be pieced together. I want to be able to say: clarify this, fill that gap, explain that contradiction. Why does the client state that? Did the client see or merely presume that? It is my intention with a first draft of a client statement to pull it to pieces. What the client has said must be pinned down precisely. If Derek writes in the statement 'I was travelling at 20 m.p.h.', I will challenge him: 'Is that the client's estimate? Did he have a speedometer? Please indicate in the statement the basis for the ''fact''.' Similarly if Derek's first draft says 'The car saw me and appeared to slow down, but suddenly it turned right across my path', I will ask for clarifications such as: 'Do you mean the car, or the driver saw him? What led the client to believe that he had been seen? Did the car then stop? If so how long for? Show me on a map where the car was and where the client was at this point? When did the car start to turn?' I believe it is my job as supervisor to be extraordinarily pernickety and demanding. This is the best opportunity I ever have, when clarifying a statement, to get the student to discover the difference between vagueness and clarity, assertion and fact, evidence and belief. Nothing should be written down which is potentially relevant to any potential fact in dispute without checking: Who said that? How do you know? At the backs of our minds we must be thinking: How do we prove that? How will it stand up in court?

I recall a case involving a debt. These clients alleged they had organised sightseeing tours for conference participants. Two clients gave instructions to two students about a series of events, most of which consisted of telephone coversations and casual meetings. Out of this we were instructed to claim for breach of contract. It took five weeks to get a clearly crafted statement of exactly what the terms of the contract were and exactly how and when the breach occurred. The client came in or was phoned for clarification about six times before the statement was ready for approval.

Once it was ready, we sent a letter before action, containing just a one-paragraph recital of the allegations. Almost disappointingly payment in full was received by return. It could be argued that all that work was wasted. Not so: the student learned to found the claim on allegations clearly set out, agreed with the client, and as complete as could be. The student was moved from a woolly approach to facts towards a precise approach.

This attention to detail is unavoidable. I have to get my student's work up to my own standard because I am acting as the client's solicitor. I probably have to exceed my own standards, in fact: since I was not in the interview, I have to learn everything vicariously, and it has to make sense from what I see on paper. This attention to detail does not happen elsewhere on a law degree. It is unlikely to happen in a training contract, for it is presumed by that stage that the student has learned to think and explain and analyse. Where else does a tutor work with a student word by word, fact by fact, allegation by allegation, omission by omission? I would not give the same attention to a draft assignment, or indeed in marking an assignment. Real work gives both me and the student a huge increase in motivation to focus on detail. Perhaps this is because student and tutor are on each other's side. I am not assessing the student when I go through the draft statement or when I question whether she has got all the information needed. Nor am I criticising ('Your attempts were worth 47.98 per cent, you lousy student; take my advice and your mark will improve to 53.52 per cent'). Together we are carrying out a task. We share an interest in doing it well.

In Mr Wheeler's case, the result of the attempt to document our client's instructions adequately actually led to the following letter from Derek:

Dear Mr Wheeler

Since your initial interview I have visited the scene of the accident on
Heaton Road. I am, however, having difficulty understanding how the
accident exactly happened as the road layout appears to differ slightly from
your description.

I would be grateful if you could attend the Student Law Office on [date
and time] in order to clarify some of the information with which you have
provided me. If this is not possible you should contact the office in order
to make an alternative appointment.

Yours sincerely

It so happens that I do not like the tone of 'you should'. My preference is for a
more respectful approach such as 'would you kindly . . .?' But that is only a
matter of preference — worth debating — and such a letter can certainly be
effective. The important point is that the student was learning to investigate facts,
not just rely on what he is told by the client. Derek's attendance note states:

During the first interview the client stated that the driver had been turning
into Mundella Terrace when he had crashed into the side of her car [this
drafting could be improved, with clearer identification of who the 'he' and
the 'her' refer to]. On inspecting the scene, however, I discovered that this
would have been impossible as cars are unable to turn into Mundella
Terrace from Heaton Road.

However, the client stated that he had been mistaken in the first interview.
The car was not turning into Mundella Terrace, but was turning into
Meldon Terrace when he crashed into it.

The client also verified other details — the speed he was travelling on his
bicycle was approximately 20 m.p.h. and the weather conditions were dry
with good visibility.

Further details of costs incurred due to the accident were also given —
costs of parts for the client's bicycle came to £76.50; loss of earnings
because of the missed weekend at officer training core [sic] total £45.00.

Derek established the positions of the car and cycle at different times and his
successor Carol went to take photographs, which were disclosed in accord-
ance with the court's directions, and used in evidence at the arbitration.

Preparing a claim

The letter before action brought no response, and Derek prepared for the issue of proceedings. Research was needed on quantum, to establish the likely size of the claim. (Would it be worth applying for legal aid? Should the claim be limited in value[37] to enable it to go to arbitration and avoid a costs risk on losing?) He would need a medical report, both for the research, and for the issue of proceedings. I had to bite my tongue so that he could discover these procedural requirements for himself.

Not for the last time things did not now go according to plan. The doctors lost Mr Wheeler's medical notes. These things always happen — later the court lost the file — but if you want a student to learn about how the system of justice actually works, you could never bring it home with simulation or description. For four months nothing could happen on the case except Mr Wheeler and Derek together chasing the doctors to find the notes and provide a report. Here is, however, one of the frustrations of real client work. The case cannot be made to proceed at the rate best suited to Derek's learning. On this case at our weekly review meetings all he could report was 'still no sight of the medical report'. However, since he was working together with other students in a firm of four, he could be getting on with other work, learning from discussions about other cases and, if he wished, could take on a further case.[38]

There were preparatory steps that Derek overlooked during the lull. The driver had not answered our letter. We had had no contact with the insurers. We could have sought a police accident report, from which details of the driver's insurers could be obtained, as well as any statement from the driver.

---

[37] At the time of writing this limit is £3,000, or £1,000 for personal injury actions.

[38] The problem of regulating the flow of real-client work to match the educational year is probably insoluble. We never expected that it would take four months to locate the notes. If Derek took on another case during the lull, it might have demanded an enormous amount of work at the same time as the Wheeler case came back to life. Worse still, both cases, and many others, could outlive their predicted lifespan to become acute when I was planning a holiday. At Northumbria we are moving towards a solution of this problem: we have trainee solicitors who assist with casework during periods where students are not available to benefit. We have also employed a solicitor to assist with case management. The ultimate solution may be to expand the office so that it carries out a year-round legal service, generating funds from legal aid and cases won, or perhaps from block grants, to meet the additional expense incurred. We would then have a supply of cases, or case tasks, for students to work on. Would they lose the sense of being in charge of their own cases, however? In the meantime we have to ensure that any case that is not completed while the students are available can be referred on or, if necessary, ditched without a referral: a retainer letter warns clients from the start that this might happen.

Witnesses could have been identified and interviewed. Instead Derek spent March catching up, and learning that next time these steps could have been taken earlier.[39] He then found a witness and wrote to her, but the letter was returned marked 'gone away'. This might have been avoided by earlier action. Could anything be done? Derek himself suggested going round to see if any neighbours knew where the witness had moved to, and was successful in obtaining her address.

Now we had the medical report, Derek could issue proceedings. The biggest part of that was to draft particulars of claim. I am even more pernickety over the quality of the particulars of claim than I am over the statement of the client. In the present case, Derek drafted particulars which required almost no alteration. Sometimes a student has to be reminded of the requirements for pleadings set out in the White Book, and of the penalty for not pleading the case (being barred from adducing evidence of facts not pleaded and running the risk of being struck out, for instance).[40]

Another issue arises. Mr Wheeler could not afford the court fee. Occasionally it can happen that a case which is worth running on education grounds can collapse because the client cannot find the court fee. Is it ethical to subsidise the client's fee? The Law Office did earn a small amount from legal aid income and costs. But if we use it we are then providing one party to a dispute an advantage which the other party may not have. Is that ethical? The driver's case would be prepared by an insurance company. I discussed with Derek and colleagues the ethics of subsidising the client. The students, as is common, were eager to continue with the case.

Proceedings were issued,[41] and a solicitor surfaced for the driver. His attitude was pugnacious from the start. A reply to an early letter from us indicates the tone of the defence:

> We thank you for your letter of 20th April, and are surprisingly aware of the case of *Mattocks* v *Mann* not *Maltocks and Mann* as your letter refers.

---

[39] I have no record or recollection of why I allowed the time to pass without contacting the police. A charitable explanation is that I was giving Derek room to make mistakes. More likely, I forgot to check the file for myself and ask the obvious question: What else needs to be done?
[40] Formal pleadings are not essential in an arbitration, of course, but perfecting them demonstrates to the court and the opponent that the Student Law Office is a professional office, and gives the client and the student adviser confidence that the case is properly prepared.
[41] But the court sent the papers back first time, erroneously stating that we had paid the wrong fee. The court had failed to notice that we expressly limited the claim to £1,000, and therefore the fee then payable was correct. It is important for students to learn about these slight but irritating imperfections of the court system. Otherwise they may still believe that the law they have learned can simply be applied. Mistakes, delays, hassles, costs, are part of the legal system too.

[We thank the solicitor for an excellent opportunity to discuss with the students whether cheap point-scoring is appropriate in professional work, and conclude that despite the sarcasm we will remain polite rather than respond to the sarcasm.]

We are quite prepared to argue that *Mattocks* is not authority for your client's claim to have his bus fares paid from now until Doomsday.

We note your invitation to share the cost of the police accident abstract but we are not prepared to share the cost of it as it is the plaintiff's place to prepare his case.

If you obtain a copy you will no doubt disclose it in due course.

Yours faithfully

A later letter contains the following gem:

It is to be regretted as it is noted that your Law Clinic purports to be some form of training ground for future solicitors, that you seem divorced from the reality of handling claims on an efficient and economic basis.

Our reply, which I decided had to come from me and not the student, contained the following, and more:

I note with interest your comments on the different approaches of practice and academia. When this case is disposed of I shall be happy to enter into further discussion of this and you would be welcome to visit this office.

We had deliberately limited the claim to £1,000 to have the case, if defended, dealt with in arbitration. The court nevertheless gave standard directions rather than referring it to the small claims jurisdiction. By the time this was rectified, at the request of the defence, it was September, and a new student was assigned to the case.

We wanted to get the case heard or settled, but were encountering what seemed like obstinacy[42] and unwillingness to cooperate on the other side. On

---

[42] This is my choice of words, and reflects a growing sense of anger. There was, when the case finally came to court, no real defence. The case was being defended in a way which would have frightened off the unrepresented litigant. It was not being fought on its merits. I will probably never learn to become calm and impartial, and the best I can do is examine my feelings in discussion with my students, and to ensure that we all recognise the danger, when feelings about the opponent arise, of responding inappropriately. We must behave like professionals, even if we feel like cave dwellers.

our attempt to have the matter set down, with a time estimate of one and a half hours, the defence insisted on three, because of legal arguments over the period for which Mr Wheeler could claim bus fares while unable to pay for the repair of his cycle. The new student, Carol, was presented with a golden opportunity to look at issues of justice, law and expediency. The sum at the centre of this proposed dispute was £2.50 per week. At what point, we needed to check, could the defence insist that Mr Wheeler cut his losses? Was Mr Wheeler entitled to have his bus fare met until the defendant paid the cost of the cycle repair? We had cited a case suggesting that if the defendant could not afford the repair (in that case to a car) then the defendant would have to meet the weekly cost of a hire car.[43]

Were we (and Mr Wheeler) really willing to slug this one out in court? We agreed to ask Mr Wheeler whether a figure could be proposed to the other side to avoid the legal argument. The client agreed on eight weeks of bus fares. Carol proposed this without prejudice, to which the opponents replied with a curmudgeonly 'Why eight?' But after a further exchange of correspondence, which we threatened to show the judge on the question of costs, they finally agreed if found liable to pay eight weeks' bus fares.[44] What had Carol learned here? Perhaps, cynically, how easy it was for a solicitor paid by an insurance company to make work for himself[45] — at the very least this added to the possible range of styles of litigation that Carol could emulate in her later professional life. Certainly she learned that there may be more important objectives, in this case getting the case moving, than winning on every issue every time. In any event, Mr Wheeler agreed that he could have afforded to get the bike repaired after eight weeks, so any other line of argument would have collapsed in court. 'Facts' always need rechecking, especially as trial approaches.

On the way to arbitration, the defendant threw a final spanner in the works by making a payment into court. This is not allowed by the rules relating to small claims. However, neither Carol nor I spotted that the rules had only recently changed to disallow such a payment, and we advised an anguished client over his prospects and the risk of costs on losing or failing to beat it.

[43] *Mattocks* v *Mann* [1993] RTR 13.
[44] Costs can be awarded in an arbitration where a party has behaved unreasonably in the conduct of the litigation, County Court Rules 1981, ord. 19. It was unlikely Carol could have discovered this in the time available for reply, and therefore at this stage of the case a certain amount of directed research was needed.
[45] The file is thick with letters, for example, querying Mr Wheeler's tax and grant status, querying a 25 pence discrepancy between the cycle repair estimate and requiring the plaintiff to prove the cost of the cycle repair at the arbitration.

Unable to sleep easily with such a prospect, given that this would put a winning plaintiff who failed to beat the payment into court into a worse position than a losing plaintiff, who would not be liable to any costs, I rang the district judge on our advisory committee. He advised me that it would be most unlikely that an order for costs would be made on failing to beat the payment in (he too appeared to be unaware at the time that a payment in was in fact disallowed by the rules). Three months later the case was listed for hearing before the same judge; Carol and colleagues had to make a swift ethical decision — did we need to declare to the other side this earlier consultation with the district judge, albeit that we knew it could not affect his impartiality? We concluded we must, and as a result the matter was relisted before another judge on the same day.

Preparing for the judge

We need to go back in time, since the real learning took place in the weeks of final preparation. The payment in was £250. Special damages were £65 (agreed) and £75 not agreed but confidently predicted (we did not imagine the other side would be able to contradict the bicycle repair invoice with any better evidence). To beat the payment in we had to find just under £110 for the pain and suffering part of the damages (interest from accident to payment in making up the difference). Where to start? First, we had to get the case into real winning shape. Secondly, we had to get the submissions on quantum ready for the court, which meant researching similar precedents in relation to pain and suffering and loss of amenity.

When I first learned the facts of the case, I had no doubt we had an obvious winner. I had taken accident referrals from the London Cycling Campaign for some years, and had never needed a final hearing. We had, by now, a police accident report in which the defendant confirmed the facts Mr Wheeler had given us, adding 'I just did not see him'. We had an independent witness statement in line with our understanding of the facts. Why were the opponents fighting and, as it turned out, instructing a barrister to appear? Why was the case not settling? Greater fees, says the cynic, or maybe trying to frighten the plaintiff into accepting a paltry amount; or did they perhaps have a secret line of argument or evidence up their sleeve, which would reduce the plaintiff's case to tatters? Would they have the equivalent of the secret video (the one which shows the plaintiff in an unguarded moment free of the debilitating symptoms the claim is based on)? We could not anticipate what this might be. But the case for the plaintiff needed testing.

In all cases heading for court we stage a mock hearing. In this case it was patently necessary. We wrongly thought the payment into court was putting us at risk on costs, and we rightly (but in the event wrongly) feared the other side had strengths and we had weaknesses that we had yet to uncover. Role-plays of real cases provide fabulous learning opportunities and provide an example of one way in which simulation and real-client work can build on each other. Student colleagues have to study, and then become, witnesses; this involves them in thorough analysis of facts, and creation of hypotheses about unknown aspects of the case. Student advocates prepare the opposing case, so we are almost as conversant with it as with our own. Submissions and witness examinations can be practised. Lines of argument and questioning which work can be retained; others can be modified. Of course the real hearing goes completely differently, but every one of the questions Carol tried out on the mock witnesses served a useful purpose. Feedback — nowadays we would use video — enabled Carol to evaluate and improve her performance.

We are talking of a claim too small for legal aid; but we are talking days and days of student preparation, with a good deal of staff time thrown in. A colleague volunteered to play the role of the district judge; students working on other cases had to drop their work and assist with this one; questions, in particular for cross-examination, had to be written, refined, planned on the basis of 'What if she says this rather than that in reply?' Staff and student time was needed for observation and feedback.

If the essence of advocacy is preparation and, despite what happens often in practice, I have yet to hear anyone state the contrary, Carol's preparation for the real event was almost a guarantee of a good performance. Her opening speech, for example, was carefully crafted, even down to alternatives of the gender of the judge and the layout of the room. Here is her beginning:

> I am Miss — and appear on behalf of the plaintiff, Mr Wheeler. I ask your permission Sir/Madam to consult during the hearing with Mr Brayne on my right/left who is my supervisor in the Law Office.[46]

> The plaintiff alleges that on the 19th October at approximately 12.30 p.m. a collision occurred which was caused by the defendant's negligence. As

---

[46] As a matter of courtesy we always inform the court in advance that the case will be conducted by a student accompanied by a supervisor. In the present case this was a waste of time as the court could not find the file with the letter and the judge could only proceed after a new file was created just before the hearing by photocopying parts of ours. We also asked the court and the opponent for permission for other students who had assisted with the case to sit in. The judge had no objection, but the defendant objected.

a result the plaintiff suffered injury, damage and loss. The accident
occurred at the junction with Meldon Terrace, which can be seen on the
map.

And she then goes on to outline the issues which will be in dispute:

> The defence have agreed special damages subject to liability in relation to
> the plaintiff's loss of earnings from a training weekend with the officer
> training corps. . . . Damage to the bike has not been agreed unless the
> defence will agree at this stage.

She goes on to state who she will be calling, and her intention to use
photographs and a plan which have been previously disclosed (omitting to
remind the court that they have lost their own copies).

In examination in chief she has two pages of questions, ending with 'Thank
you, Mr Wheeler; I have no further questions for you at present'.

Anticipating that Mr Wheeler would be cross-examined about the bicycle
repair, since the defence refused to agree this point, re-examination questions
are also prepared on this topic. It turns out that no objection is made to his
evidence and the questions could be shelved. Re-examination was required,
on the day, on two wholly unexpected issues. Mr Wheeler was skilfully led
to admitting that he may have been overtaking the witness's car on the inside
just before the accident. And he was led with less skill into a suggestion that
he had tried to intimidate the defendant when he visited her that night to ask
about repairs to his bike. Our watertight case seemed to be leaking with the
admission of overtaking on the inside, and my own help in supplying
questions for re-examination was called for. (Or was it? This is always the
debate about letting the student take charge. Personally I found it hard
enough to be in court on a case I had prepared together with the students and
the client over several months, and keeping my mouth shut. To ask me not
to supply written suggestions to the student at her hour of need was to ask
me for superhuman restraint.) On re-examination Carol was able to establish
that there was no overtaking on the inside or anywhere else, and this point
was added to the questions to the plaintiff's witness.

We had learned, with hindsight, that there were parts of the story that we had
not properly explored with the plaintiff. This is not a criticism, simply a
recognition that perfect anticipation of all angles on the case is difficult, but
it should remain the goal. Perhaps something we should do when we close

files is to ask students for a short account headed: 'What we should have done differently'.

Questions for cross-examination were probably the hardest to prepare, and the most important. Carol was reminded of the need to put each part of her case to the opposing witness, and to ensure that everything the plaintiff disagreed with was challenged. Most, but not all, of such material could be anticipated from the defendant's statement to the police and the role-play we had conducted. But not all. The result of having detailed questions prepared was that Carol had an enormous psychological advantage over the defence witness. Many lawyers, myself included, get into debate and argument with witnesses. This gives the witness the upper hand. With Carol it was almost like a boxing match, with powerful questions raining down one after the other, and the witness did not know what was coming next because a question did not necessarily follow on as a result of her last answer. Here is a sequence worthy of Perry Mason (those who started watching American TV after the sixties may prefer to compare Carol to Johnny Cochrane, or whoever the current media performer in court is).

Are you aware, Mrs —, which road user has right of way in this situation, where one person wants to turn right across the main road and the path of the oncoming traffic?

May I refer you to section 97 of the Highway Code which states when turning right wait until there is a safe gap between you and any oncoming vehicle? [Show code.]

Mr Wheeler therefore had right of way in this situation, did he not?

At what point did you see Mr Wheeler?

Why then did you cross his right of way?

In your statement to the police you say that you did not see Mr Wheeler prior to the collision, yet you suggest he was travelling very fast.

If Mr Wheeler was travelling very fast, why did you not wait, as you should have done, for the oncoming traffic to pass?

These questions, delivered in a slow non-emotional tone, led to the defendant becoming exasperated and ultimately aggressive. While this was not the aim, such behaviour from one party could only help the other to gain sympathy. The use of prepared questions enabled Carol to remain, in fact, calmer than I know I would have done, and the witness's aggression might, under my own cross-examination, have appeared to have been provoked by me.

Finally Carol had prepared a closing speech summarising the evidence heard at court. I always advocate this approach. Prepare your examination and cross-examination so that it supports your closing address, then be ready to delete and amend those submissions that are not in the end sustainable in the light of the evidence heard. She had detailed submissions on quantum ready, derived from research into Kemp and Kemp, which gave her an advantage over the defence, who were unprepared on this issue.

Judgment was given without delay for the plaintiff, and without the prepared closing speech being necessary. Submissions on quantum were not challenged (beating the payment into court by almost £500, a satisfying outcome). But to the surprise of the court and the defence, Carol was immediately ready with her application for interest on damages, pursuant to the Supreme Court Act 1981, s. 35A, and the County Courts Act 1984, s. 69. The defence seemed to think this was unfair. Carol was undeflected as she had her authority, with a yellow Post-It inserted into the relevant page of the Green Book.[47] Again victory was ours, and a few pounds were gained. Even as the district judge was packing the papers, Carol was ready with her next application, for witness expenses of £29 pursuant to the County Court Rules 1981, ord. 19, r. 4. This took everyone by surprise. The district judge declined to award more than £5, despite the clear language of the rule. Perhaps Carol's research, with which I fully agreed, had caused her to make the first such application ever before this judge.

We had prepared an argument resisting a costs order just in case we lost the case or failed to beat the payment in. Perhaps, in the light of the clear admission by the defendant that she had not seen the plaintiff, we should have been ready with a costs application under ord. 19; the defence had been doomed to failure from the moment that this was admitted. An application could even have been entertained for a wasted costs order against the solicitor personally. However, we had not prepared this point, and therefore were content to retreat with the satisfaction of a victory to assist the client in the spending of a few pounds of his damages in a nearby pub.

---

[47] *The County Court Practice* (London: Butterworth, annual).

Moving house: some lessons to learn, or the nightmare scenario

The first of the studies focused on the learning experience of students in terms of their understanding and appreciation of the law in the context of professional practice. The next looks principally at the extent to which the clinical method facilitates students' comprehension of legal theory and the potential for the integration of the clinical approach within the overall curriculum of the law programme. Case study two has been taken from the files of the Law Clinic at Sheffield Hallam University and the facts have been only slightly altered to preserve confidentiality and to allow for a debate on some important ethical considerations.[48]

The facts

The facts are nice and simple. The client, whom we shall call Simon Payne, was moving house. Completion of his sale and purchase was scheduled for 1 May. In anticipation of the move the client contacted some removal companies for quotations covering the cost of taking his furniture and personal possessions from the house he was selling (in Reading) to his newly purchased home (in Sheffield). Not knowing whom to contact Mr Payne selected three removal companies from the Yellow Pages telephone directory, all of whom provided him with written quotations of the cost of the planned removals. As will be seen the student advisers in the Law Clinic had to carry out detailed factual research based on these initial instructions but for present purposes it is enough to know that Mr Payne decided to go for the cheapest of the three quotations provided by a company called One-Stop Removals (just under £300).

One-Stop's managing director, Mr Lawton, spoke to Mr Payne the day before the moving day to say there was a problem, as the removal lorry that was to carry Mr Payne's property had been delayed overseas and he could no longer guarantee that the removals would go ahead on the scheduled day. Mr Payne was very concerned as the buyer of his house in Reading was planning to move in on 1 May. After a heated exchange with Mr Lawton, Mr Payne decided to ask another company to move him and he cancelled the contract

---

[48] Although the facts of this case were mainly as recounted above some additional facts have been included from another case handled by the Law Clinic in the same year that illustrate important ethical issues for the students, the supervisors and the clinic as a whole. It seemed convenient to amalgamate the two cases under the one heading to best illustrate the scope of clinical work in such a context. If, like badly hung wallpaper, the join is too visible, and the facts become improbable, please have a good laugh at our imperfections as writers and see what you can learn from us anyway as clinical teachers.

with One-Stop. At short notice and at a higher price (around £500) Smith's Transport collected Mr Payne's belongings and with a great deal of last-minute rearranging the move took place on 1 May.

Mr Payne consulted the Law Clinic with two main queries: first, did he have the right to claim from One-Stop the additional charges and incidental expenses incurred as a result of the change to another removal company, and second, was he entitled to refuse to pay One-Stop anything in the circumstances? Mr Lawton of One-Stop had threatened to sue Mr Payne for cancelling the contract.

The clinic system, the investigation and the learning process

The case came to the Law Clinic through one of the clinic's open sessions.[49] The student advisers on the day when Mr Payne came to the clinic were Angela and Wayne. Angela was a standard school entrant in her second year on the LLB programme and Wayne was a mature student in his final year of study. They had been allocated to the rota for that particular day.

The facts as set out above come from the file record.[50] (As in any legal practice a full note is taken of each stage of the process from the initial interview through telephone calls and letters to the detail of any court hearing or negotiated settlement.)

It is standard procedure in the Law Clinic at Sheffield Hallam for one of the student advisers to leave the interview room to consult with the clinic supervisor at the end of the initial interview and for the other adviser to remain with the client. The purpose of this is to allow the supervisor to get an overview of the case and to discuss with the student what should be done next. Invariably this results in the student returning to the client to elicit more information and/or to inform the client that a letter will be sent with some preliminary advice to the client, or making arrangements for another meeting, as soon as possible (normally within five working days). The system was introduced to allow for some quality control at an early stage. The supervisors do not sit in on the actual interviews unless a student requests, and the client permits it.

---

[49] The Law Clinic at Sheffield Hallam opens twice a week — Mondays 12–2 and Wednesdays 2–4 during term-time — when clients can call on a drop-in basis to discuss their problems and seek initial advice. Apart from referrals from other agencies this is the main way in which the clinic attracts clients. Once a case has been taken on clients are seen at times convenient to them and their adviser/supervisor.

[50] The actual file record is not set out for reasons of brevity and space. Examples of verbatim records, accounts and file documents are, however, included in case study 1.

Mr Payne was told that an advice letter would be sent to him and a further appointment might have to be made to discuss the matter further if it was felt that the clinic was able to take the matter on and if Mr Payne wished the clinic to represent him. All clients are informed both orally and in writing (by being given an information sheet) of the working practices and policies of the clinic. The educational goals of the clinic determine what cases the clinic becomes involved in. Where the clinic feels unable to represent, the client may ask to be referred elsewhere, often into private practice or other suitable agency.

As will be stressed at several points in this book a fundamental premise that the clinic operates on (whether real-client or not) is that the student must take direct (if closely supervised) responsibility for the case he or she handles. Time and opportunity must, if the experience is to be maximised, be given to enable the student to incur the experience of doing and to reflect on that experience. An important device to this end is the regular meeting between supervisor and student, or in the case of the Law Clinic at Sheffield Hallam between the supervisor and the student firm. At these meetings all of the 'firm's' cases are discussed and strategies agreed upon to progress those cases. In Mr Payne's case an initial discussion took place at the end of the open advice session between the supervisor (Richard), Angela and Wayne. It was then followed by the weekly 'firm's' meeting at which the case was discussed and a plan of action agreed.

There are several pedagogic and ethical issues arising in this case. But let's start by looking at the way in which the analysis of the case was handled. How did the students identify and address the legal and other considerations? Both recognised the subject area of the problem. It was a case involving contracts. This was volunteered by the students when asked by Richard for their first reactions. Angela and Wayne had already studied contract in their first year. Lessons had been well learnt (there must be something to commend the conventional lecture approach) for both were able to at least recite the formula that had to be applied. Had a legally binding contract (or contracts) been concluded? If so, who were the parties and what were the terms? Had any of those terms been broken or were likely to be broken? What loss, if any, had been suffered? What remedies were applicable? This was a start.

Without dragging the reader through a lesson in the basic principles of contract law, suffice it to say that Richard, Angela and Wayne were agreed that there was probably a binding contract between the client and One-Stop although none of us knew at that time exactly when the contract had been concluded nor what its exact terms were.

The first task for Angela and Wayne to address was the formulation of research questions. What needed to be investigated? To aid the students in this often complex process a form is used in the Sheffield clinic on which the student advisers are required to record what it is they are researching, how they intend to and in fact do carry out the research, what is discovered and whether this answers satisfactorily the question first raised. Put another way, do the results of the research build and fit the theory of the case?[51]

The team meetings and individual supervision sessions ran at first rather like a highly interactive tutorial in contract law.[52] The students tried to identify the legal issues at stake and the research that was now necessitated. The fundamental contractual principles of offer, acceptance, consideration and intention to create legal relations were well understood and could be applied with accuracy to the case before us. This much had been understood and retained from first-year studies (although the students struggled to recall the appropriate authorities). What about contractual terms, breach and remedies? Not only did the students find it difficult to recall what they had studied, in some cases only six months before, but also they could not relate the theory to the facts now before them.

With guidance and some prompting the students were able to identify three significant areas of enquiry that need both factual and legal investigation:

---

[51] The concept of the theory of the case arose and has been developed in the USA and is well explained in Berger and Bindman, *From Evidence to Proof* (West Publishing, 1983). There may well be a series of sub-theories in a case as well as an overall theory. In either instance the theory is a proposition that has to be tested against the evidence (factual research) and the law (legal research). If the answers fit the theory advanced, the lawyer can advise the client in confidence that all that can be done, outside of actual litigation, has been done. If the results of the research do not fit the theory then either the theory is wrong and the client has no case or the theory needs adapting and retesting. The concept of the theory works well in the context of contentious work. It does not translate so readily to non-contentious matters, for example, conveyancing, where past facts and legal interpretation are seldom in dispute. A transaction can of course become the subject of litigation and the lawyer who is, say, drafting legal documents must, so far as he or she is able, ensure that the client's interests are protected in the event of a dispute arising. This is discussed in an applied sense in Brayne and Grimes, *Professional Skills for Lawyers* (London: Butterworths, 1994), ch. 4.

[52] Team meetings are an integral part of the work of the Sheffield and Northumbria clinics. Students are allocated to a firm — a group of four, five or six students — who meet their supervisor on a weekly basis when all that firm's cases are discussed and an action plan agreed upon. This includes the student advisers who are responsible for the case and the other firm members. Individual sessions with the advisers are held whenever the student requests this or the supervisor considers it necessary.

(a)   What was said by both sides in the period leading up to the conclusion of the contract — that is, what were the terms of the contract and what representations if any were relied upon in this process? Was any of the pre-contractual stage recorded in writing? Was there a written contract or any subsequent correspondence?

(b)   What were the full circumstances leading up to the removal company's difficulties in discharging the obligations? Did they have a legally justifiable excuse for their failure to collect the household possessions as promised?

(c)   Given the facts discovered in these further investigations could the client recover damages in anticipation of the breach and was he then excused from making any payment to the defaulting removers?

With gaps in the factual account evident, it was clearly necessary to ask the client to come back for a second interview before any advice could be dispensed. This was done and Angela and Wayne came out of the interview armed with a great deal more information. This added not only to their understanding of what must now be done and of the advice that might be given but also to the complexity of the case. Because they had focused on the research issues prior to the second interview, they were able to ask far more pertinent questions of Mr Payne — questions that were essential to the formulation of the eventual advice and, as it turned out, to protracted and successful litigation.

The following facts now emerged:

Mr Payne had been attracted by the lowest of three quotations. He produced a letter from the company setting out the quoted price but which contained a proviso that the collection of his belongings was dependent upon the lorry which was to be used arriving on time from another job. Mr Payne wanted reassurance from One-Stop that they could guarantee completing the removals on the day in question (as he was contractually obliged to complete his sale then) and he was reassured by One-Stop's managing director that he (Mr Payne) could rely on One-Stop and that they would be able to complete the move on time. It was only with such a reassurance that Mr Payne concluded the contract. In correspondence with the company received after the events on the day before the removal, Mr Payne was sent a copy of a contract (which he had not seen before) which contained a limitation clause excluding the company from liability for any circumstance beyond their control. They now maintained that the lorry had been delayed in Italy owing to industrial action and were relying on the exemption clause.

Armed with these new facts and having consulted a variety of sources for their research (in this case the students' research form indicated that they used *Halsbury's Laws*; several cases, notably on frustration of contract; contract law texts; and their own lecture notes from the previous year(s)) Angela and Wayne were able to draft an advice letter to the client, which (after several attempts) was approved by Richard and dispatched. The advice contained a brief description of the client's contractual rights on the facts as understood by the clinic and the recommendation that a letter before action be sent to One-Stop demanding compensation. The letter also addressed the client-care issues required of any private practice, including the consequences of litigation, particularly in terms of costs, the likely length and nature of any proceedings and the basis upon which the clinic would represent.[53] Mr Payne accepted this advice and the letter before action was sent.

Other facts and additional theories and research tasks would emerge in the course of litigation.

Some reflections on the case so far

This was clearly a case that offered much in terms of learning for the students. It was a case that embodied virtually every aspect of the law of contract with the exception perhaps of duress, undue influence and illegality. It touched on, to a greater or lesser extent, the formation of contract, contractual terms, misrepresentation, exemption clauses, anticipatory breach, rescission and damages. These were all issues that the students had studied before but there was now the opportunity to put the theory into context and apply knowledge. By a favourable coincidence the supervisor (whose other main teaching interest was contract law) had introduced into the degree's contract course a simulated clinical element and the link therefore between the real-client clinic and so-called theoretical study had already been established. Although this attempt at integrating the clinical approach with a core part of the law curriculum was in an experimental stage, the potential for development here and elsewhere in the programme (for example, on the landlord and tenant option — the clinic has many cases involving tenants) was and is immense.

---

[53] The requirement to supply these details applies to all solicitors in private practice (Solicitors' Practice Rules 1990, r. 15). The rules do not require it to be done by letter, but this is good practice, as client and solicitor can have a complete record of what the arrangements for handling the case will be. Surprisingly, employed solicitors such as clinical supervisors are exempt from this rule, but that is of course no reason to ignore best practice.

There was an additional dimension. None of the students had yet studied civil procedure, evidence or advocacy. This case offered the opportunity to examine most aspects of civil litigation applicable to claims of such a size as well as the chance, should the case go so far (as it did), of advocacy, for the student has the right of audience in such arbitration proceedings. There was, as it transpired in this case, the added twist of an appeal! The fact that this was new territory for the students did not present such an obstacle as might be thought, for with a strongly planned and structured research strategy the students were equipped with the tools and discipline to discover what was needed, with the safety net of faculty staff who were legally qualified practitioners to oversee the process.

Finally, the case provided material for general discussion. In the planning and practice of the various stages of advocacy the whole of the student body involved in the clinic (including first-year students shadowing in the clinic) were able to watch and contribute to the exercise. The contrast between the use of a real case as opposed to fictional simulation added a dimension to the proceedings and was much appreciated by supervisors and students alike.

An important point should be made here. It transpired that this case was, despite its relatively small commercial value (under £3000 and therefore a small claim), very complex in legal terms. That complexity added colour and excitement, even though it was not essential to provide the learning experience that is at the heart of clinical work. A simpler case would also have provided the opportunity for the students to learn by doing and many of the cases taken on by the Sheffield clinic are far more straightforward. Mr Payne's case went beyond this to demonstrate vividly the link between the clinical approach and the mainstream curriculum. It also brought out significant ethical considerations. It is to these that we can now turn.

Ethics in practice

This case, with some minor modifications to the facts (the introduction of one issue arising in a case that the clinic was also handling at the time) gives rise to three important ethical considerations that can be generalised as follows:

(a)   the relationship between the solicitor and the client, in particular, issues of confidentiality and client care;
(b)   the relationship between the solicitor and the client's opponent, where, as in this case, the defendant was unrepresented; and

(c) the relationship between the solicitor and the court where the student was, under supervision, the advocate.

Several developments took place that resulted in a wide-ranging discussion on ethical issues both by the student advisers, their firm and the whole clinic.

Students are made aware at a very early stage in the clinical programme of the professional obligations incumbent on them and the clinic in terms of establishing and maintaining the expected and necessary standards of professionalism.[54] The Payne case demonstrated the full range of these obligations including the meaning of and need for the preservation of confidentiality and client-care considerations in a litigious case such as this.[55]

It was the relationship between the clinic and the defendant company that gave rise to some considerable debate both in terms of the conduct of the case and in the clinic's own position on a conflict of interest point.

One-Stop responded to the clinic's letter before action with a robust denial. This was in part focused on the alleged legal argument that as the delay of the lorry was caused by circumstances beyond their control, they could not reasonably be expected to be held responsible and further, that as Mr Payne had cancelled the contract without due cause, he owed them for failure to pay the moneys due under the contract. The rest of their response revealed an interesting point which caused the clinic some initial difficulty. It transpired that the company had a history of taking Sheffield Hallam University students on placement. The company said it was quite improper for the clinic to represent a client when the opponent was linked to the University in such a way. Further it was suggested that if the clinic did not withdraw from the case the company would complain to senior management at the university and to the Law Society on grounds of professional impropriety. The threat was used that no further placement students would be taken. It was also maintained that by representing the client the clinic was behaving in an unfair way for it had the intention and resources to embark on litigation as an academic exercise, whereas for the company there were acute financial considerations that made such small-scale court action highly

---

[54] Every student receives at the outset of the clinic option a handbook in which these standards are made explicit. In addition, before they can start work in the clinic they must attend an induction programme, which deals amongst other things with professional standards, ethical issues, working practices and office procedures.

[55] In fact the client gave his consent to the case being used in other contexts including classroom simulations. Other aspects of the case revealed above, however, have imposed an obligation on the writer to maintain anonymity.

unattractive. As the case was to be heard by way of arbitration there was little likelihood of costs being awarded even if the company were successful in defending the claim. The clinic was accused of abusing the judicial process.

As if the substantive law was not enough for the student advisers to contend with the discussions now had to include the ethical and profession dimensions requiring both additional research and, as it transpired, some internal memo writing and negotiation.

What were the ethical issues here? They fell into three main parts:

(a)   whether there was an actual or potential conflict of interest;
(b)   whether it was professionally acceptable to represent where the values were small and the other side said it was not economically viable for them to be represented;
(c)   what duties were incumbent on the clinic when dealing with an unrepresented defendant who (as it later transpired) had a very poor grasp of both law and procedure.

It may not have taken a practitioner too long to respond to these points but the students were in no position to dispatch the allegations to where they belonged. Practice manuals, Law Society regulations and policy documents and the university's own rules were consulted.

The clinic came to the conclusion that just because the company was known to the university (but not previously to the clinic) this was no reason for refusing to take on or continue to act in a case. Indeed to decline to act for a client whom the clinic was already representing itself gave rise to professional practice and ethical issues, particularly where the clinic was on the court record.[56]

As can be imagined the university was concerned at the implications of the development but agreed with the proposed (and then implemented) decision of the clinic, that it was quite proper on a professional basis for the clinic to continue to represent and that a polite explanation should be given to the defendant describing the purpose of the clinic, the obligation owed to the client and the advisability of the defendant having legal representation.

---

[56] As a result of this experience, however, the clinic made its initial questioning of the client and its own cross-referencing system more comprehensive to limit further the possibility of the clinic representing a client where there was a possible conflict of interest.

On the issues of both legal representation and abuse of process it was of course entirely a matter for the defendant to take up. In the latter instance the company could seek an order for costs from the court although the clinic indicated that this would be resisted as in our view it was quite proper for us to represent despite the value of the case concerned. It has to be said that the university's management were receptive to the clinic's view of the matter. If they had directed the clinic to withdraw from the case a real issue of conflict would have arisen: does the employed solicitor put the employer's wishes or the client's instructions first? This would be another opportunity to explore the boundaries of legal ethics and professional responsibility.[57]

Throughout these developments Angela and Wayne, together with their firm and the other clinic students, took part in the necessary work and attendant discussions with commitment and fascination and we had not even begun to prepare for trial. This was a learning experience for all of us that combined the intellectual and applied study of law and practice coupled with wider ethical concerns of the solicitor's role in relation to his or her client, as well as raising the role of the lawyer in a wider community sense. The clinic engaged (as it has done many times since) in the 'it's not fair' debate — the one where the student's view of what is just does not necessarily follow reality.

Happy endings

It only remains to inform you, the reader, of the outcome. Following a rule that can only be described as 'Sod's Law' the case was listed for hearing during the students' vacation. Neither Angela nor Wayne were, with great and mutual disappointment (but it is suspected with some relief), able to go to court.[58] Exceptionally the supervisor, Richard, appeared, using the material that the student advisers had so carefully prepared and following their advocacy plan and theory of the case (that is, that Mr Payne was entitled to damages to the extent of his losses, almost £300). The district judge found for Mr Payne.

---

[57] The answer, of course, is to be found in the solicitors' conduct rules. Principle 15.04 in the *Guide to the Professional Conduct of Solicitors* states: 'A solicitor must not act, or must decline to act further, where there is a conflict of interests between: . . . (b) the solicitor's firm and the client . . .'. Does this rule apply to employed solicitors? According to the Employed Solicitors code 1990, 1(b): 'Despite anything in this code employed solicitors must not act in any situation where they would be precluded from acting by an actual or potential conflict of interest'.

[58] The inability of the student advisers to attend court was exceptional. In our experience students seldom turn down a chance of advocacy. In this instance both had other commitments. In any event students represent only if they and the supervisor consider it appropriate.

But that was not the end of the story. One-Stop appealed to a judge in chambers, out of time and on grounds that appeared to have little merit.[59] The students prepared and conducted a chambers application and the case was directed back to the county court arbitrator with directions that he formally consider the question of frustration. The judge had read the notes of the initial hearing and was not satisfied that all the legal issues in this respect had been addressed. He also took a liberal view of the appeal being out of time, perhaps because the defendant wasn't represented. In fact the district judge had carefully considered frustration and had ruled that following the cited case of *Davis Contractors Ltd v Fareham UDC*[60] the defendant company knew of the commercial risks of the business and could not rely on frustration when the reality of the situation became less advantageous for it. What the district judge did not apparently do was to record this fully in his trial notes.

At the reconvened hearing, with Wayne as advocate, the district judge carefully considered submissions from both sides and ruled again (and with full reasons) in the plaintiff's favour. He also commended the Law Clinic and the students on their preparation and presentation — the icing on the proverbial cake! The defendent company did pay up but not before the deadline set in the court order. The student advisers were therefore required to do more research on the enforcement of judgments.

The last will and testament

The second of the case studies from the Sheffield clinic was, at least on the face of it, less exciting, and less involved. But it demonstrates well the process of learning, the link with the law curriculum and some important ethical considerations.

The facts

Again this was a case that came to the clinic through the open rota session. The students on duty were Claire and Louise.

The client, Helen Johnson, was a mature student who wished to make a will.[61] During the initial interview it transpired that Ms Johnson was a single

---

[59] While this may be an objective fact, the temptation to get personally involved and emotional when discussing the opponent's behaviour is strong. The same feelings of anger come through the file records in our first case study, above, at Northumbria.
[60] [1956] AC 696.
[61] The facts of this case are based on a combination of two cases the clinic handled in the same year. They have been put together to illustrate the value of non-contentious or transactional work in a clinical setting. Names and details have been altered to preserve confidentiality.

parent living temporarily with her parents. She was divorced from her child's father. At the time of the divorce neither Ms Johnson nor her then husband had any resources, so the only financial issue had been maintenance for their child.

Now, however, Ms Johnson was due to inherit a substantial sum from her grandfather, who was very elderly and in poor health. She wanted to make a will which would leave this inheritance and her other property (modest savings and her personal belongings) to her child, who was 12 years old. There was some urgency in the mind of the client in that her grandfather was in poor health and Ms Johnson wanted the will completed before she might inherit any legacy. She was concerned that if she died her daughter should be well provided for. And she wanted to ensure that her former husband (who had remarried) could not claim any part of the estate.

Learning from scratch

In Mr Payne's case there was already a body of knowledge amongst the students on contract law. This needed shaping and developing but it was in essence a case for reinforcing understanding. The case of the will was different: neither student advisers had taken equity and trusts. Some of their firm's members were third-year students who had taken equity and trusts, but there had been little overt reference to wills and probate in that syllabus and they too felt no better prepared to deal with the case.

However, if a systematic clinical approach is worth anything it is in the way that research methods are both designed and entrenched. With the safety net of qualified supervision, students can and regularly do embark on research into areas that they have not yet studied. The sense of confidence that is engendered by this, coupled with a thorough and disciplined approach, more than compensates for any initial inexperience.

Claire and Louise therefore set about identifying the issues that required research and what additional facts, if any, they required. The following were seen to be the pertinent questions following the firm's discussions and some preliminary reading in the practitioners' loose-leaf reference manuals in the clinic's library:

    (a)   Who could make a will and what were the legal requirements?
    (b)   Under what circumstances could the validity or content of a will be challenged?

(c)   Who would care for the testator's daughter and how could this be provided for in the will?

(d)   What safeguards could be put in the will to ensure that the testator's wishes were carried out?

The supervisor asked the extent of the anticipated inheritance. The student advisers had not deemed it appropriate to ask so direct a question. Why did it matter anyway? One of the firm's members said that if the sum was large it might necessitate the advice of a person or institution expert in investment matters and whether such a person or body should have a trustee role in the will. The advisers agreed that in order to advise the client fully this question needed to be asked.

At the subsequent interview the client was apparently highly embarrassed to reveal such details but when the reason behind the question was explained Ms Johnson said she thought the sum was around £10,000. The question also arose about the carers for Ms Johnson's daughter. Who would assume the day-to-day responsibility and be empowered to take the major decisions about her upbringing with the attendant powers that it would be necessary to grant?

Claire and Louise reported back to the firm with more information. It transpired that Ms Johnson had a younger brother whom she trusted and her father had a banking background. She was happy to appoint her mother, father and brother as joint executors and testamentary guardians. She was grateful for the tact shown by the advisers during the interviews.

Having identified the issues and researched as far as the research strategy and client's goals required, the client could be advised. Part of the advice was on the legal requirements in respect of the content and form of an effective will. Part concerned the possibility of challenge. In this respect the advisers had discovered that a dependant can petition the court if he or she feels that a will does not make reasonable financial provision but that in the circumstances (having consulted relevant authorities, both statutory and case law, and having utilised the search facility of LEXIS) students and supervisors agreed that this was highly unlikely to succeed even if technically it could not be prevented.

The task now was to draft a will. At this point several books of precedents were consulted. Now Claire and Louise knew what it was that they needed they could make sense of such practitioners' aids. To use these before would

have been to follow words without the necessary understanding — a
dangerous practice!

The draft will was finally approved after some minor amendments. The will
was executed (the student advisers enjoying being the witnesses to it) and
the matter completed.

Matters ethical

Client care was again a major consideration, although no issues arose that
were not covered by the clinic's standard rules of procedure. The need for
an efficient and professional service, characterised by good solicitor–client
communication was, and is, a constant theme in the clinic.

The preservation of confidentiality was also important and arose in two
contexts. First, keeping private the personal details of the client. In the course
of giving her instructions the client needed constant reassurance that the
particulars of her family and property would be kept within the confines of
the clinic and not revealed to other members of the student body. As has been
seen, the extent to which the student advisers felt that they could question
the client on personal matters also arose. This helped them clarify the
difference between asking questions for professional purposes and asking
questions out of pure curiosity.

Secondly, the client proved quite difficult to contact and had given her
parents' address as a contact point. When trying to contact her what
messages if any could the student advisers leave and what could they say to
anyone, other than the client, asking who was calling and why? It is part of
the standard practice of the clinic to ask clients whether the clinic can leave
messages for them and if so what, if anything, of substance can be revealed.
In this case the client simply asked that if she were not available a message
asking her to contact the clinic, but no more, could be left at her parents'
address, by fax or phone. To reveal the reason for the call would have been
a breach of confidentiality. Without the client's consent to simply leave a
message saying that the client had called would have been in breach of this
fundamental rule. The client has the right not to have his or her business
(including having gone to see a solicitor) revealed.

The client's instructions to complete the will at the earliest opportunity gave
cause for debate as the best interests of the client are paramount and yet the
students would need time to learn from the exercise and to draft the will

professionally. The clinic had already encountered several cases where the immediacy of the need mitigated against any real learning opportunity. Examples include court hearing dates that are imminent but where the client has only just consulted the clinic, or cases requiring urgent action, such as emergency applications for injunctions in the case of domestic violence. In such cases the clinic normally refers, with the client's consent, to another agency. In this case, although there was a pressing need, it was felt that the case could be properly handled in serving both the client's interests and those of the students. The client agreed that although the case might take a little longer than one might expect in private practice the slight delay was not prejudicial to the case and, if it ever were, a referral could be made.

The other matter which had to be taken into account concerned the types of work that the clinic undertook. A policy decision had been taken at a very early stage in the clinic's operation not to deal with transactional matters that were well provided for by private practice. There were two reasons for this. First, the clinic had decided not to hold a client account.[62] This excluded many transactions from the potential caseload. Secondly, the clinic enjoyed a good relationship with the local legal profession who would come into regular contact with the clinic in the course of its work and who would presumably not appreciate the clinic effectively taking work away from them. The profession was closely involved in the clinic through the advisory committee structure. As a result the clinic did not handle matrimonial cases with a financial aspect beyond child maintenance nor did it deal in the buying and selling aspect of conveyancing or probate. As the guiding principle of the clinic is its pedagogic function, only cases which had a learning value were undertaken. The making of wills was seen to be a valuable vehicle for study (issues of property, equity and trusts as well as legal skills such as interviewing and drafting are involved) but, as in other aspects of the clinic's work, only a few cases of one kind are needed to provide both the range and quality of work to serve the educational aims.

Assessment in the in-house clinic

We have stressed on several occasions in this book that the clinical ethos demands that assessment be part of the learning process. The clinical setting facilitates this development.

It might assist both student and teacher readers to know something of the assessment regime used at Northumbria and Sheffield Hallam in their

---

[62] It seemed an unnecessary complication and responsibility, at least in the formative years of the clinic, to hold clients' money. There would have also been additional insurance implications.

real-client clinics, from which the three case studies set out above emanated. We start with Sheffield Hallam.

The Law Clinic is an elective available to years 2 and 3 on the LLB degree. It is a fully weighted (20 credit) unit running for both semesters of the academic year. The unit's aims and anticipated learning outcomes are clearly stated in the Unit Outline and Law Clinic Handbook. These are:

Aims:
1. To develop an understanding of the role of law and lawyers in society.
2. To develop an understanding of the substantive rules and procedure through experiential learning.
3. To develop specific legal skills as outlined in the Rationale.

Anticipated learning outcomes:
On completion of the unit, the students will be able to:

(a) explain the conduct of case management;
(b) handle legal documents and explain their relevance and application;
(c) demonstrate lawyering skills as identified in the Rationale;
   . . .
(d) explain the role of law and lawyers in society;
(e) apply knowledge and understanding of legal rules in practical situations.

Students are asked at the beginning of the unit to complete a personal profile which details their previous experience and career intentions. They are also required to sign an undertaking to acknowledge the academic and professional obligations expected of them. The personal profile is referred to and expanded upon at various stages of the unit and is used as a formal mechanism for recording the student's progress. These prerequisites and this process are a rather crude version of a learning contract. Considerable work still needs to be done to ensure that the contract becomes an integral part of learning and reflects the active involvement of the student in the design and implementation of the assessment requirements.

The actual assessment of the unit is based on two elements: the portfolio of work and the overall performance and participation of the student in the clinic in its day-to-day operation. The elements are equally weighted.

The portfolio consists of:

(a)   a diary or log which records the detail of the student's activities;

(b)   a case study exploring the legal, ethical and practical issues arising in one case that the student was involved in; and

(c)   a critical self-appraisal of the student's experiences in the clinic. Students are expected to show in the portfolio that they have met the anticipated learning outcomes documented in the Unit Outline.

The assessment of the student's performance and participation in the clinic is based on weekly discussions with the students collectively (in their firms), with the students individually on an informal basis, and on at least two formal occasions when the student is asked for his or her own assessment of performance and is given feedback by staff (which is recorded). Staff keep a monthly log of student performance and participation.

Once the portfolio of work has been completed staff meet with students on an individual basis to discuss a final grading. Although technically the examination board reserves the right to make the final determination, staff in the Law Clinic do endeavour to reach agreement with students on their grading. This is not always an easy or pleasurable task but is part of a visible commitment to make assessment formative and to engage the students in a discussion, one in which the student is given the opportunity to present justification for a particular grading and to challenge the staff to justify their own positions. From personal experience I confirm that the assessment process, although time consuming, appears to work, in the sense that staff and students take the task seriously and it produces high-quality results. Cynics may suggest that it is in the interests of both staff and students to agree high marks and that such an outcome is made more inevitable by the personalising of the process. This disregards the close observance of assessment criteria, the professionalism of the staff (and students) and the fact that when students work hard (as clinical experience seems to show) they might be expected to do well. It also begs the question of the objectivity of assessment methods used in more conventional teaching areas.

Students receive a grading on the same scheme as for any other law unit, that is a percentage mark falling within a band on the 1st to 3rd class honours and pass scale.

At Sheffield Hallam we would be the first to admit that we are only beginning to address the complex issues implicit in assessment. Closer definition of criteria and greater use of the students in the process (including the introduction of group and peer assessment) are all ongoing challenges for both staff and students.[63]

We look now at assessment at Northumbria. The sheer size of the programme there is a challenge. We needed to come up with consistent standards across 13 supervisors, each looking after students whose cases were in different specialisms and whose clients provided more or less demanding work from students. While we are the last people — perhaps literally — to champion the reliability of conventional exam and coursework assessments, there is a great deal of comfort in parcelling up all the scripts and sending them to an external examiner and thinking, 'There — that is the sum total of all the evidence on which the assessment will be based, and all of it can be checked'. Of course that does not achieve reliability, because the person marking or checking scripts is still applying different criteria at different times to different students' answers; and is affected by mood or prejudice and by response to the student's style, handwriting or choice of content. The only problem is that universities really like assessment procedures that, in the end, get reduced to a mark out of 100 and can be debated (in some universities with the students' names remaining anonymous) in a serious examination board. Clinical programmes have to conform and find a mark out of 100 to throw into that melting pot.

At Northumbria clinical work was not graded for the first nine of my 11 years there. We just gave students a pass or a fail (never, after warning conversations, did a fail actually need to be recorded). High-quality work was carried out and students saw the rewards in the improvement to their references and career prospects. But eventually we agreed, with the start of the integrated degree, that the importance of clinical work should be reflected in a mark which counts along with traditional subjects towards the degree.

To give a flavour of how it worked (in 1995–96) I include a slightly altered assessment for one of my own students. There is not space — and perhaps it would be asking too much of the reader — to include the portfolio of work

---

[63] The assessment regime for 1997/98 is:

(a)   performance (lawyering skills, understanding legal concepts, analysis of law and facts, problem-solving strategies) and participation (group work, assuming responsibility, attendance and management, ethics) count for 50 per cent of marks.

(b)   portfolio of work (critical awareness, grasp of legal concepts, research, relating theory to practice, learning from mistakes, ethics) counts for 50 per cent of marks.

A trial scheme for 1998/99 may be implemented that will allocate a percentage to each individually assessed topic (those topics appearing in parentheses above). At present the marking is impressionistic, based on the criteria identified above.

on which the comments are based, and of course some is based on video material. What you get below is my own commentary, and perhaps the issue you will recognise is how much is based on my own subjective judgment of Lawrence's performance.

The assessment portfolio on which the assessment below is based was submitted after the student had a chance to submit and discuss a draft. The statement of what will be required is given out at the beginning of the year.

Lawrence F.

Introduction
A very conscientious student, reliable, a good member of the team.

Written communication
[We asked students to select a formal and informal document from the portfolio of work during the year. The supervisor assessed these in the light of subjective knowledge of the student's other written communications during the year. The student is required to include all drafts and a commentary on the process by which the final version was arrived at.]

Letter: incidentally reveals, in the commentary, Lawrence's tendency to avoid unpleasant facts ('passed away'). He needed some encouragement to tell this client potentially bad news as well as the straightforward information, e.g., raising the possibility of a need to see her own interests as separate from those of her husband. As a result his drafting was sometimes less direct than I would encourage.

Commentary shows good awareness of own defects, notably the legalistic language in the drafts. Typical of his approach he welcomed assistance and improved his work as a result. The final draft is helpful to the client. I think it could be simpler, perhaps because I am not totally persuaded that Lawrence really grasps the law in this area.

Particulars of claim: This involved adapting a draft in the light of counsel's detailed advice. Well done, though as Lawrence admits not a very onerous task.

10/15

File and case management
[This is based on a file memorandum prepared by the student (not just for the purpose of assessment — in theory) to update and plan further progress on a particular case.]

Memorandum is a good one, and had the client been contactable would have served as a good basis for future case management. Needed assistance in making the facts adequately clear: tendency to ambiguity or incompleteness in first draft.

11/15

Interviewing
[This assessment is based on a student's selection of a video-recorded interview, preferably one with a known client for which he was able to prepare. At least as much weight also goes to the student's own analysis of how he performed. A difficult issue is the relative rewards to be given to a student who — achieving all of our learning objectives — gives a perhaps mediocre performance and recognises this in the reflection, compared with the outstanding student who interviews well and has not so much to reflect on and could indeed sound complacent if the reflection were accurate. I come down in favour of a slight weighting in favour of the actual performance, but would still consider that real learning during and after the interview could be evidence for a first-class mark.]

Very thorough preparation of background law and facts needed. On tape he establishes a good relationship, covers the ground and explains well what he has prepared. Clearly establishes facts he needs, as the statement shows. A certain amount of awkwardness, however, some of which is picked up in the analysis. I feel Lawrence has made a good go at client interviewing, and still has a lot to learn, particularly in trying to become more client centred.

10/15

Research
[This is one of the most crucial areas in clinical work. If we are to sustain our claim for being student centred and achieving independent learning then we must give sufficient weight to students' research outcomes. The example below does not reflect this importance in the amount of consideration I gave the research work Lawrence carried out. I find when I search

for an example that shows my grading in a better light that I did not go into any more detail in the assessment of any other of my students that year. (However, this is summative assessment: much of the formative assessment — the part which helps the student to improve — takes place weekly or even more often in the case discussions.)]

Research into CICB scheme in preparation for initial interview. Thorough and accurate, albeit not demanding; fully documented.

11/15

Law Office procedures and participation
[This item of assessment is included to give rewards for conscientious and professional behaviour. Strict adherence to our procedures is vital with so many inexperienced advisers, and so much scope for mistakes. Note that I give full marks, which is contrary to convention in academic marking, but I consider there was nothing further Lawrence could have done in the course of the year to demonstrate his professionalism and conscientious- ness. What message would it give out if that was rewarded with less than 100%?]

Lawrence's self-appraisal is accurate, his attendance was 100% and there is no aspect of his firm involvement or adherence to procedures that I could criticise.

10/10

Critical commentary
[Each student is required to write a short piece evaluating his or her work and learning in the clinical programme. There was much debate — with me in the minority — when deciding what weighting to give to this self-evaluation and what contents to expect. What I wanted, and failed to get, was, in keeping with the tenor of this book, that clinical work is not just about performance; it is about evaluation of learning and putting into context. What we assessed, shown in the example below, does not explicitly reward and require a consideration of what it all means, why law works in this context and fails in that, how things could be better. That kind of learning takes place, of course, but since we did not assess it we could not reasonably insist on students getting out books on jurisprudence or statutory interpretation or sociology of law. They expected to be

rewarded for their performances as lawyers, and their reflection on that performance. Perhaps this can be justified within a vocational degree, but it is not enough within a conventional degree where students are not just learning to be lawyers.]

A frank and useful examination of what Lawrence did, and what he learned. He has tried and, given the lack of explicit tuition in this area, done well at going beyond the level of 'What skills did I learn?' The account also reflects Lawrence's personal commitment to hard work and learning.

22/30

Total 74

Here we have a first-class performance, and a better mark in fact than Lawrence achieved in his other subjects. Are we distorting the outcome by giving such good marks to a 'second-class student'? I answer this in two ways — if rhetorical questions amount to answers!

(a) If he meets our learning outcomes can we do other than reward him highly? (Were they the wrong outcomes if a second-class student can achieve first-class results?)

(b) What are we doing labelling students as 'first-class' and 'second-class'?

(c) (I've thought of a further even more important rhetorical question): What do we academics so hate about high achievement by large numbers of students anyway? Let's rejoice. To show that it's not a way of handing out high marks to everyone without any differentiation, I include the assessment profile, without further commentary, of the student who was doing the least well that year (in my subjective opinion).

Bill H.

Introduction
This student was unreliable to the extent of requiring a warning of the risk of failing. Things improved once he got stuck into a case that he was enthused about, but earlier in the year I felt obliged to transfer from him a case that required urgent attention which he was not giving it. Despite these problems his work was often good.

Written communication
Letter: very good, clear drafting.

Draft partnership agreement: good use of precedent.

(Has failed to document what assistance he got on the letter, but in fact the quality of the document is largely his own work.)

13/15

File and case management
This file review is unfocused, and would be unhelpful to anyone not familiar with the file. It perhaps results from Bill's poor involvement with the firm and tendency to work in isolation. He did not produce any other file reviews.

4/15

Interviewing
Good planning and helpful written outcome. Self-awareness from watching the video: too laid back and not engaging the clients fully. He gives the impression (but I do not think it is the reality) of not really being interested in the clients.

8/15

Research
A satisfactory research process, apart from what I consider to be undue reliance on the opinions of others rather than going to the source of the authority.

8/15

Law Office procedure and participation
This was poor, and Bill's account suggests things improved further than they did. Even at the end I was never confident that Bill would be at a meeting, or, if not, would let me know. Adherence to procedures OK.

3/10

Critical commentary
Shows awareness of the very bad start he made to the year, and indeed is
a very accurate account showing awareness of weaknesses and strengths.
However, his claim that after he realised and admitted his problems he
became a fully participative member of the firm is wishful thinking.

Overall this is a very good and honest report showing a commendable
awareness of the firm's work and his own.

17/30

Total 53

Perhaps the two biggest issues around the assessment of real-client clinics
are the questions of comparability between students, and the decision of what
we seek to reward. Let's open them both up again briefly before we conclude
this chapter.

Can we assess fairly and reliably?

Before answering this question there is a more important question. It is the
question of validity. We could very easily assess students with 100 per cent
reliability (meaning different assessors, or even a computer, always getting
the same result for each answer) if we designed our assessments (and
therefore learning outcomes) with that uppermost. Factual recall of simple
information lends itself to that kind of assessment: 'In *Carlill* v *Bubonic
Plague Corporation* the reward for catching influenza was (a) £100, (b) a trip
to Disneyworld, (c) free enrolment on a clinical law course?' Assessment of
skills of performing complex tasks and exercising critical judgment is hard
to reduce to repeatable and quantifiable performance measures. It requires
judgment by the assessor. Validity, we suggest, is the starting point for
assessment: it is more important to assess unreliably the attributes we believe
in a student learning than to assess reliably things that aren't of value for a
student to have achieved.

Having got that off my chest, I wish to avoid apologising for unreliability.
Which academic has not returned to a script, or marked the work already
assessed by a colleague, and come up with a staggering difference? Which
academic has not looked at a pile of marked scripts and thought: 'I think I
was a bit unfair to the ones I looked at at first, but I can't go through them
all again without having a nervous breakdown'? There's even the story,

probably true for every academic, of marking a piece of plagiarised work (but not knowing it to be such, even sometimes the marker's own) and giving it a devastating grade, or marking the work of a student who copied another student and giving the two wildly different marks.

In clinical work cheating is impossible. No student can impersonate in the interview — the client would notice, even if the supervisor was asleep and failed to spot it. Reflection can only be on your own performance. So in clinical assessment we have eliminated one huge headache.

But yes, there is a measure of subjectivity and unreliability in clinical assessment. When I was at Northumbria the head of school was more inclined to judge a clinical performance on conventional grading levels than I was, and so less likely to go into the 80s or 90s. Even if we tried to agree on how to approach the task we ended up 10 or more marks apart on actual students. But who is to say we would not do this marking essays or adjudicating the Eurovision Song Contest?

What do we seek to reward?

This is the crucial question. Students are very bright. With their limited time they will focus on their grades, their careers and, we hope, their enjoyment. Give them learning objectives that are not assessed and those objectives will only be achieved in a haphazard way. One of the challenges ahead for clinical legal education is to give students an immersion into learning through doing and then take them back into their academic roles — getting books and papers to read and essays to write on what they are learning about the law in their practice. This may result in lessening the amount of casework, or eating into the coverage of other subjects to allow time for teaching and learning and assessing these outcomes. We have a way to go in achieving this yet.

Some final pitfalls and anecdotes from an in-house clinic

The problems of getting absorbed in client service and forgetting learning objectives are, we hope, evident already. Problems in standardising assessment we just looked at. Problems of resourcing are only too well known. Is there yet another problem? Of course there is.

By taking a problem as a learning exercise and working on it in depth, while providing a service to the client, there is a risk of doing too much for the client. This is not meant in a patronising way, but first-hand experience suggests that a client may have been better not to have received free legal work. We give two examples from Hugh's time at Northumbria. The facts are disguised.

Mr Hope had bought a car. According to our instructions Mr Hope had been clearly misled about this model before agreeing to buy it, so it looked, after some legal research by the students, like a good case. Mr Hope was really pleased with this advice, as he had already issued a summons. The students got to work on improving and filing the amended particulars of claim.

Two years later the students had learned a little but the case, on the evidence now gathered, was less winnable, and Mr Hope's enthusiasm had turned into a desire to extract himself from a time-consuming and risky court action: risky because if he lost he would be liable for the opponent's costs. Indeed he did lose the case. He did pay the costs. Free legal advice and assistance was not good for him. If he had had to pay to go on with the case he might have backed out earlier. (Of course in the light of such experiences we now know to advise a client in such a situation that it may be better not to proceed, or might even refuse to take on the case. But we thought it was winnable.)

I am reminded about another case, that of Mrs Marquez. She was facing possession proceedings. But the landlords had served the wrong Housing Act notice before the tenancy was granted, and compounded the error by failing to show on the face of the pleadings that there was any ground in law to obtain possession. On instruction we obtained legal aid and held off possession for over a year, to the consternation of the landlords and their exasperated solicitors. It was a good learning experience, since the students were able to learn a lot about housing law from their own researches, and from observing the stream of mistakes made by our opponents. But in the end we had to cave in. Once the landlords, eventually, got their case in order there was little point in further defence. Was this an appropriate use of public resources? Any good solicitor in private practice would have used legal aid to achieve the same result, if so instructed, but we were not such a solicitor. We were a law school. I admit that I do not know the 'right' answer, but I would probably do the same again if such a good learning opportunity presented itself for student use. And undoubtedly the client would do the same again, since her gratitude was the most emotional and sincere I have ever observed, despite the final result. And this meant that she wanted my help every time she had any other legal problem.

If you provide a service, that generates its own problems, since it is hard to turn down requests for more time on the telephone to listen to the latest legal problem an old satisfied customer is suffering.

I finish with a final anecdote. On the day of the clinical conference run by Northumbria in 1992, which turned out to lead to the development of the Clinical Legal Education Organisation, my co-director of the Student Law Office suddenly had to abandon us and rush to court. A terminally ill 'client' was in the county court claiming we had promised to represent him. No records were available, but naturally we could not just say: 'Not our problem'. It appeared that he had made a phone call, talked to a student who had, without leaving a record or talking to a supervisor, agreed to giving legal help. In a sense all was well that ended well, and the case was settled at court, the 'client' pleased and a disaster avoided. In-house programmes need the most meticulous supervision. Mistakes can occur. Students must be reminded constantly that they are to take no step without consultation, ever.[64]

That mistake never recurred. No insurance claim has ever been made, to my knowledge, in relation to a UK clinical programme, nor any complaint to a professional body. But to the solicitor supervisor, you need no reminding that your neck is on the block if there is a problem. Which may make agency placements, the topic of the next chapter, more attractive than previously thought.

Conclusion

This chapter is not a how to do it manual. Both of us could write a separate chapter on the dos and don'ts, from our experience, of running an in-house clinic. We haven't offered that here. We would rather talk to people and offer what guidance we can than say: this is how to do it (which would be to suggest there is a right way, which there is not). The appendix to this chapter, CLEO's model standards for a real-client programme, will provide the beginnings of the 'how to do it' guidance.

What this chapter has been about is giving a flavour of what goes on in two clinics and in three real cases.

---

[64] Lessons learned through this type of experience have led to improvements in office procedures, and anyone wanting to set up a programme is welcome to consult either of the authors of this chapter or CLEO and to see copies of the office manuals we have developed to try to avert future errors of this sort.

On an operational level the cases show the need for compliance with the professional obligations incumbent on solicitors. Although the clinics at Newcastle and Sheffield feature many differences in their organisation and procedures both necessarily share the principle of orderly and structured approaches to all aspects of clinic work. The common use of forms, the reliance on an induction process, the articulated importance of research (both techniques and strategies), and the reliance upon regular and frequent meetings between the student advisers and the supervising staff, all combine to ensure, so far as is possible, that the exacting standards rightly expected of practising lawyers are met.

As a learning experience the real-client, in-house, solicitors' practice is very much at the sharp end of legal education. It provides a unique opportunity to study law in a context that is personally challenging and engaging, and which, if properly structured, provides a complement to the rest of the student's studies.

These clinics offer the chance for students to deal directly with a wide range of legal and practice issues, some of which they have encountered in class elsewhere, others of which are new to them. By using the methods described in this chapter the students can learn from the doing and the reflecting on the doing (provided this is actively supported as part of the pedagogic process) in both instances.

The whole is also about how lawyers behave and should behave and what law means in an everyday as well as a jurisprudential sense. The authors of this chapter hope that not only have we contributed to producing better lawyers in a technical sense but that we have also challenged the students to criticise constructively what they found around them.

At an undergraduate level the clinic has much to offer but its value will not be maximised unless and until there is effective integration with the rest of the curriculum. Our case studies do, we believe, demonstrate the potential for this and its importance within the learning environment that is the law school.

Appendix: model standards in clinical legal education (CLEO 1995)[65]

Purpose

These standards are intended to serve three different but related purposes:

- to promote good (and sometimes professionally required) practice in clinical programmes
- to provide a base from which clinical programmes can be established
- to give assistance and protection to both staff and students, particularly on the operational context of clinical work.

The model standards have been devised by the Clinical Legal Education Organisation (CLEO), which is a representative body of those practising or with an interest in clinical legal education. They are intended as a guide to clinical practice. Individual institutions will have their own specific ideas and requirements. These standards are intended to provide a benchmark for those active in or setting up clinics and reflect the wide experience of those already running clinics both in the UK and abroad. The standards are applicable to both undergraduate and vocational postgraduate courses.

CLEO proposes to produce model standards for the different manifestations of clinical teaching and learning including live-client[66] clinics, simulated clinics and placements.

The first edition of these standards addresses live-client clinical programmes and address three issues:

- educational objectives and learning outcomes
- professional requirements
- operational practice.

Educational objectives and learning outcomes

This section is based on the premise that the educational value of any unit (clinical or otherwise) needs to be clearly identified. This is necessary so that both staff and students understand what the unit is attempting to achieve and what is required of participants in the conduct of that unit.

---

65 Updated in October 1997 by the authors as to references only. The body of the text remains as adopted.
66 We have reproduced here the use of the term live-client rather than our preferred term, real-client.

The broad aims of live-client clinics are:

- to enhance the students' learning experience and understanding of the substantive law, legal process, ethics and the role of law in society
- to produce students who can take the learning experience offered by live-client clinics and reflect upon how and why cases were progressed and how this fits into the overall context of their legal studies
- to empower the students to become proactive in the process of learning
- to provide formative assessment methods which are in themselves a strategic and integral part of the learning experience
- to enable students to develop skills, both transferable and law specific, that enable students to better progress their legal education.

Learning outcomes are those objectives that the students are expected to achieve by undertaking the unit and the process by which those objectives will be achieved. Those outcomes should take into account the academic level of study the student is engaged in and the individual requirements that the students may have in terms of progression towards those outcomes.

It is not the intention of CLEO to prescribe what learning outcomes should appear in each clinical programme. An example of a clinical unit's objectives and learning outcomes might read:

This unit is designed to introduce students to the concept of live-client, in-house clinical legal education.

Students will be exposed, under close supervision, to unstructured legal problems arising from a live-client base. It is expected that through such exposure, students will reflect on and demonstrate a better understanding of the role of law and lawyers in society and of the substantive rules of law and procedure that they will have to apply during the programme. Those participating in the unit should also acquire lawyering skills (drafting, research, advocacy, interviewing and negotiation) as well as those skills that can be described as transferable (including: communication, problem solving, teamwork, organisational and study skills, and the use of new technology).

Students will be assigned to 'firms' (small groups) and the knowledge, skills and expertise of the students are expected to be shared within the firm. This is of particular relevance where a firm consists of both second and third-year students.

Although this option may be of specific interest to those students who wish to follow careers in the legal profession, it is expected that other students will also gain from the clinical experience.

Assessment is inextricably linked (if not driven by) learning outcomes. Those designing clinical programmes need to examine the pedagogic aim of assessment on the unit and identify the subject of the assessment (is it extent of knowledge of legal rules, concepts, skills and/or procedures that is being assessed?).

The form of the assessment should also be clearly set out so that both staff and students understand what is expected. Is the assessment to be by way of examination (seen or unseen); assessment of coursework (assignments, reports, presentations, portfolios); by staff, peer or self; oral or written, or on a continual basis; pass/fail or graded? It is suggested that whatever form(s) assessment take(s) it should be formative in nature so that it becomes an integral part of the learning experience.

An assessment model might read as follows:

Each student will produce a portfolio of work consisting of:

1   A journal listing the student's activity in clinic-related work, with details (subject to the rules of confidentiality) of the cases on which he or she has been involved.
2   A case study detailing one of the cases for which the student has been responsible.
3   A reflective critique of the student's experience in the law clinic, written from that student's perspective.

The portfolio of work will be submitted by week 8 of the second semester.

The supervising staff will also monitor the progress of the students' performances in the law clinic and will assess their performance on a continuing basis.

The supervisors will meet with the students at the end of each semester to discuss assessment. The content of the student's portfolio and the student's performances in the law clinic will be equally weighted for assessment purposes. The supervisors will take into account the student's own view as to the standard of his or her performance in the law clinic and will also ask for the views of that student's co-firm members. Subject to the jurisdiction of the school's examination boards, the decision of the supervisors will, however, be final.

Integration of clinical work within degree or vocational programmes is seen by CLEO as essential to the service of the pedagogic aims of clinical programmes. If clinical education has intellectual worth, it is in the extent to which it enables students to better understand concepts and principles of law and the context within which these operate. It is important that clinical programmes complement and are complemented by the rest of the course of study taken. Thus, clinics should be integrated within that course so that the pedagogic aims can be both set and achieved.

The following are suggested as pointers to whether and how such integration can be achieved:

- that clinics be a validated part of the course of study, including criteria for assessment
- that clinics be available across the years of study. The choice between making such courses optional or compulsory is a matter for each institution and will depend on available resourcing
- that the skills implicit in clinical work be linked with and used in other units on the course of study, in so far as they assist students in achieving the learning outcome for that unit
- that, subject to principles of confidentiality, material originating in the clinic be used to develop, through case study and simulation, the substance of other course units
- that staff involved in clinical programmes have a direct input into one or more of the other course units. This encourages best use of resources and enables the issues ensuing in clinical work and other units to be cross-referenced and explored. In addition, it prevents clinics from being hived-off as vocational activity and disconnected from the 'regular' faculty.

The educational purpose and service provided by clinics throw up potential conflict and tension for clinical programmes. Should a clinic identify particular client groups, act only in certain cases, or represent everyone who comes through the door? are questions that have historically troubled designers and providers of such schemes.

It is CLEO's view that, however much the clinic wishes to advise and assist those members of the community who have unmet legal need (for example, in relation to housing, social security or immigration), the principal aim of clinical programmes is educational. It is the needs of the student that must dictate which clients are assisted and in what areas. This can give rise to difficult decisions, especially where the potential client has real and often urgent needs. If the clinic is clear about why it is operating, other decisions follow more logically (if no easier to implement). It should be stressed that once a client is advised and/or represented then a professional standard of care and service is applicable. Some of the important issues relating to this are explored in the sections on professional requirements and operational practice.

Professional requirements

Live-client clinics can take a variety of forms, ranging from advice only, through assistance and partial representation to fully fledged solicitors' practices. The clinics may also be in-house or run through an external agency (such as a free representation unit or law centre). In each case there are implications, and in some instances requirements, in terms of standards and rules of professional practice.

CLEO suggests that the standards set out below will ensure compliance with such professional rules in clinics where this is a requirement. In other cases the standards represent good practice and can be followed accordingly. It should be stressed that the standards set down a minimum requirement and one that might be exceeded where resourcing and pedagogic aims permit.

The professional requirements are set out in summarised form. The relevant professional practice rule can be found in: *Guide to the Professional Conduct of Solicitors* (London: Law Society, 1996) as amended and *Code of Conduct of the Bar of England and Wales* (London: General Council of the Bar, 1990) as amended.

Although the issues listed below are set down in the context of professional requirements, they are also highly pertinent to operational practice and will also be raised in that context where relevant.

Supervision

- All clinics should be supervised by a person who is competent and experienced in both the substantive law and practice of the subject matters serviced by the clinic.

- A person or persons should be named as supervisor(s) or director(s) of the clinic.
- In the case of clinics holding themselves out as solicitors' practices, overall supervision must be provided by a solicitor who holds a practising certificate and who has at least three years' certificated post-qualification experience and a solicitor who holds a practising certificate must be in attendance at the clinic at all times that the clinic is open to the public.
- Supervision includes not only monitoring the activities of clinic students but also includes client records, the clinic diary, correspondence (in and out) and the general conduct of the office and its staff.

Stationery and publicity

- All notepaper, compliments slips and other stationery and law clinic publicity should identify:

  — the nature and extent of the clinic's services
  — that students provide the service under supervision
  — who the supervisor(s) or director(s) are
  — name, address, telephone, fax number, e-mail address (if applicable)
  — whether the clinic offers legal aid.

- A standard client-care letter must be given to every client which states:

  — the nature and extent of the clinic's services
  — that students provide the service under supervision
  — that the clinic's service is based on client confidentiality
  — if legal aid is generally available
  — who is handling the matter
  — who is supervising the matter
  — what complaints procedure is available to clients
  — the position so far as indemnity insurance is concerned
  — if assistance beyond advice is given, the extent of the assistance and how any costs or disbursements will be met.

- Each client must be given (within 14 days of interview and as early as the case necessitates it) an initial advice letter which states:

  — a summary of the facts of the case so far as the clinic understands them
  — the advice to the client (including whether or not the clinic is in a position to assist further)

— if the case requires further action and if the client wishes the clinic to help and if the clinic is able to do so, the terms on which the clinic can represent or assist.

• Each client for whom the clinic acts (beyond the initial advice letter) must be given and return signed a clinic retainer form indicating that the client understands the terms of the clinic's service and agrees to them.

Insurance   All clinics should be insured against the risk of liability arising in respect of advice, assistance and/or representation given to clients, and general third-party liability. In the case of solicitors' practice clinics, this must satisfy the terms of the Solicitors' Practice Rules and related codes of practice. Cover should explicitly extend to students and supervisors.

Confidentiality   Staff and students must be aware of the need for adviser/ client confidentiality. To this end:

• the room(s) and facilities used by the clinic must ensure that the clients' case details remain confidential to the clinic
• client interviewing must be conducted in a room to which only supervisors and advising students have access during interview sessions
• all case records, both current and completed, must be securely stored and accessible only by supervisors and advising students
• all supervisors and students must be trained on the issue of confidentiality and its practice and this must be done by an induction course at which attendance is compulsory, reinforced by a clinic manual that deals with the issue comprehensively
• other facilities for contacting clients (telephone, fax, DX, computer disks, e-mail, etc) must be operated to conform to the required level of confidentiality
• all publicity, discussion, assessment and supervision of law clinic work must ensure compliance with the overriding principle of confidentiality
• facilities for the proper destruction and disposal of confidential waste must be set up.

Ethics   Supervisors and students must be aware of the profession's expectations and requirements so far as the ethical issues are concerned. This should be addressed in the clinic manual and in the induction course.

A professional standard of service   Even though the service is provided by students (under supervision) there is only one standard ultimately which the clinic can be judged by — the standard applicable to any competent practising lawyer. This is explored in greater detail in the following section on operational practice.

Conflict of interest Supervisors and students must be aware of the professional rules relating to conflict of interest and must be able to recognise both actual and potential conflicts and act accordingly. This issue should be addressed in the clinic manual and in the induction course.

Operational practice

A number of standards are suggested in this section. These are divided into those CLEO regards as essential (or minimum) standards and those that are recommended (from the experience of clinicians in the UK and abroad).

They are produced in summary form and cover the following:

Supervision and staffing

Minimum:

- Staff must be allocated a realistic timetabled allowance for supervision and other clinic-related duties. Experience has shown that 12 students taking a clinical option over two semesters require supervision of at least 8 hours per week. Supervision continues outside of term-time.
- A ratio of no more than 12 students to each supervisor. US models advocate eight to one presuming the staff is dedicated largely to the clinical programme. CLEO suggests that, provided a minimum of 8 hours supervisor–student contact is timetabled, it should be possible to discharge the proper supervisory function and free that staff person for some other (limited) 'regular' faculty teaching, research or administration.
- At least two supervisors should be assigned to each clinic. This ensures cover and continuity.
- A supervisor must be available every time the clinic is open to the public, including when client interviews are taking place. (This must be a solicitor with a practising certificate for solicitor clinics.)
- No advice should be given by students unless it has been discussed and approved by a supervisor (note requirement again for solicitor clinics). This includes advice given in interview or via the telephone, fax or e-mail.
- Correspondence addressed to the clinic must be opened, read and allocated to students by a supervisor (note requirement again for solicitor clinics).

- Correspondence sent by the clinic must be read, approved, countersigned and dispatched by a supervisor (note requirement again for solicitor clinics).
- Each clinic should have access to administrative and clerical support or word processing or typing facilities and client confidentiality should be preserved.
- Faculty staff (academic, administrative and clerical) should be informed of who the clinic supervisors are, what their availability is and when the clinic is open to clients.
- Contingency plans must be in place to cover supervision of the clinic and its students in the event of absence of supervisors or students and during such period of the year when student attendance is not guaranteed (e.g., examination periods, vacations, etc.).
- Non-solicitor-qualified staff, whose involvement in the clinic is to be invited and welcomed, must (in the case of solicitor clinics) and ought (in the case of other clinics) be generally supervised by a solicitor holding a practising certificate.

Recommended:

- It is recommended that administrative and clerical support be provided in the form of a full or part-time person who is dedicated to the clinic. CLEO's experience is that this not only aids the processing of paperwork but adds invaluable continuity to the clinic's operation. It also replicates the organisation of legal practice.
- Appointments should be entered into an appointments diary by the supervisor or by the student with the knowledge and approval of the supervisor.

Maintenance of files and records

Minimum:

- Records must be kept of all stages of a case including:

  — record of interview(s)
  — record of telephone, fax or e-mail communications
  — record of research
  — record of court or tribunal attendance
  — record of preparation
  — record of documents given to or by the clinic should be kept on each client's file (or a general file if a client's file has not yet been

opened) in chronological order and tagged and on a form used to record that transaction in all clinic cases.

- All correspondence sent and received by the clinic should be kept in chronological order and tagged on the appropriate file.
- No client's file should be removed from the clinic without the express authority of the supervisor.
- All court pleadings, client's documents, experts' reports, legal aid papers and other relevant materials, excluding correspondence, should be kept on the appropriate file in document wallets and labelled with details of contents.
- A limitation period diary should be maintained containing the expiry dates of relevant periods and timetables relating to ongoing litigation. This may be part of the general diary provided the relevant entries are clearly marked.
- The date and time of court appointments should be entered in the clinic diary.
- A system of recording and referencing cases must be set up and maintained, for example, a general file and daybook can be kept which records the initial visit or call to the clinic by the client and the outcome of that visit. Each client can be given a reference number that appears on the client's file as and when it is opened. The reference number should include the reference to the student or firm handling the case and the supervisor responsible for it. In addition, a record card can be kept on each client's file containing personal details of the client (name, address, date of birth, etc.), special instructions as to contact and confidentiality, and a summary of every stage through which the case has progressed. In this way it will be possible for a supervisor or student not familiar with that case to discover relatively quickly what has happened and what the last development was.

Recommended:

- A file may be maintained on cards listing each client reference number and address. This can be used readily to trace client details.

Premises

Minimum:

- The clinic should have premises that are accessible to persons including those with disability.

- The premises should afford facilities for the conduct of reception duties, interviews, telephone contact and the general conduct of a client's case, in secure conditions that preserve the principle of confidentiality.
- The premises must provide students with sufficient space to conduct necessary research and to manage cases whilst preserving the principle of confidentiality.
- The premises should be signed and identified as clinic premises.

Recommended:

- The premises should consist of a reception area, waiting room and an interview room, all of which should afford security and preserve confidentiality.
- The premises should contain a focal point where students can be debriefed, discuss cases and receive notices.
- Facilities for offering basic hospitality to clients (e.g., tea, coffee) should be made available, including access to a toilet or washroom.

Equipment

Minimum:

The clinic should have:

- a dedicated telephone line or extension to ensure confidentiality. The telephone should have access to an external line
- facilities for the secure storage of files and records
- desks and chairs for interviewing and working on clients' cases
- word-processing facilities
- a library of basic practitioner texts and reference materials, or access to such, whilst preserving confidentiality
- workable and efficient arrangements for the payment of expenses, e.g., court fees, travelling costs, experts' reports. This could either be through the maintenance of a law clinic office account or by payment from the institution's payments department. In the latter case it must be capable of responding to the law clinic's needs, e.g., payment of court fees (delay may prejudice the case)
- a clinic manual which clearly sets out the recommended pedagogic objectives, the operational rules and the professional standards and duties.

Recommended:

The clinic should have:

- an answering machine, fax and photocopying facilities
- a full set of forms (legal aid, court, etc.) relevant to the clinic
- e-mail
- a dedicated budget covering predicted expenses and contingency fund
- LEXIS and CD-ROM access
- document trays into which all correspondence (having been checked by the supervisor) and notes for students are placed. Students should check the trays daily. One tray per student group or firm (see under 'student activity') has been found to be sufficient.

Funding

Minimum:

- Dedicated funding underwritten by the institution (hard money) sufficient for the completion of the period over which the clinic is to operate (i.e., teaching period).
- A contingency fund earmarked to enable unforeseen expenditure to be met.
- Where appropriate use of the legal aid fund to be made.

Recommended:

- That wherever external moneys are attracted (soft money), this be backed pound for pound by hard money.
- In the event of funding being cut or withdrawn that at least three months' notice be given to enable the orderly winding down of work.

Student activity

Minimum:

- All students must attend an induction programme which covers the operational practice of the clinic.
- All students should agree in writing to the terms of the law clinic's practice — to this end a contract setting out the expectations of the law clinic and its students should be used.

- It is a fundamental objective of clinical practice to give students formative feedback on their clinical work. A profile of each student should be kept that records their expectations, their adjudged perform-ance and the ways in which this performance can be improved.
- A minimum of two students should be responsible for each client or case. This offers protection to the student and provides continuity.
- A meeting of supervisor and students should take place weekly to review case progress.

Recommended:

- An induction programme should be held as an intensive day's course.
- An induction manual and/or clinic manual should be prepared and distributed to all participating students containing a summary of all salient clinic procedures, professional duties and obligation, and rules of practice.
- Students should be encouraged to become involved in group work to foster support and to share responsibility. To this end the allocation of students into teams or firms is, in the experience of CLEO, a useful device. Firms of, say, six students can share a caseload. Firm meetings should be held weekly, in addition to the supervision of individual students in the conduct of their cases.
- Although students can and ought to rely on the supervisors' judgment and control over cases, the initial responsibility should be the students'. This fosters a sense of professionalism and adds to the nature of the learning experience.
- Students should check their firm's tray daily.

Referrals to other agencies

Minimum:

- The clinic should have an understood and workable system of referral when it is unable to offer further services to a client or is unable to accept instructions initially.
- A letter of introduction from the clinic to the referred agency should be provided.
- If a client is eligible for, and the clinic uses, legal aid, the green form (under the advice and assistance scheme) should not be used by the clinic if the referred agency is likely to make use of the scheme.

Recommended:

- A list of local agencies, including solicitors, should be kept in the clinic and referrals made from this list.
- A record should be kept on the client's file or a general file of all referrals made (this information is very useful — see under 'management').

Management

Minimum:

- The clinic, as a validated unit on the degree or vocational programme, will be technically managed by the board or persons responsible for that programme. Supervisors must ensure that client confidentiality is preserved even though academic management rests elsewhere.
- As and when necessary, the supervisors (or director if such a hierarchy is used) will report to the board or persons responsible. In any event, the supervisors will produce an annual report setting out the details of the clinic's activities during the past academic year. Such a report should include:

  — a description of the aims and objectives of the programme
  — statistics on number and types of cases, outcomes, students' results, referrals to other agencies (including solicitors) and comparisons with previous years
  — reflections on progress and/or difficulties experienced.

Recommended:

- An advisory committee should be set up including those representing students, supervisors, academic staff and managers, representatives from the local Law Society, representatives of advice and other similar agencies (e.g., CAB, tenants' associations, trade unions), the courts and the profession.

  In the experience of CLEO, not only will this be a source of useful advice and guidance, but it will provide an important link with academia, advice agencies and the profession. Some clinical programmes have received a rather sceptical response from local practitioners, some doubtful of the quality of service that students can deliver and others with an eye towards the competition. The advisory panel serves to allay fears and foster support and understanding. A record of the number of referrals made by clinics to private practice is persuasive that clinics in fact generate work for local solicitors rather than take work away. The connection with practice is also useful as it raises the profile of the students. Some have reported that their clinical experience has been noted by prospective employers when shortlisting and interviewing.

The advisory panel should meet at least twice yearly.

- The daily management of the clinic should be organised with a rota of supervisors and students who cover particular functions. If the clinic has open drop-in sessions a rota is essential to ensure that each session is adequately staffed and to spread the work equitably amongst the students.
- During vacation periods a skeleton rota should be operated to ensure adequate staffing levels. Most clinics run down caseloads during the latter part of the term to keep vacation work at a minimum (although for those cases running during the vacation, a professional standard of management and supervision is still required).

Training

Minimum:

- Clinics should build into their programmes mechanisms to support and build on the experiential learning of the live-client work. This can be termed 'training', although CLEO prefers the view that such mechanisms are not targeted at vocational objectives but support the general educational aims of the programme.
- The training programme should be planned in advance so as to complement the learning experience at the appropriate stage of development.

Recommended:

- A weekly training workshop, compulsory for all clinic students, should be held, dedicated to a particular topic, e.g., interviewing or advocacy. The workshop can be led by an expert in that field with or without case studies and/or simulations. A common clinical experience is to use the facts of existing clinic cases and to simulate the particular issue (e.g., drafting) within that context.
- The training programme should be documented in a manual.

Review of clinical programmes

Minimum:

- An annual report of the clinic's activities should be prepared, produced and widely distributed.

Recommended:

- Regular bulletins on the clinic's activity should be issued.
- A slot should be dedicated, in faculty or departmental meetings, to the clinic for a report-back on the progress of the clinic, in terms of its aims and objectives and the implications for the degree or vocational programme of the clinic's activities
- Membership of CLEO. This will enable clinical teachers to keep in contact with others interested and active in the field. Through the journal published by CLEO scholarly and topical debate can be conducted. CLEO can be contacted c/o The Administrator, Law Clinic, Sheffield Hallam University.
- A list should be created on e-mail to enable contact to be made and maintained by those engaged in clinical practice.

The ability of students to work effectively on their own and in groups, the development of skills in communication, presentation and investigation, improvement of self-confidence and enjoyment in their studies are also all part of the clinical product.

To these ends the clinic works and nowhere is this perhaps better illustrated than in the live-client, in-house solicitor clinic.

4

Working with other agencies

Introduction

Chapter 3 described clinical activity in a university-based in-house clinic. The advantage of this approach is apparent: students work side by side with university staff who are able to maximise the learning experience through their own close participation. In spite of this, the in-house clinic is not a financially viable option for all institutions. This chapter looks at alternative models of clinical legal education, where students gain their experience by working with other agencies. The first section contains: a description of the external placement programme offered by Queen's University of Belfast; a case study which will provide some insight into the nature of the work and learning of students participating in this type of programme and the way in which the clinical activity complements the rest of the course of study; and some suggestions as to how students can get the most out of this form of clinical activity. The second section explores the use of longer placements, either in the context of a sandwich course, or by undertaking vacation placements. The third section considers a significantly different approach whereby students may become involved in the drafting of legislation. The final section moves from the context of undergraduate work and suggests a way in which work with another agency can enrich the vocational stage of legal education.

External placements as a course on an LLB degree

Introduction to the Queen's programme

> It was as if for three years you had been learning how to swim from
> reading books alone, not from actually getting into the water. Then all of
> a sudden you are thrown into the deep end and told to swim. I think by
> the end of the first week I was learning how to swim, but it was more of
> a doggy paddle than an Olympic freestyle. . . . By the end of the course I
> had learned to swim, but not to the extent that I did not need lifeguards or
> that I could take off my waterwings. (Gerard — a final year student
> following a placement at Law Centre (NI))

Queen's University of Belfast has offered undergraduate students the opportunity to participate in clinical activity since 1980. The clinical law course
is currently offered as an optional module to final-year law students who have
completed the faculty's welfare law module. It consists of two components:

(a)   a placement at a local advice centre;
(b)   a legal information project for a local voluntary organisation.

The discussion that follows focuses on the work that the students do on their
placements.

Placements   Students participating in the Queen's programme attend placements in local advice centres one morning or afternoon per week for the first
12 weeks of the first semester.[1] In a typical year we place 12 students in five
different advice centres. The biggest source of placements is Law Centre
(NI), who accommodate six students every year. The other placements
include Citizens' Advice Bureaux and a number of independent local advice
centres. All placements are in welfare rights agencies. However, the precise
nature of the case work varies from placement to placement. In generalist
advice centres such as Citizens' Advice Bureaux, the students undertake a
variety of work, including housing, consumer, social security and employment law. In other centres work is specialised: for example, the students
placed at the Law Centre concentrate on social security appeal tribunals.

Casework   On placement the students undertake live casework with real
clients. This includes interviewing, writing letters, making telephone calls on

---

[1] Some of the students' work will, however, inevitably fall outside the fixed placement time:
e.g., tribunal hearings, domiciliary visits etc.

the client's behalf, completing application forms and appeal papers, applying for legal aid, advice and assistance, and liaising with government departments and statutory bodies. In many instances, the cases involve representation at tribunals or the small claims court. It is impossible to give an exact figure of the total number of cases the students handle per year because many of the students are placed in centres which have a drop-in policy rather than a system of appointments. However, in 1995–96 12 students provided tribunal representation to over 40 clients.

The work on placement is the linchpin of the clinical programme. It is not enough for students to shadow advisers or to perform routine office duties. Students must have direct responsibility for clients, as we have learned that the level of learning is directly linked to the degree of participation in the case. This is not to say that the students are left to their own devices. They are supervised on their placement by a designated member of the advice centre. In addition, each of the two university tutors takes specific responsibility for supervising individual students.[2] These students meet weekly in a group with their tutor to discuss their cases. These sessions are highly participative as the students are genuinely interested in each other's cases as well as being eager to share their own experience with the group. The students also have regular consultations with their tutor on a one-to-one basis to discuss individual cases. Finally the course draws on the general expertise of the faculty by encouraging students to consult individual members of staff regarding cases that are within their particular area of expertise.[3]

Assessment   The work on placement is assessed in two ways:[4]

(a)   Students are asked to submit two case reports which they consider to be representative of the work they have undertaken on their placement. These count for 50 per cent of their final mark in the subject. The assessment is based on five factors: the investigation of the facts; the legal analysis; the case handling; the critical analysis; and the presentation.

(b)   Students are required to keep a learning journal from the first day of the placement. This counts for 25 per cent of the final mark.[5] The learning

---

[2] Each of us supervises six to eight students per year.
[3] These consultations usually involve consumer, contract or family law queries. The members of staff whose advice is sought are always happy to help. The work required is usually minimal. However, at one stage, when we had a greater proportion of small claims work, a colleague who specialised in consumer law was given a teaching allocation for clinical law consultations.
[4] For a full description of the methods of assessment, see Lundy, 'The assessment of clinical legal education: an illustration' (1995) 29 Law Teach 311.
[5] The remaining 25 per cent of the mark goes on the 'Law in the Community' project.

journal consists of one typed A4 sheet on which the student describes and evaluates his or her learning on placement in a particular week. At the end of the course the weekly journals are returned to the students and they are given one week to submit a two-page summary of their learning experience on the course with the weekly sheets appended. The following criteria are relevant to the assessment of the learning journals: the amount and breadth of the work undertaken; how well the student has used the placement time; the extent of the student's reflection on the learning experience; and the quality of the presentation of the work records and summary.

The total mark awarded in clinical law contributes directly to the student's final degree classification in the same manner as all other final-year modules.

Casework on placement: an illustration

In order to provide an insight into the learning experience of a student on placement, I have chosen to use one of the case reports submitted by a student for assessment. The student, Carolyn, was on placement in a Citizens' Advice Bureau. The case is typical in that it involved an appeal to a social security appeal tribunal. The issue was relatively simple. The claimant was refused the benefit of income support because she was considered to be 'living together as husband and wife' with a male friend, who had offered her a place to live while she was temporarily homeless. The effect of this was that she was deemed to be dependent on him for support, or rather that their joint resources/needs would be the basis for entitlement. The case reports which the students submit for assessment are divided into distinct sections: worksheet, facts, legal analysis, courses of action, hearing, outcome and critical analysis. I propose to consider Carolyn's case under each of these headings. The text which follows includes quotations from Carolyn's account in her case report and my own general observations about the opportunities for learning which were presented, drawing on further examples from other students' work.

Living together as husband and wife?

Worksheet At the start of the case report students summarise the work which they have done on the case: interviews, letters, telephone calls and attendance at hearings. They also detail the time spent on each activity.

1/11/94: received papers from SSAT [social security appeal tribunal]. Discussed case with supervisor and agreed to provide representation (45 minutes).

8/11/94: attempted to contact client by phone as she had failed to keep an appointment to meet me (30 minutes).

15/11/94: Still no contact with client. Worked through the adjudication officer's submission point by point and photocopied relevant commissioners' decisions (2 hours).

22/11/94: Telephoned tribunal service. Appeal set for 26 November. Receive a letter from client saying she will be at advice centre the next day (15 minutes).

23/11/94: Client fails to turn up again. Discuss case with tribunals adviser[6] (3 hours).

25/11/94: Meet client for first time. Prepare her for questions she will be asked at tribunal. Revise my submission in light of new information (two and a half hours).

26/11/94: Tribunal hearing (three hours).

The time-span of this case is fairly short. There are only four weeks from the date Carolyn received the papers to the case's conclusion. This is fairly typical in that many clients only seek advice when the date of the hearing is imminent. Although this may not seem ideal to the learning process, it actually suits the clinical law students as they can pick up and complete a case within the allotted course time.

The other point which is fairly typical is the client's repeated failure to turn up for meetings. This can be a problem in advice centres which operate a drop-in policy. What is interesting is that the student was immediately forming a negative impression of the client. She thought that her time was being wasted and that the client would probably withdraw before the hearing. The student persisted only because she realised that the case was interesting and would provide fertile ground for the critical analysis which is crucial to the assessment. The academic pressures tempered the natural human reaction. In the end, her patience paid off. Moreover, her growing resentment evaporated when she met the client and had a better appreciation of the client's very difficult circumstances. The students' changing perceptions of their clients can be traced in their weekly journals. By the end of the placement many students describe how they have learnt the 'Don't judge a book by its cover' lesson.

I have learnt a lot about myself, some of which has surprised me. On one occasion in particular I doubted the credence of a client who turned out to

---

[6] The tribunals adviser was a person specifically employed by CABx to provide support to bureaux undertaking representation at tribunal.

have a very meritorious case. I was annoyed at myself for doing this and I have since approached my cases with a more open mind. (Neil)

Other students claim to have become 'case-hardened'.

Clinical law changes your views about lawyers. Charges that I had once raised against others (i.e., of case hardening and cynicism) were now applicable to me. Whereas before I was sympathetic, now I was sceptical. This was a natural incidence from involvement in the law. But this should not be the case. . . . The fact that I am able to identify this is at least a comforting thought.

In both instances, the students have addressed an important issue, the way in which their own perfectly natural human reaction to another individual can impact upon their attitude towards a case. These students have realised that an important step towards professional objectivity is an awareness of their own potential for prejudice. In sharing their attitudes and prejudices they can explore what is and is not good professional practice and begin to understand the role of human weakness in the delivery of justice.

Fact investigation   Individual cases give students the opportunity to develop their fact-finding skills through interviewing and investigation (e.g., letters and phone calls to doctors, employers etc.). Students are given credit where they provide a clear statement of the relevant facts as described by the client. Carolyn's summary of the client's instructions was as follows.

In June 1994 the claimant suffered depression due to unemployment and the break-up of a long-term relationship. She was advised by her friends to move in with a family friend, Mr Kelly, until she could find her feet again. She moved in with him on 17 June 1994. Unable to find work in the area, she applied for income support. While filling in part 8 of the form it was suggested to her by the clerk that she change her 'No' answer to the question 'Do you or your partner live with parents, relatives or friends as part of their family?' to a 'Yes' answer. There was no explanation as to the implications that this would have upon her claim and she readily admitted that Mr Kelly lived at the same address.

However, the claimant and Mr Kelly led independent lives. She had her own room in the house and did her own cooking and cleaning. She used her own bedlinen and towels. They did not pool money, Although rent-free, the client met her own expenses and contributed to the bills. For these purposes she had borrowed money from another friend, Miss Murphy. The claimant and Mr Kelly rarely socialised together and only then as part of a group. The claimant insisted that they did not have a sexual relationship. By the time of the hearing the claimant had found employment and had moved into her own house.

Lowry has observed that through clinical casework students realise that facts do not present themselves in the logical and orderly manner in which they appear in the law reports and casebooks.[7] Students are used to getting the facts handed to them in an easily managed format. This can develop their ability to separate the relevant from the irrelevant to some extent but it does not help them to acquire fact-finding skills. Real life does not come so neatly packaged, a fact that students quickly realise:

> Sometimes it is difficult to pin down the question let alone the answer in an interview. Clients may not be sure how they want to be helped and what the clients want is of prime importance. Hence an interview may drift towards solving one problem only to discover that the client's real need is quite different. Information is often withheld for personal reasons only to be revealed at the end of the interview, completely altering the complexion of the case. (Mark)

Students often describe their early interviews as unstructured and long-winded. They frequently need to contact the client afterwards for further information. However, with experience, interviewing skills show a marked improvement.

> I feel that my ability to gain and retain relevant detail from a mass of disorganised material is very much improved — one of my most improved skills. (Martin)

In Carolyn's case the information needed was relatively straightforward but difficult to obtain in the absence of direct contact with the client. Initially all she had to go on was the information in the official case papers. Her learning journal includes the comment:

> I started preparing for the case with the help of 'Mesher',[8] though this is more difficult with only half the facts available. I suppose coping with an unreliable client is part of the learning process.

---

[7] D. R. Lowry, 'A plea for clinical law' (1972) 50 Can Bar Rev 183.
[8] This is J. Mesher, *CPAG's Income-Related Benefits: The Legislation*, which is published annually.

In the group discussion we discussed the available material. Carolyn gave the group a summary of the legal position (see the next section) and we identified the areas where more information was needed. Gaps in instructions can only be identified if the student understands the legal provisions to which they relate. In this way the distinction between the facts and the legal analysis in the case report headings is somewhat artificial. The two are considered separately for convenience: it makes the case report easier to read and to assess. In practice, the facts and the legal analysis are inextricably linked.[9] Students need the basic facts in order to identify the appropriate legal provisions. However, it is only when the law is identified and properly understood that the student is in a position to establish which facts are truly relevant. In this way students learn to marry factual with legal analysis.

By the time Carolyn managed to get an interview with the client she knew exactly what was needed. It was important to identify factors which indicated a platonic relationship. Carloyn's summary focuses on three key issues: domestic arrangements, financial arrangements and the existence of a sexual relationship. As can be seen from her summary, relevant detail included cooking, socialising, finance, sleeping arrangements and ownership of bedlinen.[10]

The complicating factor in this case was that the facts were of a highly personal nature, particularly those relating to the couple's sexual relationship or rather the lack of it. Official guidance prohibits adjudication officers from asking direct questions on this issue. When the client was not asked about it, she did not volunteer information. Her failure to mention it was construed as a tacit admission. The student had to raise the issue with her and explain its significance. Social security cases often involve highly personal details, often of a medical nature. It is common for students (who are generally in their early 20s) to record their discomfort when asking older people questions about intimate matters. One student, Martina, described her strategy for coping with such situations as follows:

> The client was getting very upset talking about some fairly harrowing family history. There is nothing I can do but reassure her that I know how difficult it is to talk about it while at the same time getting all of the relevant information from her. At least now I do not go into a day-long depression after hearing about some people's problems and thus try to avoid any kind of question that might upset them.

---

[9] See further under the section on legal analysis, page XX below.
[10] The issue about bedlinen was identified by a fellow adviser who had recently been involved in a similar case at tribunal.

Carolyn's account of the case does not mention discomfort on her part. This may have been due to the fact that she was a mature student herself and was of a similar age to the claimant. Her key concern was for the client who would have to discuss this in front of a tribunal.

The client's embarrassment was compounded by the involvement of her friend, Mr Kelly. It was clear that her case would be helped by evidence from him to the effect that they were not living together. The client was initially reluctant to draw him in, particularly on the issue of the sexual relationship, but agreed to ask him to attend as a witness when Carolyn explained that the case would turn on her credibility and his evidence in support would help her case. Real cases regularly highlight this important legal distinction — the difference between an assertion of fact and evidence. Carolyn believed that her client was telling the truth but saw the value in providing external proof. For these purposes she asked the client to put together three further pieces of evidence: a letter from her friend, Miss Murphy, stating that she was lending her money; a letter from her GP confirming that she had been suffering from depression; and a letter from her estate agent confirming that she was now renting her own flat.

I never cease to be amazed by the students' ingenuity and degree of maturity when it comes to establishing the facts and providing evidence. This is in spite of the fact that it is the one area which their law degree probably does least to address. Two cases illustrate this point. The first involved an overpayment of benefit where a claimant was alleged to have been 'doing the double'. He had been observed by two social security fraud officers allegedly selling something to a woman at whose house he had called. The student who was over six feet tall went to the house and took a photograph of himself beside the hedge to show that the hedge was at least eight feet tall and that the officers could not possibly have seen anything from the place where they said they had made their observations. The case was successful. In the second case, the client wished to sue a dressmaker who had taken up the sleeves on her coat by three inches too much, thereby rendering it unwearable. In order to commence proceedings in the small claims court, the students had to get the dressmaker's full name. She was known to the client as Lily, the name above the shop door. In group discussions, the students suggested all sorts of ways of getting the surname: telephone directory, companies registry, land registry etc. None of these proved successful. Lily was a sole trader and rented premises from a landlord who was not prepared to give out her name. To the students the case seemed hopeless, stymied by a minor technicality. In the end the student took a bus to the shop knowing that it was closed. She went into the shop next door saying that she had something to send to Lily (which of course was true in a way) but did not know her surname. She got the surname and was successful in the subsequent proceedings.

Legal analysis   As is the case in most undergraduate degree courses, clinical law aims to develop students' abilities in legal research, analysis and writing. Students are expected to provide a full and accurate statement of the legal issues pertaining to the case. Carolyn's case study set out the relevant legislation. The case was going to turn on whether the client and Mr Kelly were 'living together as husband and wife'. This statutory phrase was the subject of an important Social Security Commissioner's decision, R(SB) 17/81. This case states that the following criteria are relevant to the issue: stability of the relationship, financial support, sexual relationship, children and public acknowledgment of the relationship. Carolyn analysed each in turn, highlighting the facts which she believed would suggest that none of these factors were present in her client's relationship with Mr Kelly. In summary she stated:

> The basis of my argument would rest on the failure of the Benefits Agency to discharge the burden of proving that this was a cohabiting couple when all the evidence pointed to the contrary. This was a temporary arrangement and no more. The factors in R(SB) 17/81 were not present.

During her research, she also discovered another relevant decision, R(SB) 35/85 where a depressed man moved in with a female friend during a difficult period and the Commissioner said that it was important to look at the reasons why the two people were living together. In the light of this, Carolyn decided to emphasise the circumstances which preceded her client's move to Mr Kelly's home.

It is in the application of the law to a set of real facts that students can begin to see the relevance of their previous learning. Sometimes they are able to employ knowledge gained elsewhere in their studies. More often casework brings home to students the significance of the skills of finding, understanding and applying the law. Through Carolyn's previous study of welfare law she was aware of R(SB) 17/81. However, she was able to use her research skills to find other relevant decisions and she was also in a position to apply the law to the facts to the advantage of her client. A key objective of the clinical law course is to enable students to see the value of these previously acquired skills. Laws change and knowledge becomes outdated but the usefulness of these skills endures. It can be difficult to get this point across, particularly if students have become accustomed to lectures and exams which target specific knowledge rather than applied skills. In this respect, clinical activity is particularly instructive. Learning journals frequently recount the student's new-found appreciation of the value of these aspects of their previous study.

> Although I found the idea of sifting through the legislation and case law daunting, in fact this was one of the skills that came to hand easiest. This was the area where my academic training was most transferable. (Mark)

> My approach to statute and case law has changed substantially. They are no longer words on a page which you photocopy for a tutorial but forget to read. They are tremendously real and frighteningly relevant. . . . Studying the Social Security Acts in welfare law was one thing. Building a disability living allowance claim around them is another thing entirely. (Martin)

Case handling   Having ascertained the facts and the legal position, students must decide how to proceed in the case. In some cases the course of action will be predetermined. This was largely true in Carolyn's case. The client had already appealed and simply required someone to represent her at the tribunal. However, Carolyn still had to exercise judgement over the evidence to be presented at the tribunal. She had put together several pieces of evidence: the witness, Mr Kelly; a letter from Miss Murphy; a letter from the estate agent; and the letter from the client's GP. In the end she decided not to submit the doctor's letter. The doctor had simply stated that the client was receiving (unspecified) treatment. Carolyn considered that this did not add anything to the evidence and in fact might give the impression that the client was not being taken seriously by the doctor. Carolyn elected to omit it, thereby demonstrating an awareness of the significance of tactics in the presentation of evidence.

The case handling is an important part of the assessment process. Students are required to consider the options and explain their reasons for advocating a particular course of action. However, it would be misleading to give the impression that cases are always well handled. Two minor horrors come to mind instantly.

The first was a housing case. The claimant was living in premises which were in a pitiful state and, having discussed the case with his supervisor, the student decided to see if the client could get the flat rent-restricted. Through a technicality, the premises were not eligible for this. The landlord was angered by the tenant's decision to take action and served notice to quit. The client was rendered temporarily homeless but eventually found new improved premises. Although in fact not too much damage was done (the client has always intended to move out rather than pay what he considered to be an exorbitant rent), it was clear that the student had given advice in an area outside his and our capabilities. The mistake which we made was to abdicate responsibility to the placement supervisor when faced with a complicated area of law with which we were unfamiliar. Unfortunately our confidence in the supervisor was misplaced.

The second case was also badly handled but in a different way. The client was in major debt to a number of bodies. The student used a computer program to do a creditor assessment, i.e., a distribution of available income between the respective creditors. This automatically produced standard letters to the creditors setting out how much the client was prepared to pay them per week. One of the letters came out something like this: 'I owe you £200. In view of my income, I am prepared to pay you £0 per week. I hope this is acceptable.' The student's common sense must have temporarily deserted her because she sent the letter. Not surprisingly, she got a reply saying: 'No it was bloody well not acceptable'. The lesson this time was that all of the student's correspondence should be read before being sent out.[11] It would be impractical for the students to delay their correspondence so as to let the university supervisor check it. It is also unnecessary given that the placement supervisor is on hand and can provide this level of supervision. This is the agreed practice in all the advice centres with whom we now work.

Hearing If a case goes to a tribunal, the student will normally give an account of the hearing in the learning journal. This is the one area where experiences can be drastically different. Students will frequently refer to the manner in which the hearing was handled by the chairperson, a factor which can have an important bearing on the case. In Carolyn's case the personality of the chairperson did not play an important role. His identity, however, did. What follows is her account of the tribunal:

> We were called punctually at 10 a.m. However, due to common rather than legal courtesy, the chairman had to declare an interest. It appeared that he was in the same choral society as my client. Not surprisingly, this event

---

[11] This would almost certainly have been picked up by tutors in an in-house clinic where all correspondence is checked before being sent out.

rather threw the client who was embarrassed and upset. To avoid prolong-
ing the agony further, I asked if it was possible to be seen by the other
panel who were sitting that day. The chairman agreed but we did have a
long wait. In fact the wait did no harm because only having met the client
once and never having seen Mr Kelly until the day of the tribunal, it gave
me a further opportunity to run the case through with them. However, the
wait did add to the client's anxiety and by the time we appeared before
the second panel she was quite tearful.

To begin with I brought the panel up to date with the changes in the material
facts regarding the client's circumstances regarding her work and new flat.
This illustrated that it was anticipated that a change in circumstances would
occur. Following this, the chair asked the client about the reasons for her
move to Mr Kelly's house. In describing her state at the time, the client
became quite upset and for the rest of the proceedings I had my arm around
her, both as a comfort and because I was afraid she might make a quick exit.
It was quite difficult handing out copies of the documents one-handed. I
even passed out some of my personal copies. Fortunately we were not
asked for medical evidence about the client's depression.

The next area of questioning concerned their domestic arrangements and
the issue of bedlinen was picked up. The client gave the impression of
being someone who was none too domesticated and stated that she would
simply clear up after herself. She described how she would never ask Mr
Kelly for financial assistance, that he was doing enough now and that she
felt obliged to recompense him for expenses incurred.

At this point I asked if it were possible to raise the issue of how the income
support form had been filled in. The presenting officer conceded that the
nature of the form and time considerations could account for the clerk's
suggestion as to how to fill in part 8.

Mr Kelly proved to be a convincing witness. He stated that this was not
the first time he had helped out a friend. He also confirmed the circumstances which led to the client's residence in his home. To this I added
that the temporary nature was borne out by the subsequent facts and that
those facts bore a striking resemblance to those in R(SB) 35/85.

Finally I indicated the parties' willingness to be explicit about their lack
of a sexual relationship and how if they had only known about the
relevance of the issue, they would have had no difficulty addressing it.

There is no such thing as a typical social security hearing. The procedure is very much at the discretion of the chair and the strict rules of evidence do not apply. This in itself provides fertile ground for learning. Students cannot go into a tribunal with set expectations but must be prepared to be flexible. Each tribunal presents its own individual experience. Examples from the past include: clients who have lost their temper and threatened the panel; clients who have run out; presenting officers who have deserted their *amicus curiae* role and engaged in cross-examination of the claimant; and, of course, clients who change their story during the hearing.

One student, Sinead, had a particularly gruesome case involving an overpayment of social security arising out of changes in mortgage interest rates. During interviews the client claimed that he was not aware of the changes in the rates due to stress and difficult personal circumstances. Sinead's learning journal records her suspicions about the truth of this but the client persisted with his account. At the tribunal, after close questioning, the client admitted that he had known all along about the falling interest rates but felt that the tribunal was worth a go. He actually put it to the tribunal that they would have done the same in his circumstances! Sinead stated that this was contrary to her previous instructions and that, given the new information, she had nothing further to submit. She later identified the incident as being one of the key learning experiences of her placement. What did she learn? Quite clearly, it highlighted the potential difference between the client's instructions and the actual truth. However, the experience also encouraged her to have more faith in her own judgment: her initial misgivings proved to be sound. However, one of Sinead's key concerns was that the client's conduct reflected on her: she thought that the tribunal might think that she had colluded in the deception. She was reassured that this type of incident occurs regularly and that tribunals are fully aware of the fact that there may be nothing a representative can do when a client has deliberately set out to mislead both the adviser and the tribunal.

Sinead's case also contributed to an interesting group discussion on the ethical and practical issues involved in representing a client whom you believe to be untruthful.[12] The group discussed strategies for drawing out the truth as well as what should be done when a client indicates an intention to mislead the tribunal. Fortunately this last issue has not yet arisen in practice.

Tribunal hearings are the aspect of the course which students find most daunting. However, in the end they are invariably the part of the course from which the students derive most satisfaction.

---

[12] For a discussion of these issues, see further chapter 6.

Tribunal representation tests all your talents. You have to be able to think on your feet but what I have learnt more than anything is that statutes and cases take on a realism that I had never before experienced in my study of the law. (Neil)

Participation in the process also allows students to see the value of competent representation:

There was a lot of panicking going on in the waiting room among the people without representation, especially the elderly as they tried to make sense of a huge amount of information. This brought home to me the huge difference that representation can make not only to a client's success but also to their perception that they have had a fair hearing. (Martina)

Outcome   Carolyn's appeal was successful. The client received a backdated award of income support. The reasons for the decision were:

We accept the claimant's evidence finding her to be a truthful witness. On the basis of the same we conclude that there is no relationship of married couple between herself and Mr Kelly. The factors in R(SB) 17/81 are not present.

The chairperson's written evidence also specifically referred to R(SB) 35/85, the case Carolyn unearthed during her research. Carolyn's own reaction to the outcome was simple:

The client had an expectation of justice . . . I was relieved not to disillusion her.

The client later wrote to tell Carolyn that she had managed to get full-time employment and finished by saying:

Many thanks for all your help and patience. I wish you every success with your studies and work.

The student's mark in the clinical law course does not depend on whether a case has a successful outcome or not. However, there is no doubt that students like a happy ending. One student described a 'win' at his last tribunal as 'the icing on the clinical law cake'. However, the experience can have a bigger impact when students believe that their client was unfortunate to lose. This is particularly true when students have come face to face with the hardship of life on benefits for the first time. Students may go into a hearing worrying about themselves but they usually emerge with real concern for the impact the decision has had on their client.

As the course progressed I learned a little professional humility and perspective. I had always known but only now felt that the central issues were the client's, not mine; that success and failure were to be judged on whether my client got a fair hearing and just settlement, and not on whether my submissions and speeches impressed the panel. And as I realised this, I found that the stress no longer upset me, though it was still there. In this way the course has had a much more fundamental effect on me than I had imagined it would when I began. (Martin)

Critical analysis Clinical work gives students the opportunity to develop many new skills. These range from time recording and filing to interviewing and representation. However, a primary objective of the clinical course is to enable students to put previous learning into practice. The case reports are designed to allow students to demonstrate the skills which they have acquired during the rest of their study, particularly legal research, analysis and writing. The last section of the case report, the critical analysis, is also intended to both complement and reinforce previous learning. The degree at Queen's has a strong critical and jurisprudential flavour. In welfare law students learn about the social security legislation and administrative structures. However, the theme of the course is the State's response to poverty through legislation. We encourage students to examine the relationship between State, society and the individual through a consideration of the social, political and economic contexts in which the law operates. This process is continued in the clinical programme.[13] Students have highlighted instances where they consider the law to be unclear, ineffective or unjust. Alternatively the critique can focus on the legal process: access difficulties, resource and power imbalances, prejudices and procedural barriers to justice. The casework gives students a unique opportunity to observe the law in practice. By evaluating and contextualising this experience, students are provided with a further valuable opportunity for learning.

Carolyn's case raised a number of interesting issues. She began with an analysis of the policy rationale behind the 'living together' test, observing that:

---

[13] We are not always successful in our efforts to encourage students to seek the links between critical theory and practice. One student concluded that: 'Knowing what Rawls and Raz think is of no practical use to people with real problems'!

Long before the notion of back to basics was seeking to influence society,
the government's aim was that it should not treat an unmarried couple
more favourably than a married couple as to do so would undermine the
institution of marriage.

Carolyn agreed with the rationale behind the rule, acknowledging that to do
otherwise would put married couples at a disadvantage. However, while
agreeing with the substance of the law, she had difficulty with the way in
which it was being implemented in practice:

At first, I tended to sympathise with any adjudication officer forbidden to
ask direct questions [about sexual relationships]. However, on reflection I
tend to feel that it has become a little too convenient to avoid the subject.
. . . it seems easier for the Agency to make the assumption [about
cohabitation] and then rectify later if someone makes a fuss, instead of
attempting to ascertain the correct situation in the first place. . . .

A paradox has been created behind the façade of the avoidance of 'sexual
snooping'. Where this issue is avoided it tips the balance in favour of
'living together as husband and wife' because without unequivocal denial,
the combined effect of the other evidence is not strong enough to avoid
the label.

The experience also prompted her to draw comparisons with other areas of
law which she had studied:

In equity the expectation of maintenance or an equitable share of property
is dependent on an unmarried partner showing that there has been a
contribution in money or kind. . . . Therein lies a contrast between public
law and private law. Where the State has to come up with the money, the
situation changes. Social security law automatically treats the income and
capital of one partner as for the benefit of the other.

Law degrees tend to compartmentalise legal knowledge: it may make
administrative sense to teach contract and tort in separate packages.
However, real-life cases often cut across these academic boundaries. Thus
clinical activity can help students to see the links between various areas of
law. Carolyn's case did not actually involve principles of equity, but her
work on the social security provisions did encourage her to look for similar
provisions in other areas of law and to differentiate between the various
approaches adopted.

Carolyn's analysis also highlighted what she considered to be an anomaly in the law: that is the fact that if the claimant had been in a stable homosexual relationship, she would have been assessed individually. In the group discussion, the students saw this as a further example of the State using social security legislation to reinforce its own moral norms. Carolyn concluded that:

> What made this case so interesting for me was the possibility of a government agency ascribing to someone behaviour which the parties felt reflected on their own private moral attitudes. At the same time the Benefits Agency's approach only reflects what is common practice in society. . . . During our studies we have discussed ideas about justice and public and private morality. This case encompassed aspects of all three.

Zander has identified one of the key objectives of clinical legal education as its potential 'to use real-life situations as a vehicle for clearer insights into the nature of law and its functions'.[14] There is no doubt that the placement gives students a unique opportunity to observe the law in practice. Every year I give a lecture on income support which includes the 'living together as husband and wife' test. The year before her placement Carolyn probably sat in that lecture copying my words on to paper. A year later she had acquired a depth of understanding of the law in theory which enabled her not only to pursue a successful appeal but also to produce the above commentary. She also had a keen understanding of the effect which legal proceedings can have on real people.

Making the most of an external placement

Students can and often do act as volunteers in welfare rights agencies. While this is undoubtedly valuable, it cannot properly be described as clinical legal education.[15] The key to its transformation from a useful voluntary activity to a form of clinical legal education lies in the way in which the opportunities for learning presented by the placement are harnessed. Underpinning this are a number of other factors, some of which are purely practical in nature. The following paragraphs examine how students can get the maximum value out of an external placement. In practice, this hinges on three things: the quality of the placement; the role of the university tutor; and your own input as students.

---

[14] Zander, 'Clinical legal education' (1983) 133 NLJ 183.
[15] See A. Boone, M. Jeeves and J. MacFarlane, 'Clinical anatomy: towards a working definition of clinical legal education' (1987) 21 Law Teach 61 at p. 68.

What to expect of your placement The key to a successful external programme lies in the provision of quality placements. Most advice centres will be interested in taking a student. However, not all are suitable. The following list will give you a rough guide of what to look for in a placement:

(a) The advice centre must have an adequate caseload, including client representation service. There is no point in you going to a centre where the advice workers themselves do not have enough to do. Your needs will not be high on their list of priorities. In a busy office, there will be a greater variety of work to do and you are likely to be given a higher degree of responsibility.

(b) The centre must have a permanent member of staff who is willing to provide you with supervision and advice. The supervisor should have a good grasp of the educational objectives and requirements of the course. The supervisors we use regularly reserve cases which raise interesting issues for the students and encourage the critical process through discussion and suggestions.

(c) The supervisor must also be willing to let you take responsibility for your own cases, not simply shadow or act as a research assistant to one of the advisers.

(d) The centre must have adequate indemnity insurance to cover your work. It is surprising how many advice centres are operating without this cover, unable to afford the premiums. The insurance is important for your protection as well as that of the centre — and the client.

(e) The centre must be within a reasonable travelling distance and you must feel comfortable working in the area in which the centre is situated.[16]

What to expect of university staff The university tutor plays a number of roles. First, he or she is there to prepare you for your placement. This does not mean giving you a crash course on all the areas of law which you are likely to encounter on your placement: this is where your previous study and research capability come in. However, as all of the placements are in welfare rights agencies, we have made welfare law a prerequisite for clinical law students. This ensures that students have a basic knowledge of social security benefits and administrative structures. It also gives them experience and confidence in handling the complicated statutory instruments which contain the detail of social security entitlement. Students are also required to participate in an interviewing skills workshop and an induction day where professional advisers speak about issues such as confidentiality and tribunal procedure.

---

[16] In Northern Ireland, sectarian divisions mean that we have to address another problem: ensuring students are placed in advice centres where they feel safe.

Secondly, the supervisor is there to advise you. You should expect to meet your supervisor regularly for one-to-one discussions about your cases. The tutor should not only be keeping you on the right track when it comes to a particular case but should be giving you constructive advice on your own work and potential for development. Without these built-in opportunities for discussion and deliberate reflection, the experience on placement would not have the same impact on the learning process. Finally the tutor is there to monitor the placement. If you do not feel comfortable about any aspect of your placement, it is to your tutor that you should turn. Difficulties do occasionally arise — for example, if the placement supervisor has been sick for a couple of weeks. The tutor should have a contingency plan for this type of situation.

What can students do to help themselves?   The attitude of a student towards a placement will also have a significant impact on its ultimate educational value. First of all students should be prepared to treat their placement and their clients with professional respect. In particular we insist upon two things:

(a)   Students should attend the placement at the specified time. If they are not able to attend or are going to be late, they must give the centre reasonable notice.

(b)   Students must respect the clients' confidentiality. They should also treat the information given to them with respect. Among other things, this means not using their client's story to get a laugh at the client's expense in the union bar and not leaving case files in places where the unauthorised might get access to them.

Secondly, you will maximise the value of your placement if you view it not just as some sort of work experience but as an opportunity for self-growth. More will be gained if you use the experiences as a springboard to self-reflection. The Queen's course facilitates this in three ways: the individual discussions with tutors; the group meetings; and, perhaps most importantly, the learning journal where students analyse their experience, acknowledging their strengths and making plans to address areas which they are not happy with. Kreiling has identified a primary benefit of clinical legal education to be its capacity to enable students to 'learn to learn from experience'.[17] This is a phrase which would be worth bearing in mind while you are on placement.

---

[17] K. R. Kreiling, 'Clinical education and lawyer competency: the process of learning to learn from experience through properly structured clinical supervision' (1981) 40 Md L Rev 284.

Conclusion

I should like to return to the swimming analogy which opened this section. It interested me that the student felt that he had been thrown in at the deep end.[18] Why did he feel this way when he had access to so much support? The answer probably lies in the fact that all of the advice centres we work with are stretched for resources and are often quite happy to let students get on with it. However, I also wonder whether throwing them in at the deep end is such a bad thing. No-one has drowned yet.[19] It occurred to me that what external placements lack in terms of university staff input, they might make up for in the level of responsibility afforded to students. However, I want to borrow and extend Gerard's analogy in order to shed some light on the difference between in-house clinics and external placements. It seems to me that in an in-house clinic the university staff are in the water getting wet with their students. In the placement model, the university staff are standing by the side of the pool getting occasionally splashed but seldom drenched. In each case the end result is that students become better swimmers.

Longer-term placements

The approach to placements which has been described so far in this chapter would involve you as students spending some of your time during your course working with an appropriate agency in order to broaden your experience and understanding of the law you are learning. You will have noticed the care with which supervision arrangements were made to ensure that students' experience in their placement went beyond mere work experience and contributed effectively towards their degree study. Effective supervision is crucial to any clinical work involving real clients and their problems. During the period working in the advice centre the student at Queen's had regular access to the faculty supervisor. Some universities have approached the provision of this sort of experience by arranging longer-term placements which are likely to operate on a full-time basis, possibly on a sandwich course or by arranging placements in the vacation. Where this is done regular supervision may be more difficult. It will be particularly important to establish the aims and objectives of the placement and to establish effective working contracts between the student, the law faculty and

---

[18] Another student said that she felt like 'Alice falling down the rabbit hole'.

[19] Some clients might have received better advice. However, given the nature of the student–supervisor relationship, it is likely that mistakes which are made would have made by the supervisor acting without the student. If anything, the third opinion from the university tutor can help to highlight potential problems.

the supervisor in the placement itself. This section of the chapter is inevitably more general than the others, given the variety of approaches adopted and the limited development (in the authors' view) of the fully clinical nature of such longer-term placements.

One approach is to provide a sandwich course. Three LLB courses and seven joint-honours law degrees are offered as sandwich courses.[20] The best-known and longest-established example is the degree course at Brunel University, where students undertake two placements of 22 weeks each, one at the end of the first academic year, the other in year 3. Full sandwich years are also used, the business law degree at Bournemouth University, and the BA (Law) at Sheffield Hallam, for example, running a placement throughout year 3 (40 or more weeks). Alternatively, it might operate in the context of a vacation placement between two years of the course, as with the scheme running at the University of Central Lancashire. Such vacation placements may be generalist in nature, or may concentrate on a particular area, such as the death row clinic offered through the Centre for Capital Punishment Studies at the University of Westminster.[21]

This approach gives students real experience of the practice of law. The experience of working at the same place over a significant period gives a realistic feel of what work as a lawyer involves. It would be, however, a matter for concern if placements were used as little more than work experience. There is scope for using placements of this sort to enhance the educational value of a degree by incorporating them into the overall experience of a degree course as a genuinely clinical element. For this to be effective there needs to be genuine integration of the placement experience into that of the course as a whole.

This requires attention to two elements of the placement. First, supervisors in the placement itself need to have some knowledge and understanding of the educational objectives of the placement. Secondly, positive steps need to be taken to ensure student activity which has an integrative function. I shall explore each in turn.

Supervision

One of the practical difficulties with many sandwich course or vacation placement schemes is finding employers who are willing to take placement

---

[20] P. Harris and M. Jones, 'A survey of law schools in the United Kingdom, 1996' (1997) 31 Law Teach 38 at 47.
[21] For an examination of the work of this clinic see A. Boon and P. Hodgkinson, 'Life and death in the lawyer's office: the internship in capital punishment studies' (1996) 30 Law Teach 253.

students, provide them with useful experience and, where appropriate, a reasonable income. The shortage of good placements means that they are likely to be widely spread around the country. This creates problems for active liaison between placement supervisors and academic staff. It is important, if the placement is to make a significant contribution to the educational goals of the degree, that the student gets useful experience. This goes beyond ensuring that he or she is not merely used to photocopy, but must address the variety of activities observed and carried out, and whether they relate to the educational experience sought.

Most placement (that is, external) supervisors are busy solicitors or other senior staff with heavy workloads and major responsibilities. While a few individuals might be interested in developing an academic role few are likely to be in a position to act as academic supervisors. It may be reasonable to expect an individual to be designated as the student's direct supervisor, but not to expect active tutoring. Indeed, accepting and responding to the responsibility for your own development in the placement is one of the valuable aspects of the experience for individual students. Given limited expectations of the employer, a particular responsibility falls on the placement tutor. The purpose of visits must also be considered. At Bournemouth University there are two visits during the placement year, which are predominantly pastoral in nature. Where academic queries arise there is feedback to the placement tutor, who arranges necessary input from an appropriate member of the academic staff. Certainly, it would be unwise to have to wait for a rare visit for problems to be explored and it is necessary to establish opportunities for more regular communication.

Regular visits from the placement tutor (that is, the university tutor) will be easier to organise where it is possible to place students within a reasonable distance from the university base. Where, however, students are placed all around the country the task of visiting them becomes expensive and time-consuming.[22] This, in practice, means that tutors' visits will be rare or non-existent, which in turn requires other steps to be taken to achieve a sufficient link with the educational purposes of the placement. The main way of achieving this is to provide certain required activities for students to undertake during their placement. We will consider this below, but in terms of implementation the role of tutor and placement supervisor needs to be considered here. It is desirable to ask students to keep a placement diary or reflective journal in which they record their activities and what they are

---

[22] These problems might fall into some perspective when it is recalled that one of the authors has recently established a placement programme at the University of the South Pacific, where tutors visiting students on placement may have to fly several thousand miles.

learning from them. Where there is a sandwich course placement this may be returned to the placement tutor at regular intervals, providing opportunities for feedback. This cannot be carried out so easily during vacation placements, although developments in communications and the flexibility of working practices do raise the potential for such feedback during vacation placements as well.

Where such a journal is kept, the placement supervisor may have varying degrees of input. The supervisor may simply accredit the fact of the experience in areas of work the student has been engaged in or may be willing to make some comment, or to offer feedback or advice to the student. It should, however, be recognised that this will generally be limited to the skill development and the application of knowledge, which are the areas of expertise the supervisor has. Linking with the academic programme and the broader educational objectives of the placement can only reasonably be expected of the placement tutor.

In practice, some degree of negotiation may be expected in these cases, with placement supervisors being willing to undertake various degrees of involvement in their students' learning process. The shortage of placements, however, means that the university has little leverage in such a negotiation and will generally have to accept any degree of involvement by the supervisor, however limited. Therefore it is likely that any particular placement scheme will either work on the basis of a minimal degree of supervisor involvement, or flexibly according to the interests of each individual.

Student activity

How will you as a placement student spend your time, and how will those activities link into your work on the degree course? Your main tasks will be dictated by the nature of the placement you have secured. You may be working with a high street solicitor; in a commercial or City firm; in a local government or commercial legal office; in a legal advice centre or law centre or possibly with a specialist agency of some sort. The nature of the placement and its work will obviously determine much of what you find yourself doing. Experiences will range from the relatively mundane (probably the best from the perspective of understanding the nature of the working life which lies ahead of most lawyers) to the very unusual, such as the death row internships mentioned above.[23] The nature of the placement experience should inform

---

[23] See note 21.

the nature of the student activity. That fact itself should inform you at the time of choosing your placement (whether to work in a general solicitors' practice, in a commercial office or a public body of some kind; whether to seek a primarily litigation-based experience or one working predominantly in an office). It is worth remembering that the more involved you are in the actual process of court litigation the further your own activities will be from the core activity of your supervisor. You might wish to reflect on whether you would prefer to be involved in a higher degree of responsibility for an individual activity in the relatively routine context of the office, or to be a relatively junior member of a team involved in active litigation.

The scope for committed involvement in a specialist placement can be seen in this quote from a student working on a death row placement in the USA:

> MPD [Multicounty Public Defenders' Office] was typically American in that they assumed that because you had volunteered to work, you wanted to do as much work as possible. In return they offered a significant amount of responsibility early on. This could be alarming as I soon realised when I was left to prepare a client's entire mitigation case in my first week. However, I almost always received adequate help if I asked for it, and, most importantly, only spent one morning photocopying. . . . The final major piece of work I did was the legal research for a client's petition to the US Supreme Court. Neither of the lawyers working on this case was around when I was doing this, so I was left entirely on my own.[24]

If all you do is what any junior member of staff might do, there is a risk that your placement will be nothing more than work experience. In order to guard against this a number of activities may be required by the university. At the University of Central Lancashire, where the placement operates during the summer vacation, students enter a learning contract with their university supervisor which states clearly the learning outcomes they are required to achieve. They know that their assessment will depend upon their having the necessary experience to achieve these outcomes. With this in mind they then negotiate with their placement supervisor the types of experience their placement should include, thus taking a considerable degree of responsibility for their own learning process.

Students must show competence in respect of each outcome, indicating both the work done, and a reflective attitude towards the activity. To this end the

---

[24] Boon and Hodgkinson, op. cit. (note 21) at p. 263. The quote is from Clive Baldwin, a CPE student at City University undertaking the internship in capital punishment studies with Westminster University.

outcomes go beyond competence at the identified skill and require a degree of evaluation. Thus the interviewing and negotiation skills element of the course contains two learning outcomes:

As a result of this course the student will be able to demonstrate an understanding of the skills necessary to communicate effectively with clients.

As a result of this course the student will be able to evaluate the processes involved and skills required in negotiating a settlement with other parties.[25]

The evidence to support this will consist of examples of the student's work (with genuineness accredited by the employer), the process of critical reflection being displayed in the reflective diary. Rather than simply 'doing outcomes', actually achieving learning outcomes requires the ability to stand back from your work and ask, 'How have I achieved what I have done?' and 'Why have I done it the way I have?'[26] The results of this process are presented during the term following the placement, in a portfolio which also provides the basis for assessment of students' work.

This approach provides an effective method of encouraging reflection on the learning process and providing the university with some evidence of the student's development. It is inclined, however, to be concerned centrally with skill development. Most clinical programmes are concerned also that the work experience relates in some meaningful way to the broader learning concerns of the degree course itself. There are various methods of approaching this task. One is appropriate where students undertake a final-year project and may be based on issues which arose in the placement experience. At Bournemouth University a significant proportion of the project titles chosen by students stem from such issues, providing students with an opportunity to engage in academic study of something they may have gained a real insight into during their period of work. Examples from 1995/96 include: 'An analysis of the potential effectiveness of the Woolf report in the light of recognised problems within civil litigation', 'Fraud in documentary credits', 'An assessment of the relationships in the UK construction industry in contractual terms' and 'The duty of disclosure in the criminal trial — failures of the current system and the problems of the new proposed system'. These topics were all chosen by students who had undertaken placement in solicitors' offices, experience which will no doubt have informed both their choice of project topic and their insight into their chosen subjects.

[25] Standard learning contract, University of Central Lancashire.
[26] This section drawn from S. Wheatley, *Work-based Learning for Lawyers* (forthcoming).

The keeping of a log or journal is a characteristic of many placement schemes. How they are then used varies. The internship in capital punishment studies at the University of Westminster operates through a project in the form of an academic essay on a topic negotiated before the internship. After the placement has finished students have fortnightly two-hour seminars which are used to help in the completion of their logs and paper. They must then present their paper at a conference organised towards the end of the semester and are assessed on both the content and presentation of that paper. In this way the log has the twin function of helping to organise students' thoughts about the experience as they are undergoing it and also to enable subsequent reflection on that experience in the specific context of the project topic which they have agreed.

Thus there are many ways of ensuring that placements which involve more distance from the taught course itself remain integrated with it. If there is effective supervision by a member of the faculty and a responsible person with the organisation in which the student works, and student, faculty and supervisor have proper learning contracts which ensure that the experience is genuinely educational, a real clinical experience can be achieved.

Working with other agencies to study legislation and the legislative process

So far in this book we have concentrated largely on clinical work in the context of the individual client's problem. In direct work with real clients there may have been a dispute requiring settlement, litigation or some other response. There may have been a situation where the assistance of a lawyer was needed to avoid a potential dispute. Similarly, the simulated activities have tended to revolve around individual disputes, potential or actual. Two issues are raised here. The first is that the work has tended to be with the individual client. The second is that there has been a slight tendency to work in dispute resolution rather than dispute avoidance. Both raise important issues, for an understanding of the law and how legal practitioners work.[27]

In truth much of legal theory and legal practice is in dispute avoidance. The careful drafting of contracts to ensure that no misunderstandings can arise is a classic example. Real-client work is largely dependent on the problems which are presented to the student clinic. Many people do not seek the services of the lawyer until they are in an actual difficulty, which is why

---

[27] This distinction is developed with many useful examples in S. Nathanson, *What Lawyers Do* (London: Sweet & Maxwell, 1997).

dispute resolution plays such a large part in the work of a clinic. Note that the examples we have presented to you are not exclusively of this type. You may recall students at Sheffield Hallam drafting a will and another at Northumbria advising two clients on the establishment of a taxi business. It may be that the growing reputation of these clinics might generate more work of this sort.

Similarly, most cases arising in a real-client clinic will concern individuals' problems as it is inevitably individuals who are likely to come through the door for this kind of free service. However, some law centres have also undertaken work with entire communities and assisted in campaigning as they discover the common elements of legal problems underlying many individuals' difficulties. There is scope for universities to work together with such organisations, thus exposing students to the experience of devising changes in law or practice which could improve the quality of life of many people.

Simulations, of course, free the tutor from the exigencies of which cases come through the door, but in practice have mostly been concerned with individual dispute resolution. This is probably because they reflect the main thrust of the law degrees of which they form a part. I would argue that if the study of law is to progress beyond the narrow study of pathological cases, clinical methods provide a medium for doing so.

This section presents a clinical approach towards the study of legislation and the legislative process which attempts to address both of the issues presented above. It is based on experience of a course taught at South Bank Polytechnic during the 1980s. You may notice that this programme blurs the distinction between 'simulated' and 'real-client' work which we have used elsewhere, and it is, perhaps, for you to decide whether it belongs better in one category or the other or, indeed, whether it exposes the limits to the value of these categories. What is important is that the course's approach is based on the sound educational principle that experience of a process can lead to a greater understanding of it and better retention of the knowledge learnt in the process.

Legislation is often seen as a relatively dry part of the curriculum. If it concentrates on a sterile discussion of the processes, the subject can indeed be tedious. Legislation, however, is not only the source of much of our law. The legislative process is the forum for much of the crucial political debate in the country. The clinical approach allows students an opportunity to participate in that process and to contribute to it at the point where it matters most: the committee stage.

Students take this course in the first year of their degree and work in their normal tutorial groups. Tutors have chosen a specific piece of legislation which is due to progress through Parliament during the year. They will choose a government Bill, at least some aspects of which will be controversial, and will involve the interest of one or more pressure group. I recall, for example, in 1987/88 using the Criminal Justice Bill with its proposals to abolish the defence right of peremptory challenge of jurors.

Students are prepared for the exercise by lectures on the relevant substantive law and a talk on the techniques of pressure groups: drafting amendments, including fall-back amendments, drafting briefing papers etc. They also receive a pack with the relevant parts of the Bill, the Hansard report of the second reading debate, any legislation which is being amended, Green and White Papers and any relevant reports, newspaper cuttings, government and pressure group briefings for and against.

A debate is then organised at which spokespersons from Government and Opposition present their views about the chosen clauses and students have an opportunity to discuss their arguments with them.

Students then, working in tutorial groups, prepare a critique of the government proposals. They may be supportive of them or critical of them from whatever perspective students choose to adopt. Experience suggests that the vast majority of students found themselves critical of government proposals, but the reasons for that critical view and thus the specific criticisms could vary significantly. As different tutorial groups are given different clauses to work upon, there are opportunities for individual and group presentations of their criticisms to the class as a whole.

Each tutorial group must now come to a final and formal view on what legislation in this area *should* be designed to achieve. They must then draft a clause or amendment which will achieve their objectives. Students are not expected to approach this drafting task unaided. They will already have been introduced to statutory interpretation and will thus have a basis for understanding the significance of particular wordings. By individual and collective work, with tutors acting as constructive critics, each group will arrive at their best draft.

Tutors then pass these drafts to MPs on the standing committee to which the Bill is to go for its committee stage. In many cases pressure groups or MPs themselves will have identified the same potential amendments to clauses as students have drafted, but it may be that useful ideas come to them as a result of this exercise and that the students' suggested drafts may be proposed by MPs on the standing committee as amendments to the Bill. It is highly probable that, one way or another, the substance of amendments drafted by first-year degree students are actually debated in Parliament. Where possible, students are timetabled to attend the committee stage of the Bill they have been working on and, if fortunate, may hear part of the debate on their own amendment. In any event they are supplied with copies of the relevant committee Hansards and the reports of the report and third reading stages of the Bill.

This experience is seminal and provides a better perspective from which to understand the legislative process than reading about it in books or learning it from a lecture. The depth of understanding of the issues raised by the Bill and of the significance of the precise wording of different amendments which students acquire before attending the committee stage debate produces an informed perspective from which to judge the legislative process critically. Students are in a better position to judge how correct Richard Crossman was when he said:

> . . . the whole procedure of a standing committee is insane. What is the sense of starting at the beginning and working line by line through each clause when in many cases there is no one there who understands what they mean? If we had a select committee at which I could be cross-examined on the main policy and the committee could get down to discussing the controversial issues, that would be far more constructive.[28]

The experience also helps students to understand the task of statutory interpretation more thoroughly and with greater insight. It provides experience of drafting with precision, which helps the development of precision in other writing activities and in argument. It gives an insight into the real influences on the final content of our legislation and the relationship between political systems and legislation. It also provides for an in-depth study of a particular area of substantive law which may crop up in other courses.

[28] Richard Crossman, *The Diaries of a Cabinet Minister*, vol. 1 (London: Hamish Hamilton, 1975), p. 561, quoted in S.A. Walkland (ed.) *The House of Commons in the Twentieth Century* (Oxford: Clarendon Press, 1979), p. 290.

How, as students, might you get the most out of experiences such as these? Obviously, engaging seriously with your tasks at all stages is essential, but there are certain key stages at which your approach to your task is crucial. One is where the group agrees on the objective they seek to achieve with their draft. This may not be an objective with which you agree. Indeed, if the tutor has chosen the clauses well, there are likely to be clear differences of opinion within a tutorial group. If, having argued as effectively as you can for your view of matters, the majority of the group accepts a different objective, you must turn your efforts towards the full implementation of that objective, no matter how flawed you consider it to be. This shift is inherent in representing people as a lawyer, when you may well find yourself disagreeing with a client's objectives but nevertheless putting your energies into achieving them. This is important not merely as a first stage in preparing you to become a practitioner. It also helps you with general skills such as co-operative working, communication and argument, and puts you in a better position to understand how representation in an adversarial system works.

Another key point arises when you attend the committee stage debate. Most visitors to Parliament have little background information to enable them to understand the subtleties of what is being discussed. You will. Your knowledge of the issues may well be greater than that of many of the MPs participating in the debate. You can use this privileged position to assess critically what you experience there.

Finally, you can use the experience as a basis for reflecting upon what you are learning elsewhere. Your tutor may set you such a task in the form of coursework or a seminar topic, but even if this is not done formally you will get the most out of such an experience if you consciously bring it to your other studies. For example, how does it inform your understanding of the constitutional principles on which our legal system is based? Where do power and influence lie and how does that influence your understanding of sovereignty? How effective is the system of Parliamentary scrutiny of Bills and in what ways does it matter if the Government can command a majority in the House of Commons and its committees?

Working with the Free Representation Unit on a vocational course

The previous sections have presented ways in which students studying on a law degree might gain useful clinical experience from working with other agencies. This section looks at an example of how those working on a vocational course might make use of similar types of work. It is taken from the Bar Vocational Course (BVC) at the Inns of Court School of Law (ICSL). The BVC itself is organised around a series of simulated clinical activities known as practical training exercises. Trainee barristers who have completed two thirds of this course then take two options. These options are designed to integrate the skills which students have been developing throughout the course and apply them to a new area of law in which the student has a particular interest,[29] taught over seven weeks and assessed by a simulated clinical task, perhaps involving drafting and the writing of an opinion. An alternative is the Free Representation Unit (FRU) option,[30] where instead of working through simulated cases they take on real cases in the industrial tribunals.

FRU, which is run on behalf of the Bar, is a charity providing free representation in tribunals. Most of their clients are referred by Citizens' Advice Bureaux, although some are referred by solicitors' firms. Representatives act free and are mostly students on the final year of their degree studies, CPEs, LPCs or BVC, pupil barristers and some practising barristers. BVC students are all encouraged to take on cases for FRU during their year at the ICSL, but this does not contribute to their work on the course itself. For 24 applicants (chosen by drawing lots)[31] their FRU experience may count towards their qualification itself.

Before taking out a case FRU representatives undergo weekend training in social security and industrial tribunal work. They must then carry out 'secondings'. This involves reading the papers and writing an opinion on two cases. One at least of these must proceed to a tribunal hearing at which the aspirant representative attends. The quality of the opinions must be satisfactory for the individual to become a representative. Those taking the FRU option will have completed courses in civil litigation and evidence and have developed skills of case preparation, interviewing, negotiation, advocacy, opinion writing and drafting. These will be invaluable in the experiences they encounter when they take out their own cases.

---

[29] The conventional options currently available are: company law; criminal law; employment law; European Community competition law; family law; inheritance planning; international trade; landlord and tenant; property disputes; and sale of goods and consumer credit.

[30] For a fuller discussion of this option see N. Duncan, 'On your feet in the industrial tribunal: a live clinic course for a referral profession' (1996) 2 Contemporary Issues in the Law 53.

[31] Students who apply to take the FRU option are asked to select a third option which they will do if (demand exceeding supply) they are not selected for the FRU option. I debated selecting on grounds of experience (which could deny the option to those with most to learn from it) or motivation (but why should my values override those of my students?) and settled for drawing lots as that is, at least, impartial.

This raises one of the main differences between the FRU option and the undergraduate real-client clinical courses we have looked at so far. On a vocational course the objective is to prepare students for the demands of practice. Less emphasis is therefore placed on developing the quality of the academic study of law, and more on how effectively the student represents the interests of the client.

An example can be seen from Fiona's case. Her client had been an accountant working in a moderately senior position in a company. He had disclosed some fraudulent dealings and, on alerting senior management, had been promptly sacked. With the help of a CAB he had submitted an originating application to the tribunal and his employer had claimed that the dismissal was for his own misconduct in failing to keep proper financial records. Fiona, whose experience of financial matters was limited, arranged a meeting with her client in order to explore how she might best pursue his unfair dismissal case and to work out what further information she needed. The combination of Fiona's experience of preparing cases and her client's knowledge of the accounting systems of his former employer enabled them to identify precisely the documents which were necessary in order to establish the case. She wrote to the employer requesting discovery of those documents, but received no response. She therefore sought an order of discovery from the tribunal. The employer resisted this order, so a hearing was arranged before a tribunal chairman at which Fiona had to argue why it was necessary in the interests of justice for discovery to be ordered. She succeeded in this, and the tribunal ordered those documents to be produced within 14 days.

Shortly before the expiry of that period the employer contacted the FRU office to seek to negotiate a settlement. Initially they were only prepared to offer a relatively small sum, which Fiona, having calculated what the tribunal would be likely to award and assessed the chances of success, rejected. She explained what the tribunal would award and explained that if she did not receive the necessary documents, she would apply to the tribunal to have the defence struck out. Shortly afterwards, the employer was in touch again offering the sum of £9,500, pretty much what the tribunal would have ordered on a finding of unfair dismissal. This, with her client's approval, Fiona accepted, and she then drew up a consent order to ensure that the settlement would be binding. (I do not know whether her client subsequently · informed the authorities about the fraud issue.)

This was an excellent performance and earned her a very good grade. She was assessed, not by having an assessor sitting in on all these activities, but on the basis of a file which she submitted containing anonymised papers, the plans she prepared for her client conference, the interlocutory tribunal hearing and the negotiations together with the details and the outcomes of each. The assessment criteria included the quality of her analysis of the factual situation and the strengths and weaknesses of the case, the accuracy of her legal knowledge and the effectiveness of any research she had to do; the effectiveness of her interviewing and of her use of the procedures surrounding tribunal litigation; the persuasiveness of her advocacy and the effectiveness of her negotiation skills. These contrast with those appropriate for clinical courses in the undergraduate context by being aimed squarely at the demands of practice as a barrister. Thus, there is a degree of narrowing in the objectives of the work at the vocational stage, and the clinical approach is as capable of responding to that need for narrowing as any other.

There is a risk that an option based around individuals working predominantly alone without regular tutor supervision might miss the opportunity to encourage reflection. Students are introduced to the need to reflect upon the way in which the legal system and those who work within it operate by a discussion and directed reading at the beginning of the course. They are asked to keep a reflective journal to encourage them to think about how their skills are developing and thus to optimise the value of the experience they have. This is designed to ensure that they do not simply repeat experience without learning from it, but that they engage in the cycle of learning described by Kolb.[32] This sees optimal learning deriving from reflection upon experience leading to the development of theories which help to make sense of that experience. These theories are then tested out on the next opportunity for experience. The reflective journal encourages students to learn as fully as possible from taking real cases, which, in their nature, provide for a variety of experiences interposed by opportunities for reflection.

Here is one example, from a case where it emerged that a chef had been paid without deduction of tax. The student was engaged in a telephone conversation with his client through the client's daughter, as his English was sufficiently poor to need her to act as translator. The student (who spoke the client's language to a fair degree) overheard the client resisting his wife's suggestion that he should lie about his understanding of the tax situation. He pre-empted the daughter's first statement by indicating that he had heard the conversation. His reflective journal records his thoughts about the ethical issues this raised:

---

[32] Kolb, *Experiential Learning: Experience as the Source of Learning and Development* (Englewood Cliffs, NJ, Prentice Hall). See further pp. 47–50.

In a sense I had averted an embarrassing situation by shooting first and not letting them tell me the lie. On the other hand, should I not have waited until they came back to me with an answer (albeit a lie) aimed at me? Or would that have been unethical? Maybe I was exaggerating my ethical duty and should just have pretended not to hear. But then again, maybe they should not have spoken that loudly (I could not not hear). (Tom, 1997)

This, if not typical, is an example of the ethical problems that are commonplace in the handling of real cases.[33] Reflection on the dilemmas thrown up flows naturally from the requirement to keep a journal of this sort. It is also common to find students reflecting on their learning as a whole. The end-of-course questionnaire regularly produces comments such as:

It has helped me understand civil procedure in context, fact management, conference and negotiation skills in reality and the power we possess over people's lives.

Many students describe the FRU option as the most valuable part of their course. Their responses and the quality of their work attest to the high levels of adrenalin produced by taking on a real case and the recognition that a real client depends on their care and thoroughness. It transforms their experience of simulated work and takes them on a significant step further towards preparedness for practice.

Advantages for the collaborating institutions

Earlier chapters have stressed the view that a student law clinic should, as part of a university, be predominantly concerned with educational objectives, and therefore a case which served no educational purpose would be inappropriate even if the client was very deserving of help. Where the student experience is with another agency the balance of interests is inevitably shifted. The agency gets a volunteer who has a considerable degree of legal knowledge and, where the clinic is optional, a motivation to work in this particular field. Many students who have worked with agencies as a part of their course continue to act as volunteers afterwards, which assists with the perpetual demand for advice experienced by most such agencies. It will be necessary to establish some sort of agreement between university and agency so that the university can be sure that the student will not merely be used to photocopy or file documents and the agency can rely on students being

---

[33] For further examples, see chapter 6.

available for specific hours on a regular basis. Thus an appropriate balance can be struck between the interests of the two. It may be that some training of agency staff is necessary, and this may become a developed relationship where agency staff bring their experience into other university classes, and university teachers acquire practical experience through working with the agency. Furthermore, providing a service for the community may also enhance the local reputation of the university and help it to meet aspects of its mission statement; association with the university may enhance the reputation of the advice centre.[34]

Where specific demands are made on agency staff, appropriate payment can be made. For example, the employment caseworker at FRU acts as the main source of supervision for the students on the FRU option. The ICSL and FRU have an agreement whereby ICSL meets the cost to FRU of the time the caseworker spends in supervision of students and the incidental costs such as photocopying.

Creative thinking should be able to come up with solutions which are in the interest of all involved in such a collaboration, and where circumstances do not permit the establishment of an in-house real-client clinic this is an effective alternative which can be seriously considered.

Conclusion

This chapter has presented a variety of models which may be used to link up with agencies outside the university itself. Some of the experiences (e.g., the death row and legislation experiences) are different from those which could be provided by an in-house clinic. The nature of the coordination involved differs radically from that of an in-house real-client clinic, but it generally requires less in the way of capital investment or ongoing supervision of students. Thus, where resources are limited, it may be an effective way, perhaps the only way, of introducing valuable real clinical experience. These cost savings, however, have an inherent corollary in the relative lack of control by the university. In essence, some costs are met by the placement provider as the student (ideally) provides some valuable work for that provider. This creates a tension between the immediate interests of the placement provider and the academic concerns of the university. This needs to be addressed at an early stage and the proper place of each potentially conflicting set of objectives established, preferably in an agreed document

---

[34] See further S. Rice, *A Guide to Implementing Clinical Teaching Method in the Law School Curriculum* (Sydney: Centre for Legal Education, 1996).

recording the aims and objectives of each person and organisation. A learning contract of this sort can provide the foundation for a process of regular review so that the quality of the learning experience can be assured.

The further (or longer) a student is removed from the academic environment the more likely it is that the immediate objectives of the placement provider will dominate and the experience will, while valuable as work experience, lose some of its potential as a course of clinical study. Learning contracts, careful attention to student activity, proper supervision and linking to the more conventional study of the degree are all useful tools in maintaining proper attention to those academic goals. Ultimately, however, it is your awareness, as a student undergoing experiences of this sort, of what you can gain from it, which is most likely to ensure that you achieve something of sound educational value.

5

Role-play and simulation in the clinic

Some general observations on make-believe learning experiences

Virtual reality on the computer screen has become an accepted experience for millions of children in the developed, technocratic world. We drive racing cars, plan cities, zap aliens or manage football teams at an age (old or young) and with an enthusiasm that defies the constraints of our pockets, position and expertise. The excitement and insight that we accomplish from the comfort of a chair as we attempt feats safe in the knowledge that failure is harmless beguiles with its promise of the fulfilment of actuality. Fortunately few confuse the simulated experience for the lived one. Nevertheless the interaction with the problems, surprises, and calculated challenges posed by the program composers engages parts of the brain that comics, books and instruction manuals can only tantalise.

Clinical programmes based upon simulations offer similar stimulus and excitement — with the heightened interest that participation demands action, beyond the sitting-down, push-button passivity of the virtual world. Doing law as a means to learning about law is different from learning the law by reading it.

Since many of us study law in the recognition that we may one day work with it, there is always the attraction of seeing if it works. And if our understanding of law and legal techniques is going to develop, we should be actively seeking ways to test whether an idea will float, fly or flop. For others, less sure of entering practice, clinical programmes provide the opportunity to feel what lawyering is like. Whatever a clinical course claims to offer in the student handbook, most students discover that the fusion of law with practice generates opportunities for learning which are their own. The process of engaging intellect and behaviour, of utilising law, of intervening in human affairs, and of dealing with others' approaches to oneself, challenges our preconceptions, tests our understanding and confronts our ignorance by means that cannot be achieved in more traditional teaching.

The many forms of clinical teaching offer such opportunities, whether practice or research and development is the learning objective. This chapter addresses the strengths and deficiencies of learning from simulated legal situations. Simulation is commonly regarded as a valuable part of clinical teaching, but one which is the poor relation of the real-client clinic. It undoubtedly lacks the startling and awakening encounters that are presented in the live clinic, and it misses the involvement and commitment of coping with people who have need of legal expertise. Simulation, however, can provide opportunities and advantages that real-client clinics cannot address, not least of which is the suitability of the experience for the learning task. Simulation is a real experience and can engender some of the emotions and adrenalin flows normally associated with real client work, as this account of a student about to role-play a client in a trial indicates:

> Yes it was the day of the daunting trial! I have never felt this nervous for a long time, it simply cannot be compared with anything else. As the time came closer I freaked more and more. I had a meeting with my sympathetic solicitors an hour before the actual trial. At first I was cool but as they dived into their roles and began to wander into their own world I freaked and had to go for a stroll. Yes, I hate to admit it, but it is true. I was 'getting emotional'. (S1)

Along with the other forms of clinical teaching discussed in this book, simulation has a particular role to play in the law curriculum. Indeed, whilst little is written about simulation and role-play in legal education, it is a technique or method that is widely practised by many law teachers, often by those who would neither regard themselves as clinical teachers nor recognise the label of clinician.

This chapter first discusses the part that simulations and role-play can play in the daily work of the law school. The second section considers simulation as a substantial part of an undergraduate course focusing upon law in the hands and mouths of lawyers. The course described is the second or third-year full-course option which is part of the law in practice programme at the University of Warwick.

The place for simulation in undergraduate legal education

The efforts to inculcate into lawyer behaviour a concern for the customer added momentum to the realisation that lawyer training required more than mastery of legal knowledge. Designers of vocational courses began to see lawyer work as a complex combination of abilities. Phil Jones analysed the job of lawyering as a compendium of micro skills capable of practice and improvement.[1] In order to provide practice in the skills of the lawyer, trainers devised exercises and recreated legal situations as the basis for student experiments. Better to learn from one's mistakes in the classroom than cock up in court.

This laudable development in lawyer training in England and Wales, however, accentuated an unfortunate and debilitating division in legal education. Given that the professions had been used to concentrating on what lawyers do, and the universities on what legal rules lawyers should know, the lawyer's skills were regarded as the prerogative of vocational training and knowledge of the substantive rules considered to be the business of the academy. In the university law schools, the academics insisted upon the intellectual rigour of legal analysis, which they would teach. In law offices and chambers, practitioners proclaimed their role as keepers of the keys to legal practice. The vocational–academic divide remained polarised.

The professions historically guarded the entrance gates to legal work by setting their own exams to determine entry. Initially the courses and exams run by the Law Society and Bar also concentrated upon the substance of legal rules, albeit with an emphasis upon procedure and 'practical' subjects. Not until the end of the 1980s did the vocational law programmes develop courses directed towards the behaviour of lawyers in courts and law offices,

---

[1] P. A. Jones, *Competences, Learning Outcomes and Legal Education* (London: IALS, 1994). Phil Jones distinguishes between different models of competences, adopted by a variety of vocational institutions. These include transaction-based competences adopted by the Law Society, which require the performance of the small tasks which comprise a specific legal transaction (e.g., a conveyance). An alternative model, which is closer to that which is adopted in the Warwick materials, is a more generic approach, which seeks to identify broad abilities, incorporating cognitive as well as behavioural skills (e.g., to understand the social, legal and strategic context of an advocatory performance).

and look for competence in addition to knowledge. Legal skills became objects of accomplishment for the aspirant practitioner. The vocational divide was fixed upon a muddled distinction between education and training.

This false dichotomy created an obstacle to legal education which clinical teaching is attempting to redress. The obstacle consists of a tendency for academic lawyers to shun matters practical. Whilst contextual studies have burgeoned in British law schools since the 1970s, the context of what happens to law when lawyers get their hands on it is largely ignored in degree programmes. The phenomenon is more marked in the 'old' universities, as the divergent histories of the 'old' and 'new' universities have resulted in the latter generally being more receptive to the significance of legal practice as a subject of intellectual enquiry. The failure to address the behaviour of law in the context of its practitioners has contributed to a reluctance to develop more enlightened teaching methods, particularly experiential ones. Many legal academics dislike getting students to do what lawyers do.

The emphasis upon lawyer behaviour and conduct in the legal process, however, can provide a valuable impetus both for research into the role and function of lawyers and for inquiry into the translation of social problems into legal cases. The pinnacle of legal labour as portrayed in countless films and television series was the criminal defence lawyer. Trial practice in the US became an accepted object of professional education and training. Perhaps because of the complexity of the trial process, or the seriousness of allowing tyro-lawyers loose in real trials, simulation became a popular mechanism for rehearsing the skills and challenges of the courtroom. So much so that the simulated method of teaching trial advocacy is 'virtually universal' in the US[2] and widespread in the legal practice and Bar courses in the United Kingdom.

As a teaching tool, simulation is now regarded as valuable across the range of lawyer tasks. Its value has been noted, for example, in teaching negotiation, which is a process largely hidden from public gaze, which by its nature is not highly structured or stylised, and which has few substantive or procedural rules.[3] If the essence of clinical learning is its concentration upon

---

[2] S. Lubet, 'What we should teach (but don't) when we teach trial advocacy' (1987) 37 J Legal Educ 123.
[3] G. Williams, 'Using simulation exercises for negotiation and other dispute resolution courses' (1984) 33 J Legal Educ 307.

the process of law in the interchanges between lawyer and client, lawyer and court, and court and client, and the experience of legal rules within that process, there is a need to investigate how that process relates to the broader degree syllabus. The experience for the student can be gleaned from involvement in the 'real' situation, the real-client case, or recreated in the simulated example. Simulation as a teaching process ranges from the snapshot exercise, commonly introduced into otherwise traditional teaching situations such as the seminar, to the longitudinal reconstruction of cases from interview to judgment.

Simulation is a form of make-believe. To benefit from the process participants need to play a role. Role-play has long been accepted as a valid educational and training technique. The process of inviting students to imagine another point of view, the practice of drawing a class into the experience of an otherwise uncapturable social reality can provide an opportunity through which to view the dry blandishments of a text; or to bring life to the bald descriptions of narrative. Moreover the roles that are played in these make-believe scenarios should not be fantastical or based upon reflected stereotypes. To participate as the legal representative of a client in a role-play should be to play oneself in the role of a lawyer, not to imitate one's memories of Rumpole or Kavanagh QC.

Many law teachers who might otherwise consider themselves educational traditionalists employ the clinical technique of simulation in its broadest sense. There is a wide range of simulated situations and role-plays that can be adopted to enhance any syllabus. The clinical experience, however, offers more than just a chance to play, or to take a welcome break from textual analysis. Whilst having fun should not be regarded as a vice or indulgence in the syllabus, clinical methods — real or simulated — need to be grounded on clear objectives which relate to the rest of the objectives of a course, or the remainder of the courses in the curriculum. As a student you need to be informed in advance of the experience, the educational purposes for playing. What will you get out of it? Simulations, whether a snapshot or longitudinal case, make heavy demands upon resources, especially student and staff time. Is it worth it?

These issues are addressed below — first, by considering the value (for mind and money) of a clinical exercise in a substantive law course, and then by discussing simulation as the basis for a clinical course involving a longitudinal simulation.

An example of simulation as part of a substantive law course (reliving *Donoghue* v *Stevenson*)

The law of tort(s) is an essentially common law phenomenon, invariably an essential topic for early study on the law degree, and increasingly a popular subject for inclusion in A level law. Alongside the quaint example of contractual relationships floundering in the Carbolic Smoke Ball promotion lies the decomposed snail in a Scottish ginger beer bottle as an instance of consumer vulnerability to the doctrine of privity of contract. They both provide classic examples of cases to be read, learnt and inwardly digested in the privacy of your own library space; later to be rehashed in brief exchanges with a seminar leader, before being regurgitated in the examination room.

Whilst *Donoghue* v *Stevenson* [1932] AC 562 is a seminal case in the development of the duty of care as a principal element in the tort of negligence, the dry bones of the headnote and the rigorous analysis of the *ratio* have clinging to them the rich pickings of the role of the judiciary in the mediation of commercial relationships between supplier and consumer, and the plight of the punter in the early café bar. The duty of care principle can be easily grasped as a cognitive rule. The facts of the case present a neat encapsulation of Jerome Frank's $R \times F = D$ (rule × facts = decision)[4] and are memorable for their grotesqueness. But what more can be learnt by the law student from Mrs Donoghue's gastroenteritis?

The simulated exercise that follows offers a method for reinforcing our understanding of the legal rule and the legal relevance of the surrounding facts, but additionally provides an opportunity to consider the lawyer's role in the formulation of the dispute, and the adversarial nature of the common law. It also illustrates more dramatically than the text of the case the historical significance of the decision for the consumer.[5]

Description of simulated exercise

Students are divided into two groups, Donoghues (Ds) and Stevensons (Ss). Ds are asked to prepare what they imagined would have been a statement taken by Mrs Donoghue's lawyer; Ss are asked to do the same — as if they

---

[4] J. Frank, *Courts on Trial* (1947). Jerome Frank, a leading figure in the American Realist movement, argued against the unwarranted emphasis the law schools placed upon appellate court decisions in favour of the recognition that most cases were decided upon their facts. His rather crude scientist approach to law is discussed further below.
[5] A. H. Manchester, *Modern Legal History* (London: Butterworths, 1980), p. 30.

were Stevenson's lawyer. The basic requirements of recording a witness's statement should be explained to the class — first person narrative, chronological account, recording all salient facts and details.

If desired the role-play can be developed. Students can be invited to work in pairs — one in each pair accepting a client role and being interviewed by the other concerning the experience as D or S. The context of a café in Paisley in the 1920s and the expectations or suffering of customer and proprietor can be further explored by role-playing instances in the trial. Students can be asked to prepare an opening statement, or to role-play an examination in chief. The experience of role-playing a witness can be used as a basis for exploring the difficulties from a witness's point of view, and the lawyer's control of the story. The very activity of legal role-plays encourages imagination and emphasises the significance of the lawyer's influence in extracting facts relevant to the legal narrative from the individual's narrative.

If the exercise needs to form part of a unit of assessment, the lawyers for D and S can draft either a witness statement or a proof of evidence. The piece of writing can form the basis for class discussion, teacher evaluation or peer review. By focusing upon the beginning of the case — the interview between lawyer and client — emphasis is placed upon the commonplaces of lawyering and attention is switched towards the interactions between lawyer and shop assistant rather than lawyer and lordship. The follow-up class discussion can be tailored to pursue a variety of objectives dependent upon syllabus, and level of knowledge as the exercise in figure 5.1 overleaf illustrates.

Objectives of the simulated exercise

Amongst the overall objectives of the tort course may be 'to understand the principal rules and elements of the law of tort in general and those of the tort of negligence in particular'; 'to understand the principal cases and the reasoning within them' and 'to appreciate the role of precedent and the process of distinguishing or applying facts to similar cases'. These objectives can be pursued by the traditional process of private library study accompanied by class exposition and discussion. They are also addressed in the simulated exercise, however, which can encompass additional objectives as follows:

(a)   to appreciate the social context of a landmark decision;
(b)   to understand the significance of fact in a legal case (e.g., 'opaque' quality of the ginger beer bottle);

Thinking of the issues in the case of *Donoghue* v *Stevenson* from the point
of view of either the lawyer acting for Mrs Donoghue or for Mr Stevenson
consider the following questions:

(a)   Was it important that the lawyer discovered from Mrs Donoghue
that the glass bottle was opaque? Why?

(b)   Why do you think that those advising Mrs Donoghue did not
recommend a legal action against Minchella, the café proprietor?

(c)   Would a lawyer in the USA have given her client the same advice
at that time? Why/why not?

(d)   Would it have made any difference if Mrs Donoghue's friend, who
poured the drink out, had become ill from drinking the ginger beer?
Assuming Mrs Donoghue's friend is also your client, what advice would
you give?

(e)   What advice would you give Mrs Donoghue and Mr Stevenson
following the House of Lords decision? Was there still something that Mrs
Donoghue had to prove in order to establish liability? What should Mr
Stevenson have done?

(f)   What are the laws affecting drinks manufacturers (such as Coca-
Cola) today?

(Other questions can be devised which are appropriate for the teaching
objectives of the class.)

Figure 5.1   Exercise for understanding *Donoghue* v *Stevenson*

(c)   to understand the development of the tort of negligence as duty of
manufacturer to consumer;

(d)   to appreciate the social problem resulting from the contractual
doctrine of privity;

(e)   to introduce the role of the lawyer in the factual construction of a
legal case.

Traditional, more didactic methods could also cover these additional objectives, but less effectively and probably by consuming more time, at least if
the tutor is going to spend time checking each student's comprehension. In
the simulated case, the students themselves check each other's understanding
in the interaction.

The *Donoghue* v *Stevenson* example illustrates the potential that simulations
hold for the enrichment of seminars dedicated to the understanding of

substantive rules. It is a reminder that simulation has been alive and well in many classrooms for a long time and that it is more widespread than some law teachers appreciate. The method is less familiar as a vehicle for teaching about law and legal process, however, and the next section describes the potential that simulated case studies hold as the basis for a programme directed towards an understanding of the role of lawyers in the translation of social situations into legal cases — and the nature of law as practised in office, chamber and courtroom.

Learning from experience: the educational basis for simulated casework

Beyond the reconstruction of legal incidents as vehicles for law learning in the traditional syllabus lies the potential of a more ambitious simulation project — the (re)creation of the social problem as a law 'case'. The longitudinal simulation in which students discover the role of the lawyer in the handling of a client's problem from interview to disposal is a suitable technique for exposing the legal process to student understanding.

Most importantly in the undergraduate curriculum it affords an opportunity to 'learn about' law by 'learning how'.[6] Our understanding of what law is and how it works (or fails to work) is significantly illuminated by studying its use in the hands and mouths of those who invoke its force and influence. Central in this role are lawyers; and the simulation clinic as well as the real-client clinic provides a laboratory in which law in its practised and professional context can be studied. Your concern as law students should focus, as Julian Webb proposes, on questions of the *use* and *control* of knowledge.[7] For the law student this includes both the influence that law wields over the lawyer and the power that the lawyer can wield with law.

One of the foremost critics of the false dualism between knowing and doing was Donald Schön, who eschewed the 'technical rationality' of educational programmes which concentrate upon knowledge as the study of abstract concepts and the assimilation of data.[8] Schön favoured an approach that incorporates the complexity of practice, with all the challenges that accompany a problem in the 'real' world. For the law student, the problem on paper is conventionally stripped of the uncertainties, emotions and interactions that arise in the lawyer's office, police station or courtroom. Schön articulated a

---

[6] A concept developed by Julian Webb, 'Where the action is: developing artistry in legal education' (1995) 2 International Journal of the Legal Profession 187 at p. 193.
[7] Ibid., p. 189.
[8] The work of Donald Schön was discussed further in chapter 2.

process for 'reflection in action' — through which we can learn, whether as student or seasoned professional. He invoked the idea of artistry embracing technical knowledge, experience, and imagination or creativity.[9] The process by which artistry is developed is by reflection in action — pausing to analyse the basis for our decisions and behaviour. Schön's approach to learning, in fusing the division between 'knowledge' and 'know-how', transcends a concept of practical skills as behavioural competences.

The relevance of Schön's approach for the simulated or real-client case in the law syllabus is to (re)create a social situation with legal implications as told by clients and witnesses. This provides experiences through which we can understand the role of law, with many of the complexities which accompany its use. Understanding law's role is different from knowing law, as the study of texts suggests. Understanding how law works or is worked by lawyers belongs in the undergraduate curriculum as much as it does in the vocational training programmes.

Julian Webb has analysed in greater detail the role of the longitudinal simulation within a 'practicum'.[10] Developing the work of Schön[11] in the law school context, he analyses the potential that the virtual law office holds for reflective and critical study. Those who wish to explore the processes underlying experiential learning, should consult Webb's account of the legal process course at the University of the West of England.[12]

Using simulated cases as the basis for a clinical programme

Schön's approach to learning emphasises that all situations of knowledge in action are potential learning experiences. He was eager to remind us that we are never too knowledgeable to stop learning, never fully accomplished as experts or professionals. He did not make any major distinction between the learning potential of the simulated or the real-client clinic.[13] What then are the specific benefits of simulated clinics for students?

So far this book, in concentrating upon real-client clinics, has described the advantages of the 'live' case as:

---

[9] The concept of artistry in the context of legal education is explored in Webb, op. cit. (note 6).
[10] Webb, op. cit. (note 6).
[11] D. A. Schön, *Educating the Reflective Practitioner* (San Francisco: Jossey-Bass, 1987).
[12] See C. Maughan and J. Webb, *Lawyering Skills and the Legal Process* (London: Butterworths, 1995).
[13] One advantage that Schön would have probably recognised in the simulated clinic is that students are afforded greater opportunity to 'stop and think'. The pressures experienced in the real-client clinic often prevent opportunities to reflect. See Webb, op. cit (note 6) at p. 198.

(a) excitement of the real;
(b) exposure to practical knowledge and experience (forms, practice texts, time, cost);
(c) understanding of context of legal rules in a fallible human and bureaucratic environment;
(d) flattery of client dependence;
(e) variety of activity (interviewing, visiting court, taking photos);
(f) exposure to relationships beyond the university;
(g) excitement of the unexpected and challenge of the unknown.

Elsewhere Barnhizer has added the politicising force that many clinics may exert, and there are strong arguments for introducing and maintaining live clinics for the ethical issues with which students are confronted.[14]

This chapter does not seek to suggest that simulation is an alternative to working with real clients, but that effective law learning is dependent upon employing a spectrum of teaching methods, from real-client to didactic lecture. The idea that a medical student should try out her knife on a live patient before first practising on a dummy or a corpse would receive scant support. Likewise the simulation provides a controlled environment where law students can learn about what happens in the real world with little or no risk to their clients or themselves.[15] Whilst interviewing and drafting can allow for some correction in supervision, there are obvious advantages for the student practising the process in the safety of a simulation before being 'let loose' on those seeking assistance. Indeed, simulated rehearsals of client–lawyer interactions ensure that students are well prepared and are not 'let loose'. Furthermore, as Webb points out, live casework does not allow much opportunity for its deconstruction in action, and it also veers towards an emphasis on the legal problem rather than the process of lawyering as the client's needs can eclipse the student's.[16]

Such deficiencies as the live model has derive from the tension between educational objectives and practical and professional demands of legal service. These have already been presented in the two images of the clinical teacher:

---

[14] D. Barnhizer, 'Of rat time and terminators' (1995) 45 J Legal Educ 49.
[15] Williams, op. cit. (note 3).
[16] Webb, op. cit. (note 6), at p. 214. The pity is that the traditional pupillage model developed by the Bar, failed to accommodate simulation, a failure that was only eliminated in part by the new Bar Vocational Course as introduced by the Inns of Court School of Law in 1989, and, as from 1997, provided by other institutions.

(a)   as legal fixer — ready to intervene as professional on behalf of the client to ensure successful outcome;

(b)   as pedagogic facilitator — deconstructing realities and reflecting upon lawyer practices.

The former emphasises the amateur status of the student and threatens a lower quality of service unless the student performs as puppet of the supervisor. The latter leans towards the exploitation of the client as a teaching experience and suggests conflict with a practising lawyer's primary duty to the client. The challenge is to balance the opposing tensions and to reduce their effects to an acceptable minimum — a task to which this book seeks to contribute.

Notwithstanding the acceptability and undoubted strengths of the real-client clinic, as an educational mechanism it contains some disadvantages which may be avoided in the construction of simulations. These potential disadvantages include:

(a)   students' inexperience and ignorance, which jeopardises client service;

(b)   student anxiety induced by client responsibility;

(c)   inappropriateness of case category to student knowledge or legal competence;

(d)   premature exposure to client problems;

(e)   lack of 'fit' between clinical experience and pedagogic objectives;

(f)   inadequate opportunity for reflection and research because of urgency of problem;

(g)   dependency upon awkward-to-regulate supply of clients;

(h)   increased demand upon resources — multiplicity and unpredictability of client problems requiring more student and supervisor research time;

(i)   increased demand upon resources — live clients are less available, further distanced from law school than role players; and communications are more expensive (letters, telephones).

The most effective methodological approaches are those which retain the greatest number of advantages whilst avoiding the greatest number of disadvantages. The artificial creation of experiences in simulations can address these disadvantages. There is no real-client dependency — there is no legal or other need to be addressed, only a game or exercise to join. The situation can be tailored to the educational objectives of the syllabus and the needs of the student. Moreover, the simulated experience, as Stephen

Brookfield has noted, reaches the parts that more traditional teaching methods do not:

> Both simulations and role plays . . . reproduce within the artificial classroom environment the visceral flow of feeling as it is experienced outside this setting. In simulations and role-plays, students feel the heightened sensations associated with real-life dilemmas, decisions and problems.[17]

But in moving the emphasis towards the student some of the educational advantages of live client are inevitably lost:

(a)   loss of satisfaction derived from client dependence and its replacement by drudgery of law school task;
(b)   loss of exposure to relationships outside the university;
(c)   diminution in excitement which accompanies the real thing, and absence of emotional dimension; loss of complexity;
(d)   reduction in breadth of legal and social issues to which student is exposed;
(e)   less appreciation of practical context and human influences on legal practice.

Whilst some of these advantages may not be lost completely, they explain very clearly the strengths of the real-client model. Simulation and role-play as teaching methods can replicate many of the factual situations to be confronted in the real world, and they can do so in an environment of 'safe lawyering'. Ideally, however, simulation should be viewed as an adjunct to real-client work, and as providing an opportunity to try out the techniques and approaches before venturing into a real lawyer–client relationship.

An example of simulated casework

The Law School at Warwick has offered clinical courses since 1976.[18] The current undergraduate curriculum offers one full-year and two half-year clinical courses as part of its law in practice programme. These are all second or third-year options.

---

[17] S. Brookfield, *The Skillful Teacher* (San Francisco: Jossey Bass, 1990), p. 115.
[18] For a full account of the history of the Warwick Programme see A. H. Sherr, 'Clinical legal education at Warwick and the skills movement: was clinic a creature of its time?' in G. Wilson (ed.), *Frontiers of Legal Scholarship* (Chichester: Wiley, 1995).

The main course is a full-year option, focusing on the role of lawyers and legal work and based upon simulation. One of the two half courses is for advanced study of practice and the other builds upon an internship or placement for six months in law-related work, often at a solicitors' practice or barristers' chambers. This chapter concentrates upon the methods and experiences of the main course.

The most frequently cited aspect of the course amongst students is its differentness from other courses:

> I found a place, sat back and listened. It was the start of the strangest three hours I have ever spent in terms of courses at the law school. . . .

> I was in a state of mild panic. I thought that maybe it would be best to simply drop the course and take up a subject with a classic framework; textbook; lectures, seminars; a few essays and then an exam. At least I know where I stand with that.' (B1)

Fortunately, the student persevered:

> I left the session in a very positive frame of mind. I still was not 100 per cent sure about what the course entailed, but I felt sure that it would be challenging and that it offers the opportunity for personal development in important areas.' (B1)

So do students achieve personal development? Does the Warwick programme challenge? And what does it seek to enable students to learn from its simulated experiences?

Aims and aspirations

As we explained above the broad intentions of the Warwick programme are to explore what law is through studying our own attempts to use it. The formal aims of the law in practice programme are directed towards the integration of practical experiences with the study of socio-legal and theoretical materials. The aims of the programme are:[19]

---

[19] From *An Introduction to Law in Practice* University of Warwick course materials, 1996.

> (a) To explore the role of lawyers in the transformation of social problems into legal cases.
> (b) To analyse the work and role of lawyers and to investigate the nature of the skills utilised in legal cases.
> (c) To submit the practice of law, particularly pre-court and lower-court work, to academic study and scrutiny.
> (d) To encourage innovative methods of teaching law by introducing real or simulated legal experiences into the classroom as a basis for study.
> (e) To encourage research into the workings of the law, legal processes, the legal profession and legal skills.

The study of what happens to the implementation of legal norms (whether statutory duty, private right or publicly provided benefit) in legal practice, and the nature of lawyering jobs in this process are the central concerns of the programme. Interviewing, for example, is studied both as a technique which lawyers need to accomplish for the efficient, competent and empathetic performance of their profession, and also as part of the process by which lawyers elicit and select information from a client, which conforms to the lawyer's conception of a legal problem, which their professional discourse (law) may be able to resolve. As others[20] have pointed out, clinical teaching offers a rare opportunity to reflect upon the lawyer's influence upon law.

The main full-course option is simulation based. Real-client and workplace study are now available in the two half courses although these do not involve an open door clinic.

Course structure

The course has three components — skills analysis, simulated casework and contextual studies of law in practice:

(a) The skills component acquaints students with the basic tasks of lawyering and equips them with a framework for working upon the simulated cases.
(b) The simulated cases provided examples for students to act and interact with the facts, law, parties and legal representatives in resolving a simulated dispute.

---

[20] Webb, op. cit. (note 6) and J. Hunter, 'Teaching plumbing with Periclean ideals: should it be done? Can it be done?' (1996) 30 Law Teach 330.

(c)   The contextual studies offer research and theoretical analysis with which the clinical experiences can be compared.

If students are to benefit from learning in action they need space in the syllabus to reflect upon their activities and they need different perspectives upon their role and the role of lawyers as others have seen (and written about) them. Given the fascination that doing law holds for most law students, it is important to ensure as far as possible that the activity of lawyering is conducted in an environment that supports inquiry and critique. Hence the focus upon theoretical materials as a background to practical activity signals the distinction between accomplishing lawyers' skills as technique and applied practical knowledge and understanding the effect and responsibility of the individual's practice of law as a social force. It is this potential that enables Webb, building upon Donald Schön, to hope that students can be equipped 'with the foundations of a method, a knowledge, and (we hope) a sense of ethics and social responsibility capable of surviving the transition into the real world — whether that is a world of legal practice or not'.[21]

What happens in a law in practice class at Warwick? Students attend a three-hour session each week, which is divided between the three components of the course. Each week there will usually be time spent on skills analysis, contextual critique and casework, as well as dealing with the inevitable administration which clinical teaching generates. Space is important. There needs to be room to break from whole class into small groups of two, three or four students.

There is much less emphasis placed upon lecturing and more upon students taking responsibility for their own learning. Since it is a full course for credit, contributing to the degree, there are the usual and some unusual mechanisms for assessment. Assessment is discussed in more detail below.

Skills analysis and exercise

The skills analysis involves the study and practice of the vocational skills. These classes are role-play and simulation based. We start by breaking down the macro-skills into exercises utilising situations borrowed from non-legal experiences. Taking the skill of advocacy, for example, we believe that courtroom interactions are stylised versions of everyday exchanges. People

---

[21] Webb, op. cit. (note 6) at p. 211.

are forever telling each other stories — what we did over the weekend, the movie that we saw last night, an account of Harry Enfield's latest character. Much of what happens in court is story telling, albeit constrained by convention and controlled by rules of evidence and procedure. Lawyer skills can be understood and practised with some confidence if they are viewed as versions of the commonplace and familiar. The approach is explained more fully elsewhere.[22]

As an introduction to preparing an opening speech, through the avoidance of jargon, the necessity for explanation, and the structure of oral descriptions, the class does an exercise based upon an extraterrestrial conversation. The course tutor role-plays a Martian circling the earth in oral but not visual contact with the class. Course members are asked to describe certain everyday activities to the Martian such as cleaning one's teeth, putting on a jacket, or hoovering the lounge.[23]

The resulting demonstrations are used to explore the structure of narrative in the monologue; similarities between written and verbal accounts; assumptions about the knowledge of the audiences; the demystification of abstract concepts and the importance of imagination in the evocation of common experiences in the explanation of uncommon situations. Such simple (and, dare it be admitted, fun) examples seem to provide a valuable learning vehicle:

> You really have to think about how much a Martian would understand, and bring your explanation down to that level. It's a good exercise for forcing you to structure your explanation, and to explain not only *what* certain things are, but *why* certain things are done. (B1)

Students go on to consider the difficulty of pitching the technicalities of a case appropriately for their comprehension by a lay bench or jury. What knowledge can you assume such an audience to possess? Which words will they understand? Do they know what a 'banksman' does on a building site? Understand 'security of tenure'? Or comprehend the sound of 87 decibels of the Spice Girls?

The skills topics are organised as follows:

---

[22] P. Bergman, A. H. Sherr and R. Burridge, 'Learning from experience: non legally-specific role plays' (1987) 37 J Legal Educ 535.

[23] For more details of hoovering the lounge and Martians see Bergman, Sherr and Burridge, op. cit. (note 22).

    (a)   Constructing legal problems:

        (i)   interviewing and fact finding
        (ii)   fact investigation and evidence
        (iii)   legal writing.

    (b)   Pursuing legal strategies:

        (i)   negotiation
        (ii)   advocacy
        (iii)   alternative dispute resolution.

Each skill area is accompanied by readings from key texts and is accompanied by its own objectives and self-assessment questionnaires. The texts adopted fall into two categories — articles that describe the skills and provide guidance and 'tips' on established 'good practice'; and studies that approach the skills as lawyer transactions, worthy of reflection and evaluation, susceptible to critique and challenge. Thus the class considers an excerpt from Avrom Sherr's *Client Interviewing for Lawyers*[24] on the thirteen-point plan as a structure for interviewing. Such texts and the various skills textbooks supply technical advice on how to interview. It is an objective of studying interviewing, however, that the students 'should understand the significance of the context and role of the interview'.

The raw skill and technique of extracting facts and interpreting feeling from a client or witness is therefore considered against the background of the lawyer's function as a translator of social circumstances into the stuff of a legal case. The integration of technique and analysis is achieved by considering each discrete vocational skill in the context of research and writing about its operation, function and effect. Thus the role of the lawyer as translator of the client's problem into a legal case and in serving the client is examined through Maureen Cain's study of lawyers in the county courts.[25] We enquire into the particularised knowledge that the lawyer uses in the control of clients, or rather, as Cain argues, as 'conceptual ideologists'. What actually happens in lawyer-client interviews is considered via Sherr's study of articled clerks, which also affords an example of the value of empirical research into the behaviour of lawyers.[26] Binder, Bergman and Price's notion of client-

---

[24] (London: Sweet and Maxwell, 1986).
[25] M. Cain, 'The general practice lawyer and the client: towards a radical conception' (1979) 7 Int J Sociol Law 331.
[26] A. H. Sherr, 'Lawyers and clients: the first meeting' (1986) 49 MLR 323.

centred lawyering is explored and the class ponders the tensions between client service and time-costed accounting.[27]

The practice of interviewing is experienced firstly by investigating its component micro-skills (which we analyse as listening, memorising, recalling, questioning and summarising) and rehearsing some of these in classroom exercises. Ultimately, students will conduct videotaped interviews as part of their case studies. They will be asked to complete a questionnaire about their interviews. This ensures a degree of reflection about the interview. Self and peer evaluation become an integral part of the learning process through the use of questionnaires (see below).

Similarly, fact management is studied first from the viewpoint of constructing a sound legal case, based upon admissible and persuasive testimony from witnesses and the collection of essential real evidence. The technique of analysing evidence is assisted through considering Wigmore's suggestions[28] for charting the facts and inferences which comprise evidential propositions. The job of gathering evidence is then submitted to the pitfalls and privileges of legal evidence, including consideration of the witnesses' fallibility. A quiz which probes the class's perception, memory and recall abilities is conducted as a prelude to studying excerpts from Elisabeth Loftus's work[29] on the psychological dimensions of eye witness testimony. Frank's simple equation[30] of forensic positivism ($R \times F = D$) is examined alongside Bernard Jackson's explanation of the behaviour of language in the courtroom and the significance of culture and identity in the construction of narratives.[31] The wider social theoretical context of the individual skills is achieved through personal reading and is encouraged by an emphasis in assessment upon integrating reflection upon practice with the wider readings.

The skills exercises are intended to facilitate a greater understanding of the readings about the skills, and they also may have a value beyond the requirements of the course:

> I feel that the ability to undertake practical exercises during the teaching of the course helps to stick the information in my mind incredibly well. It

---

[27] D. Binder, P. Bergman and S. Price, *Lawyers as Counsellors: A Client-Centred Approach* (St Paul: West, 1991).

[28] Wigmore's chart analysis has been revived by William Twining in 'Taking skills seriously', in N. Gold, K. Mackie and W. Twining (eds), *Learning Lawyers' Skills* (London: Butterworths, 1989).

[29] E. Loftus, *Eye Witness Testimony* (Harvard University Press, 1979).

[30] J. Frank, *Courts on Trial* (1947).

[31] B. S. Jackson, *Law, Fact and Narrative Coherence* (Roby, 1988).

has also given me more confidence, not only in writing letters and negotiation exercises, but applying this knowledge to everyday social events. (B2)

As course leaders we derive encouragement from frequent expressions of development by students on the course, often expressing an appreciation of 'doing' law, rather than theorising:

> Anyone can learn about the theory side of advocacy skills and objectives. The interesting and useful element of the law in practice course is that it takes these theories and puts them, and you, into real-life situations so that you can appreciate their practical effects for yourself. This first-hand experience is an invaluable part of really learning, understanding, remembering and developing your individual advocacy skills. More often than not you discover that you've been using these skills (well or very badly) for your entire life. Recognising them is the first step to developing them further. (D1)

This particular student is (probably unwittingly) paying homage to Donald Schön as well as affirming the transferability of the skills which he is developing.

Simulated cases

Whilst the skills topics and exercises occupy much of the weekly class time, a considerable measure of student effort goes into work on the simulated cases which provide the 'laboratory experiment' or 'practicum' for investigating law and its practice. In these cases the students perform the role of lawyers as well as role-play the witnesses, working in groups. Group work is an important aspect of the course. Students learn from each other as well as sharing problems. Group discussions perform a vital function in student learning. A group should consist of at least three members; more than five in a group allows some members to freeload on others. Since each group needs to represent a party in a case, the number and type of case are influenced by the size of the class — or the numbers in the class must be restricted to the resources available, including adequate supervision. In Warwick we have ranged between a class of 24 students, divided into three cases (each case involving two parties serviced by a group of four students), and a class of 46 students working on four separate cases (two of which involved three parties) in groups of four or five. This is the model described below.

Each student is randomly assigned to one of the following four separate case studies:

(a)   a university disciplinary hearing concerning an allegation of theft from cars;

(b)   a personal injuries action resulting from a collision between a bus and a crane;

(c)   an employment case involving an allegation of sexual harassment;

(d)   a local authority prosecution of a landlord for unlawful eviction.

These four cases involve 10 separate parties. Students are provided with a room for meeting, and a computerised case management system specially written for the course, which generates letters and other documents, records essential data, and enables supervisors to monitor progress. The class is also encouraged to record interactions with clients and witnesses on video. Each group has a weekly supervision meeting with one of the two course tutors, and students keep a weekly journal in which they record their reactions to the course. We shall describe the operation of one of the cases — the university disciplinary hearing.

The university disciplinary hearing

This represents a simple case involving allegations of theft (or attempted theft) from cars by three young people. The alleged behaviour (trying car door handles) has been observed by two security guards or police, who become prosecution witnesses. The three 'defendants' adopt a cut-throat defence. One blames the other two and claims non-involvement; the other two blame the third.

The 'case' is constructed by using other members of the class as witnesses. An effective situation can be created by showing different witnesses different versions of the same event. Hence witnesses will give factually contradictory accounts in the belief that theirs is the 'right' or 'true' explanation. This can be done by making a simple video depicting three different scenarios (or by using the set of videos prepared by the University of Warwick), each showing the activities of a group of three people walking beside a row of parked cars:

- In **video A** all three characters commit an offence. This tape is shown to the security guards or police witnesses.
- In **video B** two characters are seen to commit an offence such as trying to open car doors, or actually opening a door. The third person is innocent and distances himself/herself from the activity.

- In **video C** the third character commits an offence and the other two are
  not involved.

The simulation requires a class of at least nine students divided into three
groups of four 'solicitors', each representing one of the parties — prosecution, defendants 1 and 2, and defendant 3. The format of a university
disciplinary hearing is used because it simplifies the procedural aspects of a
criminal trial, and strips the occasion of some of the more complex rules of
evidence.

Course members from another group are assigned the various roles of clients
and witnesses:

- university registrar,
- two security guards,
- three student 'defendants'.

Each witness is supplied with a role-play, describing the background to the
events and outlining the position to be adopted. Additional witnesses can be
created if necessary, either of fact or of character, depending upon the length
of time available for the eventual hearing. Our experience is that even with
the above witnesses, it usually takes at least three hours to complete a
hearing.

The group representing the university first interview the registrar as client
and the two security guards. The interviews are recorded on video and the
group drafts witness statements. Group members are supplied with a copy of
university disciplinary regulations and draft an appropriate charge. Two of
the student defendants who disagree with the third are separately represented.
The defence groups also interview clients and witnesses. Although the
hearing is informal, preparation involves consideration of prosecution advance disclosure, and groups concentrate on the quasi-criminal nature of the
proceedings. Legal research is involved as the groups strive to identify the R
(rules) in Frank's equation:

> It was my aim this week to complete the work on hearsay and also to look
> at the aspects surrounding the defendant's shield under section 1(f)(ii) of
> the Criminal Evidence Act. (S1)

The case reinforces students' study of substantive areas of law, in this case
criminal law:

One of the main developments since last week has been our decision to 'clarify' the charge. On deciding that theft would be difficult to prove because of 'intention to permanently deprive', we decided to try the students under s. 12 of the Theft Act, taking a conveyance without authority in association with the Criminal Attempts Act. After having spent a good day's work, we discovered that s. 12 was only a summary offence, and the Criminal Attempts Act did not apply to summary offences. . . . We are back to square one. (B2)

The group eventually resolved any difficulties and confirmed its opinion on the way to proceed with the supervisor.

The supervision is an integral part of the learning process. Each week the supervisor is available to review progress on the case, approve letters and pleadings, and to give guidance on future activity. It is during the supervision that detailed points of law and procedure will be discussed and resolved as well as issues of strategy and ethics that emerge from each case.

Each case culminates in a hearing, a guarantee that the simulated approach can offer that which the real-client model cannot. Each hearing lasts between two and a half and three and a half hours, although students are urged to observe strict time constraints in dealing with the witnesses and addressing the court or tribunal. The room is arranged as realistically as can be managed in the conventional classroom. Local practitioners are invited to sit as judges. Without being asked to, students dress the part and are inventive in obtaining helpful props (security guard uniforms etc.).

All the trials are videotaped and become a major event in the student's university experience. The trial provides a shared experience for the whole class to consider the adversarial quasi-criminal process. It provides an opportunity to raise the issue of procedural and evidential safeguards and fairness, and to enquire into the justice of informal disciplinary hearings. A senior member of Warwick University's registry who participates in real disciplinary hearings sits as chair of the simulated disciplinary committee, affording a valuable opportunity to engage the executive and judicial functions of the University community.

Whilst the technique of reconstructing three different versions of reality is at first sight manipulative, it replicates the widespread experience of many contested trials where different witnesses, whether through mistake or malice, create alternative versions of events. At one level the blatant portrayal of three distinct factual accounts is a reminder that the adversarial process, with its insistence upon champions of each party's point of view, is a contest of competing narratives during which truth finding is not an objective[32] shared by all. On another it provides a foundation for a critique of Frank's $R \times F = D$ equation as students discover how difficult, and how crucial, it may be to establish the facts.

Finally, the simulated trial is valuable for the insights that it brings into the experience and interactions of the witnesses, in this case one of the students role-playing a security guard:

> I have noticed that over the time that I have spent with the group acting for the university . . . I have started to empathise with them a lot. I think this is quite an interesting point as in terms of when the time comes to giving evidence I will feel quite biased towards this group. Obviously, I think in such a case this would be a very normal reaction considering I witnessed the incident and am employed by the university. However, as a point to reflect upon later I think this would remain true of many lawyer–witness relationships. (Y1)

Contextual studies

We have already seen how the more practical parts of the course are related to readings about law and lawyers. The contextual readings which accompany the course are based upon a selection from the following topics:

(a) Legal services or legal markets?
(b) Lawyers and their clients.
(c) The rise and fall of legal aid.
(d) Analysing and researching the courtroom.
(e) Advocacy and the adversarial process.
(f) Lawyers and empowerment.
(g) Discrimination in practice.
(h) Information technology and the practice of law.
(i) Professional ethics.

Since a major objective of the course is to relate the practice of law to theories of lawyering and studies of the legal process, students are encouraged in discussion, journals and exam questions to relate their experiences

---

[32] The university trial and the unlawful eviction prosecution provide further useful examples observed by the whole class of the adversarial process. The contextual readings include Goodpaster's demolition of this as a truth finding mechanism — G. Goodpaster, 'On the theory of American adversary trial' (1991) 78 J Crim L & Criminology 118.

on the course to the prescribed readings, as illustrated in the following excerpt from a journal:

> It is interesting to consider the role of the solicitor as a social controller (as was discussed in 'The general practice lawyer and the client' by Cain) in relation to our actual case. To a degree we do have the dictatorial role in events as we are responsible for running the case and deciding how Randle's (the client) case is best presented. On the other hand, as is emphasised by the Cain article, perhaps our role is more concerned with translation of facts into a scenario which best achieves the ends dictated by the client. (E1)

It would be misleading to suggest that the fusion of theory in practice is either easily or inevitably achieved. Some students enjoy the challenge of confronting their own experiences in the light of the writings and insights of others. Some hate it. The following comments from journals illustrate that students, not course tutors, are the architects of their own learning experiences. The comments all relate to an exercise in analysing a simple theft scenario on the basis of a Wigmorean chart:[33]

> This week we reviewed the Wigmorean fact analysis charts. I think that the concept is very worthwhile and anything that can help you analyse a complex mass of facts and observations is to be welcomed. (I1)

> I have to say that whilst I could see the logic within the system itself, it is in fact learning a new language and a new way of thinking. Major thought divergence at this point in my life is not a good idea as I have just about got the hang of using words. (F1)

> Understood perfectly the benefits of breaking down the information into its component parts but found the exercise of then using symbols to represent this largely a waste of time. (M1)

How are students assessed?

The assessment has three components:

(a)   a written essay or short project for 20 per cent;

---

[33] The Wigmorean approach to evidence analysis is explained by William Twining (see note 28). Wigmore devised a scheme for breaking down the ultimate thing-to-be-proved into its constituent parts, and then identifying in chart form the facts and inferences from the available evidence which substantiate or contradict the thesis.

    (b)   a two hour exam for 40 per cent;
    (c)   casework and class work for 40 per cent.

The essay is on a topic that includes a practical dimension of law. It is assessed by the same criteria as any other piece of written work. In this there is an acknowledgement that all too often the criteria for assessing written projects are implicit, rather than explicit. Suitable criteria[34] for assessing the law in practice essays are:

    (a)   choice of topic;
    (b)   theoretical understanding;
    (c)   knowledge and understanding of law;
    (d)   contextual understanding;
    (e)   analysis and critique;
    (f)   research (library and fieldwork);
    (g)   organisation and structure;
    (h)   references and citations;
    (i)   writing style;
    (j)   presentation.

An opportunity for course teachers to assess the technical knowledge of students is provided by including a two-hour exam during which students are required to answer three questions. In the exam students are encouraged to refer to their casework as a source of examples for analysis. Typical questions from the exam paper are:

What insights into the role of the lawyer in the resolution of social problems did you gather from the simulated trial in which you took part as an advocate?

'Litigators resemble historians, and litigation is largely a process of recreating historical events.' (Binder and Bergman, *Fact Investigation*)

Discuss.

Critically evaluate EITHER Michael King's models of the criminal justice system OR Maureen Cain's analysis of lawyers as translators in the county courts. Illustrate your answer with examples from your visit to the courts and/or the simulated trials.

---

[34] I am grateful to Abdul Paliwala who devised a list of indicators from which these criteria are adapted. Abdul's indicators are used on the LLM law in development course at Warwick.

The case and class-work component makes up the final 40 per cent of the assessment. It includes work in groups, contribution in class and performances in the trials. The following criteria for assessment in this part of the course are provided:

    (a)   commitment and effort on the cases and in class;

    (b)   understanding of the content and role of the legal issues in the case;

    (c)   appreciation of the factual elements of the case including dealing with witnesses and managing other evidence;

    (d)   recognition of the context surrounding the simulations and the social and professional circumstances (including ethical matters) that might arise in practice;

    (e)   ability to reflect upon your experience and its contribution to your understanding of the role of lawyers in the resolution of social problems;

    (f)   sensitivity and imagination towards others involved in the case, including your interactions with other members of the team;

    (g)   ability to reflect upon the experience and the implications for your own development.

The first criterion, commitment and effort, is to encourage activity on the course. Since the emphasis is upon action as a mechanism for learning, the course cannot be undertaken by reliance upon accumulated knowledge but derives from engaging the exercises and simulated cases.

There are various ways in which students are able to show that they have met the criteria, and to display their progress. An important part of the learning process is the keeping of a weekly journal in which opinions, thoughts and reactions to the work can be expressed (and from which the student quotes in this chapter are derived). Tutors also have an opportunity to meet the class in small groups and discuss context, strategy and role.

Testing skills, competencies and knowledge

Learning objectives are an essential mechanism for ensuring that courses are focused and coherent. The objectives should be reflected in the criteria for assessing a course as a mechanism for evaluating how students individually have achieved the objectives set.

Whilst the Warwick course is concerned with the nature of the skills that lawyers practise, since it is not a competence-based course, individual performance of skills is not an assessed component. This is because we feel that there is a danger of basing the criteria for evaluation upon too narrow a breakdown of lawyer tasks into behavioural competences.[35] If this is done the work of a lawyer is explained as technique and student ability tends to be judged for its external display of appropriate behaviour, rather than for the content of legal knowledge or breadth and depth of analysis.

Simulation has the attraction as a teaching method that it can provide a series of largely similar experiences for successive cohorts of students. Moreover the simulation can be constructed to include elements that explore a student's approach to specific situations. Thus it can ensure that an ethical issue or rule of evidence is raised. Again there is a contrast with real-client clinics, where client problems and hence student experiences are inevitably unique.

Each course will usually set its own objectives in relation to the curriculum of a degree programme. The discipline of articulating learning objectives is a valuable mechanism for tutor reflection. Course objectives can also provide an informative review of the totality of teaching programmes and the teaching context of individual courses. Thus objectives can be set at different levels and adjusted to a varied range of tasks or skills.

As we have explained above, the class work and case studies on the law in practice course at Warwick address the conventional skills of lawyering — legal research, interviewing, case management, drafting, negotiation and advocacy. They do so in order to provide a context in which to reflect upon our involvement with law, and law's intervention in human affairs.

The broad objectives of the course are those set out at page 187. The various tasks that a lawyer performs are scrutinised as part of the enquiry into the nature of law and lawyering. Interviewing, for example, is traditionally studied as a competence that enables lawyers to ascertain the client's 'problem' in an efficient and sympathetic manner. To help students understand the skill of interviewing they are introduced to a set of learning objectives for the conduct of interviews, which are to:

(a)   understand the significance of the context and role of the interview in the translation of social problems into legal cases;
(b)   display knowledge and understanding of the implications of different interviewing approaches;

---

[35] See further note 1.

(c)   demonstrate the ability to conduct an interview sympathetically, ethically and efficiently, and with a suitably structured approach;

(d)   elicit the facts, distinguish those of legal significance and relate them to the relevant law;

(e)   advise and counsel a client on future outcomes and agree a strategy for dealing with the case;

(f)   reflect upon the experience of the interview and analyse problems, successes, and significance of the interview and review alternatives.

These objectives were originally designed as part of a research project into criteria and assessment on undergraduate law courses conducted by the now-defunct Council for National Academic Awards.[36] The research pointed towards the shortcomings of reducing learning criteria to a series of micro-skills for assessment. Such an approach is best suited to competence-based courses.

Since the Warwick course is not competence-based, the criteria are not used as tools of formal assessment. They are a teaching mechanism. When used as the basis for questionnaires which are completed by students, they perform a valuable peer and self-assessment function.

Understanding of the function and process of interviewing is assessed by examination, where the role of the interview in the translation of clients' personal histories into legal cases, and our own contribution as lawyers to the framing of those cases and the representation of our clients, can be explored.

The student perspective

On page 186 we quoted a student's apprehensions and aspirations that the challenges of the course would lead to her personal development. An explanation of the learning process and the potential that lies in the course for both personal development and course credit emerges in the comments below by past students on the course. Their comments, which are taken from their journals, focus on two of the assessment criteria for coursework — appreciation of the factual elements of the case, including dealing with witnesses and managing other evidence; and sensitivity and imagination towards others involved in the case, including interactions with other members of the team.

---

[36] P. A. Jones, op. cit. (note 1), pp. 96–109.

Rules, evidence and witnesses   Much of the early part of the skills analysis
and the casework is devoted to concentrating on the availability or otherwise
of factual information upon which a legal case may be based; and the
potential of that information as 'evidence' in a hearing. Thus issues range
from the perishability and fallibility of evidence to the selection of facts in
the construction of competing narratives.

The lessons learnt may occasionally seem obvious, although they are rarely
trivial, as this student's reflection on an interviewing exercise illustrates:

> I found it hard to concentrate on getting a clear general picture of events
> as opposed to concentrating on particular facts which, on reflection, were
> not particularly relevant. The articles on interview technique were alarm-
> ingly accurate as I found myself concentrating on one legal solution . . .
> at the expense of finding other facts which may have suggested other legal
> or non-legal solutions. I also think I let myself and my partner down by
> not paying enough attention to the time. (E1)

and as another student reflects on the effect that courtrooms have upon lay
witnesses:

> I wonder how many lawyers make it a point in helping witnesses
> overcome their negative feelings towards the court? It is easy to lose sight
> of the fact that witnesses overall do have such feelings in the first place
> and that it is the lawyer's responsibility in [sic] making the witness feel
> as comfortable as possible. (V1)

Moreover, whilst work on the cases consumes a great deal of time and
energy, it is invariably regarded as time well spent,

> These trials have been very good experiences and are of tremendous value
> to this course. My original fear that they would take up too much time has
> not been borne out in practice. On the contrary, I feel that my group
> actually spent more time on our trial than was strictly necessary because
> it was such a useful and enjoyable experience. (I1)

The same student later reflected upon the process of learning which he
considered to be occurring on the course:

> This course has been an innovative way of getting information over in a
> way that relates to practical as well as academic interest. It is easier to

learn when the actualities of the subject are there for you to experience personally, it is a good way of learning and offers a more 'in depth' and practical way of addressing issues in a meaningful way that is easily related to actual practice. (I1)

Working together Sensitivity and imagination towards others involved in the case, including other members of the group, is an important element of the case work. Group working is not usually regarded as a suitable object for evaluation in undergraduate courses. Students appreciate the difficulties from the outset:

> What frightened me most about the course was the prospect of working in a group. That is something I have not done for several years and it is not something that appealed to me. (B1)

Sometimes these fears materialise, particularly early on in the course as students find their identity in relation to the other members:

> This was not a good day! . . . When I got to the lecture I realised most of the other groups had got together during the week and prepared a formal speech and some had even typed them. I gave my group my piece of paper with my ideas on and asked for theirs. They had not written anything down so no one could present all our arguments. On deciding who should represent, after realising none of us wanted to do it, I reluctantly agreed but felt angered and embarrassed that our contribution rested solely on my meagre efforts. . . . I am angry with my group and I think they know but if it means this won't happen again then that's fine by me. (F1)

The student's plight and concern was picked up by other members of the group:

> R said she would present it, which was fine until the time actually came for her to present it and she felt like fainting. We all rallied round her. K took her place and A and I comforted her . . . She insisted on leaving though.

> After she left and during a break, the rest of my group sat down and had a good talk. We were shocked at what had happened to R. We had known she wasn't eager to present but we didn't know the extent of how she felt. (G1)

The group met together the following week and tried to reassure the upset
and disgruntled student:

> I guess it was to reassure her but it made me feel better knowing that others
> felt the same way as well, especially since we made it a point to remember
> how the others in our group felt and to be helpful whenever possible. (G1)

The group dealt with the situation well and by week 7 the same student who
had been initially aggrieved, recorded:

> The group definitely interacted on a better level today. I must admit I have
> tried to make an effort to get on with one member with whom I don't
> altogether see eye to eye. In fact once my attitude changed, so did theirs
> although I don't think we will ever be 'best buddies'. I have thought about
> this situation and believe it is quite a valuable experience in that there may
> be times in the future that I may have to work with someone with whom
> I am incompatible but obviously I will have to resolve the situation or be
> miserable and inefficient. (F1)

Group work invariably proves to be a rewarding and supportive experience,
and the ability of many students to be reflective and confront their own
difficulties is frequently borne out in their journal entries. The same student
continued later:

> This is it! . . . I have realised that good preparation makes you feel a lot
> easier about things. My biggest worry is that I will faint while making my
> speech because ever since term 1 and me drying up, it has preoccupied
> me. I have told the others that if I do, they must take over. Our group is
> working brilliantly. Nervous energy is taking over now and I want to just
> get on with it. Thursday night comes and I am feeling really confident and
> I think it is to do with the group rather than me thinking I am really good.
> (F1)

The effort and emotion expended by this student paid off evidently and the
feared 'drying up' did not occur:

> To me the trial was brilliant. To someone watching it or marking it may
> have been inadequate or a bit boring at times but to me, I would have done
> it all again the next night if I could. I thought that afterwards I would sleep
> for a week, but as it happened I could not wind down. I wasn't in a bad
> mood, ecstatic that I had done [sic] and I thought done it well. (F1)

The candour expressed in journals facilitates assessment of the criterion to display sensitivity towards the other members of the group. The self-reflection and understanding shown to others in the above extracts is likely to be reflected in a high grade. But group work often gives rise to anxiety concerning the nature of individual performance. Will I be brought down by idle members of the group? Will my efforts merely result in others getting credit? Are we assessed as a group?

The main source of evidence of groupwork (and the other criteria) comes from the weekly group meetings with the case supervisor. Individual contributions are revealed in such sessions. Course tutors towards the end of the year discuss the group performance, analyse the strengths and weaknesses of their group effort and indicate the range of grades that they have in mind. The group has the opportunity to present its own account of effort, commitment and development over the year. The second stage of casework evaluation occurs in meetings with each student during which the student's own contribution and that of other members of the group are discussed.

The essence of working together is an appreciation that whatever you do has an effect on the other members of the group. If a meeting is missed or a task not completed, the other members will usually understand — at least the first time. But if one or two members rely too much upon the efforts of others, the frustration will emerge. Often such frustrations are an integral stage in the development of a group:

> The interpersonal dynamics of the group underwent something of an upheaval today concerning when we should schedule our meeting with R. . . . Such events are in my opinion vital to develop the skill to both deal with others and to influence them in making their final decision. Whether other members of the group feel quite so positively about such matters though I'm not sure! (E1)

and:

> Last Monday when we all met we discussed the problem of certain group members not pulling their weight, not showing up for meetings interviews etc. D and I made it clear that we were not happy about it, and I think it cleared the air a lot. We decided to make a 'fresh start' and since then things have been a lot better. (B1)

The group's action described in the last excerpt was effective in encouraging a reluctant student to participate, as his own account bears witness:

Having missed the Thursday meeting with R, I did make it to the group
meeting on Monday evening. However, what awaited me was quite a
shock. Although perhaps I hadn't really been working at 100 per cent
effort, I didn't think I was being totally slack. Nevertheless the group
thought this to be the case. They said that I had missed several meetings
and was not committed enough to the case. Maybe I had been a bit lazy,
but I was still quite surprised at the ferocity of their attack.

However, in retrospect it was just the 'kick up the backside' that I needed.
It made me realise that the group had been carrying me and I hadn't been
pulling my weight lately. I also realised that I couldn't get by just inputting
into the group stupid wisecracks and jokes, that I would actually have to
do some real work, not only for myself and to get a good mark but more
importantly so I didn't let the group down. (G2)

The tendency for peer pressure to provide an impetus to those members who
might otherwise 'ride' the efforts of others is quite powerful.

Some conclusions

All in all, the trial was a very rewarding experience. It enabled us to see
the different stages in the work of lawyer, be it a solicitor or barrister. As
I come from a country where the two professions are combined, I was
especially happy to be able to go through all the procedures from
interviewing to representing in court. I have learned many practical things
through this experience. It enabled me to attempt the different stages in
the legal profession without (much) fear of making mistakes, and while
having the opportunity to receive guidance and ask questions. (L1)

This student sums up the totality of the experience. For some law teachers the
case study as test bed may be regarded as too practical for serious intellectual
inquiry. Should such prejudices still maintain, William Twining's 'Taking
skills seriously' may provide arguments to challenge them.[37] The case study
does provide an opportunity to 'put the whole thing together' and since the
majority of live cases are settled before action, and since students do not
have automatic rights of audience in this country, the case study is the only
method to ensure that all students have an opportunity to take part in a trial.

The Warwick programme seeks to combine an approach that focuses upon
the competences of practice combined with the quality of analysis and

---

[37] Op. cit. (note 28).

demonstration of comprehension of issues confronted. Since the objectives of the Warwick programme are to understand legal practice and to be reflective about its purposes and methods, competency at each skill is not an objective. Ability to perform a given task is not a requirement of the course, although inability to perform a task may be evidence of a lack of understanding. We hope thereby to overcome the deceptive discussions that divorce skills from knowledge, and to break down the divide that distances the practice of law from its learning, and the study of law from the environment of practising lawyers.

The Warwick programme is only one of several initiatives directed towards learning about law through investigating its process. Elsewhere in this book are many instances of courses which share similar aspirations on undergraduate programmes. We would argue that students should expect that all law courses in universities should offer more than a narrow insistence that the study of law is restricted to the analysis of its meaning in statute and judgment.

But perhaps the greater challenge is provided by the new vocational courses, which can be in danger of confining clinical teaching to the accomplishment of discrete performances in the sanitised setting of a lecture room. If undergraduate programmes can be accused of ignoring the practical environment of legal rules and an over-concentration upon legal reasoning as the sole object of intellectual endeavour, still more may Legal Practice Courses and the Bar Vocational Courses be restricted to teaching skills as technique. If the vocational–academic divide is really to be bridged there must be scope for the introduction of clinical content into these courses. Jill Hunter identifies the tendency of clinical skill subjects, whether real-client or simulated, 'to place far too much emphasis upon performance and far too little on intellectual enquiry of a broad conceptual kind'.[38] In her account of a course on evidence and advocacy she argues for vocational courses that reinforce 'the critical, philosophical and conceptual edge that characterises intellectual inquiry in clinical education in the law school so that students develop insights beyond the ''doing'' and the ''knowing''' in the recognition that this will promote 'the direction of legal practice beyond mere client (and/or lawyer) need and towards community needs'.[39] A similar plea has been made by David Barnhizer.[40] This chapter and the rest of this book are directed towards enhancing the student experience of learning. We have

---

[38] Op. cit. (note 20) at p. 333.
[39] Ibid. at p. 353.
[40] Op. cit. (note 14).

adopted a specific understanding of clinical learning that transfers to the student a greater responsibility for his or her learning — recognising that the law teacher's role is more mentor than messiah. More significant, however, is the notion that clinical learning, including simulated casework, embraces an ethical dimension which non-clinical teaching finds it hard to emulate.

6

Principles in practice: ethics and clinical methods

During the night of June 1972, during the United States Presidential election campaign, a security guard discovered a break-in the Watergate complex in Washington DC. The premises affected were the Democratic Party campaign headquarters. The subsequent inquiries showed that the break-in had been authorised by senior members of the Republican Party, and disclosed a slush fund supporting a network of unethical activities. This eventually led to the resignation of President Nixon.

The resignation was prompted as much as anything by the attempted cover-up of the truth and the use of senior officials to assist in that cover-up. In particular, central to the attempts to deceive the public and the judicial process were a number of lawyers at all levels of seniority in the profession. Twenty nine lawyers were eventually gaoled or disbarred as a result of their involvement in the affair. One consequence of this was a recognition in the United States of the need to address the ethical standards of the legal profession.

As a result ethics became a compulsory subject in US law degrees. But it is relatively easy, when discussing ethical problems, to arrive at unimpeachable ethical standards. It can be much more difficult to live up to them in practice.

Around this time clinical legal education methods had begun to take root in large numbers of US law schools (see chapters 1 and 7). Could working with real legal problems be a better way of getting students to become ethically literate lawyers?

By comparison, and possibly because no analogous scandal has ever come to light here, legal ethics has received relatively little attention in the law school curriculum in the United Kingdom.

Things may be about to change. In 1992 Lord Templeman addressed the annual conference of the Association of Law Teachers; drawing from his experience on the Bench he indicated the growing need for legal education to address ethical issues. The following year the Society of Public Teachers of Law adopted professional ethics as the theme of its annual conference and a section of the society has been established with this as its concern. The 1996 report by the Lord Chancellor's Advisory Committee on Legal Education and Conduct (ACLEC) not only laid considerable stress on the need for legal education to address professional ethics and conduct but also indicated that:

> Students must be made aware of the values that legal solutions carry, and of the ethical and humanitarian dimensions of law as an instrument which affects the quality of life.[1]

There are increasing pressures on lawyers which make ethical issues more current. To quote again from the ACLEC report:[2]

> As the organisations in which law is practised become larger and more complex, as competition and instability in the market for legal services increases, and as many legal practitioners experience a growing sense of insecurity, there are real dangers that professional standards will be threatened unless counterbalancing steps are taken to reinforce ethical values.

It seems probable (and, I would argue, desirable) that ethics will take on a higher profile in the law-school curriculum. If the ACLEC report is influential in how law courses are presented it is also likely that students will be engaged in active rather than passive learning.[3] As we have argued earlier in

---

[1] ACLEC, *First Report on Legal Education and Training* (1996), 1.19. Similar concerns are expressed by the US MacCrate Report (see pp. 240–1 and 251–4).
[2] Paragraph 1.19.
[3] Paragraphs 2.2 and 4.21.

this book, clinical methods provide wonderful opportunities for effective active learning. In this chapter I will briefly consider what might reasonably be covered by the concept of legal ethics, will discuss how and at what stages this might best be incorporated into the curriculum and will then explore the ways in which clinical approaches to learning can help in understanding and internalising ethical principles. I hope that this will show that the great value of clinic lies not in studying ethics as such, or in learning the codes, but in exposing students to ethical problems so as to make concrete and real the theoretical arguments which may be discussed in other classes.

An example of facing real ethical issues at law school may be seen by considering the ethics of using delay in the running of a case. It is quoted by Susan Kupfer, who teaches legal ethics at Golden Gate University, San Francisco:

> The student represented an elderly couple in a housing matter. They had successfully challenged an administrative proceeding to evict them by claiming the eviction was retaliatory for a previous challenge to a rent increase. The landlord was a college professor who was unrepresented by legal counsel.

During the 30-day period for the administrative order, the landlord mistaken-ly filed a lawsuit to evict the couple. The suit cannot be brought without the administrative certificate, which is an absolute prerequisite. The ethical issue for the student was the timing of the filing of an answer to the lawsuit. To wait until the last day on which he could answer would mean the 30 days would have run and the landlord would have lost his right to appeal and the lawsuit. The student wondered:

> Do I file in the ordinary course or wait until the very last day? In the normal case, I decided I would have filed in the ordinary course. While there is a duty owed to the client to advocate, it does not supplant the duty to myself to play fairly. . . . Was I right? I thought so then, but I'm not so sure now. How different is it to argue and win on a procedural point, unrelated to the merits, rather than capitalise within the rules on an opponent's mistake, and thus prevail?

The landlord was tipped off, hired an attorney, and pursued the administrative appeal properly.[4]

---

[4] Kupfer, *Authentic Legal Practices* (APLEC Conference Papers) (Sydney: College of Law, 1996), p. 746.

Most lawyers would feel no compunction about using the procedural advantage of delay in such a situation and their duty to their own clients (the tenants) confirms the formal correctness of this position. However, the student recognised a real conflict between his duty to his clients and the principle that issues be resolved on the merits. In this case, the fact that the landlord was unrepresented raised a further ethical question. How fair is it that one party to a dispute should receive the benefit of free legal expertise through the operation of a university law clinic while the other does not? Thus this simple, but real, problem raises not only the question of the proper application of the professional codes, but also forces a consideration of the nature of a legal system in which cases may well be resolved without the merits ever being considered. A problem like this provides a significant learning opportunity, not only for the student who encountered it but also for fellow-students able to discuss each other's cases in tutorial and supervision sessions.

Arguably, such a problem provides a much more profound experience of ethical issues than an academic discussion can ever do. Moreover, it is the experience of clinical teachers that ethical problems, far from being rare, crop up with great regularity. The experience alone, of course, is not enough. It needs to be backed up with opportunities for reflection and discussion so that the lessons of experience may be shared and learnt. This has been a significant influence on the design of the clinical courses presented in this book.

What do we mean by legal ethics?

Ethics is a major strand of philosophy. It may indeed be seen as the study of moral philosophy. As such it is involved with asking questions about the moral rightness of actions and covers all human activity. This would be a fine subject to teach and study. However, it is not what we propose here, as we are concerned with the more focused study of legal ethics.

By legal ethics we propose two fields of study: ethics and the law, and ethics and professional conduct.

Ethics and the law

In this context ethics involves a critical analysis of the ethical content of the rules and procedures encountered in law itself: so that we can test them against ethical standards (standards on which we may have clearly differing views).

This approach to the study of legal ethics may well arise in the context of a legal theory or jurisprudence course, or it might arise in legal method courses. The place where these issues find themselves is likely to influence the nature of the study adopted. In a jurisprudence course, for example, it might be common to find a highly theoretical or philosophical approach to the study of legal ethics. I recall from my own undergraduate studies a consideration of law and morality organised around the Hart–Fuller and Hart–Devlin debates.[5] I found the reading and discussions fascinating, but have retained little of the argument as I have never consciously had to apply those arguments to concrete situations. A legal method course which approaches the study of legal ethics is more likely to root that study in the experience of practice, whether from the perspective of the practitioner or the client. It is common, where ethical issues are studied in such courses, for hypotheticals to be used to stimulate discussion.

In either case there is a risk that the discussion will be dry and sterile. This is not to undermine the need for a theoretical underpinning to an ethical debate. Conclusions which are not firmly founded in a theoretical under-standing of the issues may, frankly, be dangerous as it is all too easy to find superficially attractive solutions which carry the seeds of other problems with them. However, a theoretical approach which does not engage with the problems which arise in reality may be set adrift. What is more, ideas which do not find themselves anchored by concrete examples are particularly difficult to understand and to learn about. Theory and reality are the twin foundations of the study of ethics and provide a basis for its study in context.

One of the beliefs which all the authors hold is that a crucial context of any study of substantive law is its impact on the lives of ordinary people and that any ethically based analysis of law should recognise this reality.[6] Much can be done to move in this direction by introducing class discussions of hypothetical situations. However, taking the further step of approaching a realistic but simulated problem through role-play, or to encounter the ethical problems that arise when undertaking real cases, adds all the value that has been presented elsewhere in this book for the use of clinical methods. Involvement, motivation, realism and relevance are all enhanced.

---

[5] See H. L. A. Hart, *The Concept of Law* (Oxford: Clarendon Press: 1961); Lon L. Fuller, *The Morality of Law* (New Haven: Yale University Press, 1972); H. L. A. Hart, *Law, Liberty and Morality* (London: Oxford University Press, 1963); P. Devlin, *The Enforcement of Morals* (London: Oxford University Press, 1965).
[6] See also chapter 2.

Ethics and professional conduct

By using this expression we mean more than learning the professions' codes.[7] That is, indeed, essential for those who intend to join one or other profession. However, for academic legal study which is not necessarily aimed at professional qualification, the detailed study of all elements of the codes is unnecessary, and for those who do so intend it is insufficient simply to study the existing codes. If that were all that were done, there would be little insight brought to bear upon them and an opportunity for the critical eye to be cast over the codes would be lost, as would an opportunity to keep them open to review and improvement. For the codes are not immune to criticism. The profound differences in view as to what constitutes ethical behaviour mean that any attempt to codify the conduct of lawyers must be subject to criticism. It is even the case that in certain circumstances the solicitors' and barristers' codes may not agree with each other, making some criticism inevitable. For example, when dealing with the issue of client confidentiality the solicitors' code provides certain public interest exceptions.[8] None appear in the barristers' code, which, if the client refuses to sanction disclosure, requires the barrister to withdraw and not disclose.[9] It is therefore important not merely to learn what the conduct rules are, but what impact they have and what they ought to be as well.

When should legal ethics be dealt with in the curriculum?

We would argue that an ethical perspective on specific elements of substantive law should be pervasive. Whenever students are learning an area of substantive law that study should be informed by a critical understanding of its effect on real people. That understanding is in part informed by the ethical principles we as lecturers bring to bear on each area. For example, a narrow approach to the study of the law of obligations would clearly need to address the topic of negligence, but in doing so might require only knowledge of the law of negligence. For real understanding, however, it would need to encompass an ethical consideration of the basis for and limits on the extent of liability in the present law. The context of alternative approaches (no-fault compensation schemes or compulsory insurance, for example) is also only imperfectly understood without the ethical element. Why should someone (or an insurer) suffer liability if not at fault? Why should a victim receive no

---

[7] Law Society, *Guide to the Professional Conduct of Solicitors*, 7th ed. (1996); General Council of the Bar, *Code of Conduct of the Bar of England and Wales* (1990) loose-leaf.
[8] Law Society, *Guide to the Professional Conduct of Solicitors*, 7th ed., principle 16.02.
[9] General Council of the Bar, *Code of Conduct of the Bar of England and Wales*, para. 504 (e).

compensation because fault cannot be proved? Because they cannot afford to bring the claim? Because a technicality of the rules of evidence means that an essential piece of information cannot be admitted in court? There may, of course, be excellent answers to all these questions (there are, although they conflict with each other), but they cannot be thoroughly explored without the ethical element. In doing this, value judgments need to be made explicit: those underpinning the actual law, those underpinning proposals for reform and those underpinning students' and lecturers' own preferences.

It is therefore an inherent part of the informed study of a field of law that ethical dimensions are explored as a part of that study. This element of legal ethics should, we think, be a pervasive part of the study of substantive law, whether at undergraduate or postgraduate level.

The study of professional ethics raises different questions. If the law degree is not aimed exclusively at preparing people for the legal profession it is arguable that the study of professional ethics is not necessary at that stage, even though it might be at the later vocational stage. No doubt a good *knowledge* of the law can be attained without studying professional ethics, but, as stated before, a contextual understanding of the law requires an understanding of how the profession operates. There is therefore a strong case for elements of professional ethics to be taught throughout legal education, from first degree to continuing professional development after qualification. When, recently, the issue was studied in Canada the Cotter Report[10] came to this conclusion. This is not to propose that undergraduates should learn the codes as such. Instead, undergraduate courses should introduce, where appropriate, a critical appreciation of the role lawyers have in society and the impact of their behaviour on their clients and others. This cannot be done without reference to the codes. This approach to study not only injects realism and context into what might otherwise be rather abstract. It also begins the process of encouraging a critical look at the codes, so that when a prospective lawyer comes to study the codes with the aim of learning how to behave professionally he or she does not accept their content unquestioningly. Thus a vector for constructive criticism of the codes is introduced into legal education at a relatively early stage, bringing with it a greater chance of informed development.

Few law degrees in the UK currently approach the study of ethics, and fewer still professional ethics, in any depth. What follows, therefore, is in part a plea for the enrichment of the law curriculum.

---

[10] B. Cotter, *Professional Responsibility Instruction in Canada* (Quebec, Conceptcom, 1992).

Role of clinical legal education

We have already mentioned the need for those studying the vocational courses to be familiar with the relevant code of conduct which applies to them and to develop an understanding of how it should be applied in realistic cases. The role-play elements of the LPC and BVC will provide some opportunity for that learning to take place. However, learning the codes and applying them is not enough. It can lead to an uncritical acceptance of existing practice and an unthinking approach to the application of professional standards. As we have argued, students need to understand why the codes have developed as they have and to develop a critical view of those codes.

It is also arguable that students should have participated in serious discussion of ethical principles before they encounter ethical problems in real situations. There is evidence that if this is not done the ethical element may appear unrelated to the mainstream study of law. This is suggested by Julie Macfarlane's research which, 'based on interviews with law students taking clinical courses at three undergraduate schools suggested that participation in a clinical programme tended to render students more cynical about what "going to law" could offer clients and, in many cases, transformed their personal values from belief in the legal system to something approaching scepticism'.[11] The overall structure of the ethical element in a programme therefore needs to be considered. You will see how the issue is addressed by the Columbia University 'profession of law' course, which is presented below.

Work in moral development in other fields suggests that changes in moral judgment are triggered by 'crisis', situations which force you to reconsider your beliefs.[12] This is precisely the valuable function that clinical experiences can provide, when you, as student or lecturer, are faced (either in a simulation, or when working with a real client) with uncomfortable choices. Such experiences thus achieve more than making moral dilemmas concrete. They may also provide a focus for a critical view of the legal system, the expectations of practice within it and the laws which it applies. They may also provide the 'crisis' which can stimulate serious reflection on your own moral judgment.

---

[11] J. Macfarlane: 'Look before you leap: knowledge and learning in legal skills education' (1992) 19 J Law Soc 293 at p. 306.
[12] F. Osler and A. Schlüfli: 'The thin line phenomenon: helping bank trainees form a social and moral identity', in G. Lind, H. A. Hartmann and R. Wakenhurst (eds) *Moral Development and the Social Environment* (Chicago: Precedent Pub., 1985), p. 150 at p. 166.

Use of real-client clinics

We revisit shortly the experiences of some of the students undertaking work in real-client clinics which were raised in chapters 3 and 4. We can see the ways in which ethical issues arise in respect of both the general ethical perspective on specific areas of the law and the ethical dilemmas to which practice inevitably exposes you.

A perspective on ethics

A characteristic of most real-client clinical work is that it brings students into contact with the legal problems of economically disadvantaged people. This may be a new experience for many law students and is more than a valuable learning experience. It forces exposure to the effects of social and economic inequalities which will have a far greater impact than reading about them. It also requires students to approach problems from the perspective of those dealing with this disadvantage, and thus, while not forcing any particular conclusions on individuals, does provide an experience which may challenge preconceptions. The role of the lawyer in this situation also becomes apparent. As Simon Rice has put it:

> A community legal centre is an opportunity for students to learn law critically, to see a lawyer's role in an inherently conservative system and to analyse it. Recognition of values and roles is fundamental to the purposes of clinical education.[13]

The experience of Carolyn on the clinical law course at the Queen's University of Belfast[14] gives a clear example of this. Her case, you may recall, concerned a refusal of benefits on the basis that the client was cohabiting with the man who had provided her with emergency accommo-dation. In her reflective analysis she was able to explore the ethical underpinning of the relevant rules. She found herself accepting the govern-ment's aim that unmarried couples should not be treated more favourably than married ones as this would undermine the institution of marriage. However, its implementation in practice gave her cause to worry:

> At first, I tended to sympathise with any adjudication officer forbidden to ask direct questions [about sexual relationships]. However, on reflection I

---

[13] S. Rice, *A Guide to Implementing Clinical Teaching Method in the Law School Curriculum* (Sydney: Centre for Legal Education, 1996).
[14] See page pp. 139–144 and 151–3.

tend to feel that it has become a little too convenient to avoid the subject.
. . . It seems easier for the Agency to make the assumption [about
cohabitation] and then rectify later if someone makes a fuss, instead of
attempting to ascertain the correct situation in the first place. . . .

A paradox has been created behind the façade of the avoidance of 'sexual
snooping'. Where this issue is avoided it tips the balance in favour of
'living together as husband and wife' because without unequivocal denial,
the combined effect of the other evidence is not strong enough to avoid
the label.

Carolyn was able to go further and explore the way that a homosexual
relationship would have been treated differently and thus to identify the way
in which legislation can be used to reflect society's moral norms, although
sometimes with possible unintended results (a financial advantage to those in
homosexual as opposed to heterosexual relationships). The case gave her the
opportunity to explore the ways in which the moral imperatives undermined
what might have appeared to be a more rational economic analysis based on
the fact that two (whether cohabiting or not) can live more cheaply together
than apart.

Professional ethics

Few real cases are without an ethical dimension. We will select a few
examples from the cases already described.

Martin, also at Queen's,[15] learnt from experience the development towards
being able to put his client's interest before his own:

I had always known but only now felt that the central issues were the
client's, not mine; that success and failure were to be judged on whether
my client got a fair hearing and just settlement, and not on whether my
submissions and speeches impressed the panel. And as I realised this, I
found that the stress no longer upset me, though it was still there. In this
way the course has had a much more fundamental effect on me than I had
imagined it would when I began.

In effect, he had taken critical steps towards developing a professional,
ethical and practical attitude towards practice.

---

[15] See page 151.

Carolyn had to consider how open her evidence should be in order to argue her client's best interests, yet not mislead the tribunal. She decided to withhold a medical certificate which had simply said that the client was receiving (unspecified) treatment. She formed the view that this could give the tribunal the impression that the doctor did not treat the client's problem seriously. Should such relevant evidence be withheld? Should the tribunal not have an opportunity to form their own judgment on questions of this sort? Is this not particularly problematic in proceedings which are partially inquisitorial in nature and not dominated by the adversarial assumptions which justify representatives to go as far as they may in presenting their client's case without actively misleading the tribunal? Having to face up to questions of this sort is a powerful learning device. Having to make a decision and *apply* the ethical framework ensures that the learning is deep.[16]

Confidentiality arose as an issue in the case at Sheffield Hallam, where students drafted a will for the client.[17] Professionalism was developed here as students learnt how personal details could be discussed legitimately within the clinic, but not outside, and that their inquiries of the client should not go beyond what they needed to meet her needs, for example, to satisfy understandable curiosity. The skill of limiting their messages to parents who could not be told the subject-matter of the message was another important example of ethical understanding linking with professional development.

Mr Payne's case[18] raised issues of conflict of interest. You will recall that the defendant had been in the habit of accepting the university's students on placement and this was clearly potentially embarrassing to the clinic and the university. I will not repeat here how the problem was resolved, except to draw attention to the fact that even if the answers arrived at seem reasonably obvious they do not appear so when you are in the middle of the problem and it does not present as a textbook case. This, of course, is the nature of clinical work. It is easy enough to identify the correct answer to a textbook problem, but in the real world problems do not present in that way. Each one strikes afresh and the professional development in handling it is internalised in a way no textbook problem can be. This case also raised other ethical issues, but they are presented clearly on pp. 98–101 and we will not rehearse them here.

As we can see, ethical issues arise regularly in real-client work. The experience thus teaches students that ethical problems are not rare. They are

---

[16] See chapter 2.
[17] See pp. 102–6.
[18] See pp. 92–101.

common occurrences and are an inherent part of the experience of legal practice. Also, real dilemmas will provide a basis for reflection on the most ethical way to respond, which can be the subject of discussions with other students and tutors. In this way, the experience of real-client work can provide insights which complement the discussion of ethical principles in a variety of contexts which could be chosen to be part of the mainstream curriculum. It can also provide examples which can be developed in simulations, to allow students to explore the consequences of different responses to an ethical problem.

Use of simulations

Simulations can be used in a variety of ways in teaching ethics. Traditionally, ethics has been taught in the classroom by discussion; the consideration of problems; how you would apply competing ethical solutions to a particular problem; the discussion of competing theories of ethical behaviour. This is a necessary part of learning about ethics and understanding ethical behaviour. However, it is not enough. Anyone can identify an ethical solution to a problem in a classroom. We may disagree about the most ethical solution and we may disagree about the theories which underpin the decisions we take. However, we are unlikely to be tempted actually to act unethically, a temptation which really can arise in practice, and this is where one of the principal issues for understanding ethics in the practice of law arises.

This point is made with great clarity in the introduction to Columbia University School of Law's clinical 'profession of law' course.

> When you are asked by the Multistate Professional Responsibility exam-ination or its equivalent to identify the ethically proper course of action, you will bear little cost if you select one of the more ethical options among the multiple choices provided. But the difficult — and all too frequent — ethical questions that lawyers face in daily practice arise because of substantial penalties that may accompany a choice to engage in more, rather than less, ethical behavior. Ethically impeccable behavior may harm clients' interests, diminish lawyers' income, disrupt their family lives, undermine their standing in their professional and wider communities, and even place their jobs and livelihoods at risk. Only by intuiting some of the anxieties associated with the potential costs of ethical behavior can you appreciate how difficult — and important — it is to develop a disposition and capacity to identify and follow an ethically proper course of action.

To put the same point slightly differently, you are likely to find when trying to respond to the wishes of real people, particularly working in the commercial field, that they will seek your advice, not to be told whether a particular objective or course of action is lawful/ethical or not (with the implicit agreement that it will be abandoned if not lawful), but rather how an objective may be pursued or a course of action followed without acting unlawfully. Your client may not wish to hear that in your view there is no lawful and ethical way of doing that! If that is your expressed view there may be other lawyers who can conceive of a way of achieving the objective which is arguably lawful, or at least unlikely to attract a penalty.

The following section of this chapter draws heavily upon one particular example of a clinically taught course on legal ethics: Columbia University School of Law's 'profession of law' course. It is presented as an example of how clinical methods may be integrated with other teaching approaches to apply a theoretical frame of reference to actual decisions. Simulation forms a part of the student activity and is used to address these concerns in a realistic way. The course lasts for one week and is taught intensively. Students are expected to undertake prior reading (extracts from several conflicting approaches towards the issues of legal professional ethics[19]) and establish which of a number of potentially conflicting 'ethical models' they will seek to adopt in the role-play work which follows. For example, they will be asked to consider which of the following competing goals they should adopt: to maximise the client's autonomy; to serve as the client's moral conscience; or to guarantee the justness of the outcome. This provides a theoretical basis for the work which follows, work which forces a critical consideration of the ethical approach which had initially seemed the most attractive. Before starting on the simulations students are asked to consider four situations in which lawyers are placed in difficult situations and answer three questions:

If I were to proceed as the lawyer contemplates, would I be 'lying' as most people understand that term? If so, or if not, should I proceed as the lawyer contemplates? If so, or if not, how does my conception of the lawyer's

---

[19] H. Wachtell, 'Special tender offer litigation tactics' (1977) 32 Bus Law; W. Simon, 'The ideology of advocacy' 1978 Wis L Rev 29; S. Pepper, 'The lawyer's amoral ethical role: a defense, a problem, and some possibilities' 1986 Am B Found Res J 613; D. Luban, 'The Lysistratian prerogative: a response to Stephen Pepper' 1986 Am B Found Res J 637; A. Kaufman, 'A commentary on Pepper's "The lawyer's amoral ethical role"' 1986 Am B Found Res J 651; S. Pepper, 'A rejoinder to Professors Kaufman and Luban' 1986 Am B Found Res J 657; D. Luban, *Lawyers and Justice: an Ethical Study* (Princeton University Press, 1988), pp. 21-3; W. Simon, 'Ethical discretion in lawyering' (1988) 101 Harv L Rev 1083.

appropriate role affect my answer to the question of how I should behave in each of the four situations?

To give you an idea of these situations, one is reproduced below:

> Attorney Smith is representing the plaintiff in a car accident case. The complaint asks for $500,000 in damages. The client is greatly in need of cash, fast, and has informed Smith that anything more than $50,000 settlement would be acceptable and desirable. Opposing counsel (with whom Smith has not yet discussed settlement) telephones Smith and says that the defendant is willing to settle for $75,000. Smith contemplates responding as follows: 'Well, I guess I'll let my client know about the offer, but I can tell you right now that she wants, expects and deserves to receive a lot more than $75,000'.

Having considered these four situations, students are asked to prepare a paper justifying which of the ethical approaches is the most attractive. The first class of the week follows the submission of these initial papers and allows for some discussion of the introductory readings before embarking on the simulations, which are presented below.

There are three role-plays, which place students in a variety of situations.

The corporate lawyer

The first requires you to undertake the role of a junior lawyer in a successful firm of corporate lawyers. At various stages of the simulation you are required to take on the role and decide how to respond to the situation you find yourself in. The firm's growth is in part the result of its successful representation of its major client, whose founders are good friends of the founding partners of the firm. Their financial transactions (which involve the leasing of machinery which has been bought on a loan secured by a charge on that machinery) are certified and underpinned by the legal opinions of the firm that the transactions are fully lawful.

The chief executive of the client company informs you that he has in the past performed acts of financial impropriety. (How should this affect your dealings with him? Who is your client, him or the company?) A whistle-blower employed by the client company suggests that impropriety is continuing and is then offered a surprisingly generous severance payment. The scale of the ongoing fraud which has been perpetrated becomes clearer, until eventually the senior partners of your firm decide to withdraw from representing the client. As a final sting in the tail, a friend who works for another law firm phones to say that they are being engaged by the erstwhile client and wants to know why your firm has ceased to represent them.

At each stage of this (simplified) sequence of events you have a series of ethical questions to respond to. They include a number of issues:

(a)   Should you respect confidentiality in respect of crimes committed in the past, or which are ongoing or about to be committed?
(b)   How might your decision conflict with any duty to prevent crimes?
(c)   What impact does the fact that your firm is implicated in some of the earlier fraudulent deals have on your response to these questions?
(d)   Who exactly is your client? Is it the chief executive who has admitted the former impropriety or the company he manages?
(e)   Should there be continued involvement with a client whom you believe to be engaged in criminal behaviour?

The simulation actually places students in much more detailed situations than can be indicated here and the problems are presented with great precision. In effect, students are presented with the ongoing situation and required to take decisions to resolve ethical problems at specific stages. They do so by registering answers to multiple-choice questions which, when completed, provide a record of their decisions. There are also opportunities for discussion. They are all matters to which the professional codes are relevant, but, as with most generally worded codes, finding the relevant section is insufficient. In addition it is important for students to interpret the code and to recognise that no clear answer emerges from a simple application of the wording of the code.

The public defender

The second is that of a public defender representing a client who faces the death penalty in Georgia for an alleged murder. You are presented with two crucial stages of the relationship between lawyer and client at which ethical issues arise in highly charged circumstances. The first is pre-trial, and presents you with an interview of a client in custody. The second occurs after a guilty finding and addresses issues surrounding appeal decisions.

In the first simulation the initial tension arises because your client's first language is not English. Although charged with murder, it is not alleged that

he actually carried out the killing, merely that he was an accessory
(nevertheless facing a capital penalty). Three ethical issues arise: how to deal
with a client who may be considering perjury; how to advise your client
when you recognise that he may be easily manipulated; and the role of the
lawyer's own political and moral values in representing clients.

These issues also present problems concerning the relationship between
different potential defences and the lawyer's duty to the court to ensure that
it is not misled. A video is used which presents alternative approaches to the
interview.

The first 'deals' with it by avoiding it altogether. (We have not cited an
extract from the first.) The second raises it but cuts the client off before he
gets too deeply into the potentially perjurious information:

> Lawyer (after some questioning): Look John Henry, you're not feeding me
> a line here, are you? Because I want you to know from the start: I can't
> let you get on the stand and feed the court a line!
> Client: I know that! I know all about the courts! Listen, I don't explain
> things so good, okay? *No puedo hablar inglés muy bien.* But I'm telling
> you, this is how it happened.
> L: All right, but why is it, do you think, Casey was able to throw all this
> heroin around so cheap? I know the cops busted him for dealing heroin,
> and that he arranged to get them in on the coke trade for a lesser sentence.
> But where'd he get all this freebie heroin? You're not going to tell me the
> police were supplying it?
> C: Well . . . the way I figure it, the cops didn't get the whole stash when
> they busted him. So he was using the stash to buy himself into the cocaine
> scene.
> L: The 'way you figure it' isn't going to do us much good.
> C: Did I say that? I meant he *told* me.
> L: He told you he'd been busted by the cops!?
> C: Would I be here if he did? No, he just said he had a heroin stash he
> had to get rid of — quiet like.
> L: He told you that?
> C: Yeah.
> L: Interesting. All right.

The third extract shows the lawyer initially going into detail about how she
will respond if he does attempt to mislead the court:

L: All right, John Henry. Before we go on, I think I'd better expand some more on what I told you before about my keeping the things that you say in confidence.

C: What are you talking about?

L: It's just that when you tell me things in private, I have to keep what you say a secret — unless, of course, you tell me that you're going to go out and kill someone or something like that.

C: I never said that.

L: Of course you didn't. That's just an example. But here's where it gets tricky: when you're in court, testifying under oath then you have got to tell the truth, and I can't let you lie. If you get up there and you tell a lie, and if I know or believe it to be a lie, then I have to advise you otherwise. And if you insist on telling a lie under oath, I have to withdraw as your lawyer.

C: What if you don't know I'm lying?

L: John Henry, have you been lying to me today?

C: Of course not. That was just . . . an example.

L: Very clever. But this is important. The point is, I wouldn't have any problem with you testifying to anything that was true, or things that I have no reason to believe are false. But if you tell me something in private and then you get up on the stand and testify to something different — a lie — I have to get off the case right then and there. And the judge will probably have a very bad impression of you. Do you understand that?

Each approach involves a different balance between loyalty and honesty to the client. None is purely and obviously the correct way of behaving. The practical consequences for the lawyer–client relationship and for the requirement to avoid misleading the court provide the forum for the ethical discussion that ensues. This is carried out after each video extract. You would be required to choose whether you would adopt each approach. Naturally, at all stages you would have to be able to justify the choices you make and to anticipate the probable consequences. Your work would be conducted through role-play, rather than explanation. Therefore, rather than talking about what you would say to your client you would be expected actually to say it, using the tutor or a fellow student as the client. Tutors refer students back to the reading which informed the start of the course. This provides an opportunity to explore ethical positions which retain both loyalty to the client and to the justice system.

The second stage at which you have to decide how to respond ethically in respect of this case is some time later, after the client has been convicted and sentenced to death. An appeal is under way and you receive a letter from the client asking for the appeal to be dropped and for a date for his execution to be set. A wide range of ethical problems are raised by this situation and it is an area where the codes provide little guidance. An additional factor here is the statistics which show the high proportion of ethnic minority men on death row, particularly in States which formed part of the Confederacy before the Civil War. You are required to confront your own personal attitudes and explore the extent to which it is proper to allow these to inform your responses. What is more, there is a principled argument arising, which could be the basis of a test case on the constitutionality of certain aspects of the use of the death penalty, so your ethical principles may force you to weigh up the interests of possible future defendants as well as the client himself. With these concerns in mind you have to consider how to respond if, for example, you individually were committedly opposed to the death penalty. On what ethical basis could you withdraw as the client's representative? A further issue arises when it emerges that a State-employed chaplain may have influenced the client to abandon his appeal. The role-play tasks explore these and other issues in considerable depth.[20]

Students' proposed solutions are exemplified by further video extracts which show the lawyer adopting various approaches, each of which is underpinned by a particular view of the relevant ethical considerations. A discussion of these follows, using transcripts of the video extracts and making regular reference to the professional codes of conduct. It leaves students with the realisation that the simple stricture that you should always do what the client wants, provided it is not fraudulent or illegal, does not always provide an ethically satisfying answer.

The divorce attorneys

The third situation is the culmination of the course. It requires students to act as one or other of the lawyers working in suburban practices, representing the spouses in a divorce action. As in the first scenario the interests of the firm come into play here, but in very different circumstances. The individual lawyers are junior in each firm, working in an area with which they are relatively unfamiliar (raising ethical issues in itself) and are both in a position where their future in the firm requires them to do this job well. The issues

---

[20] Those with an interest in this area should note the real clinical course operated by the Centre for Capital Punishment Studies at the University of Westminster and described in Boon and Hodgkinson, 'Life and death in the lawyers' office: the internship in capital punishment studies' (1996) 30 Law Teach 253. See also page 160.

surrounding the divorce, which is complicated by the need to consider a child of the marriage, raise different ethical issues from those of the commercial problem dealt with in the first role-play. The desire for the parties to settle the matter without undue fuss or rancour, with the child's concerns coming in here, raises interesting questions about whether each party's rights should predominate over the interests of both. Complications arise because of elements of dishonesty coming from each client and one client's racial bigotry directed towards the opposing lawyer.

The method used is to start with a video of the initial client interview. Students then work in firms representing the two clients and initially discuss the situation and the ethical issues it raises. Students then individually undertake specific roles such as communicator with the client, negotiator or 'ethics officer' (given responsibility to ensure that ethical issues do not get lost in the heat of the negotiation) as the role-play continues. The negotiation between the parties' lawyers should produce an agreement, which students undertaking the role-play present to the 'client' (the tutor who undertakes the role). Finally a debriefing session pulls the whole exercise into shape and draws students' attention to the ethical issues which arose (whether or not they were overtly dealt with in the simulation) and facilitates discussion of how they should be handled.

This third role-play is the one which fits most closely with the concept of clinical legal education which we have been using in this book. It involves the most developed role-play activity within the course, and is an important step for students who will later be meeting real clients in their law school clinics, in vacation employment or when they enter practice.

Students' reactions

This brief presentation of the course described cannot do justice to the breadth of its coverage or the depth with which it addresses the issues which arise. It may, however, be helpful to present some of the comments produced by students who have undergone the course.

This is really how issues arise. Ethics is not a separate entity.

The simulations were great hands-on experiences that I don't think could have been done on a 1 hour/week basis.

I strongly recommend this approach. Ethics seems to be a subject that can't really be taught like other courses — it is something that is learned through experience. I enjoyed it very much, and although I had thought about these issues previously, this course helped me clarify these issues and to get an idea of what it might feel like to confront them.

There were negative responses as well. Most were practical suggestions for improving the simulations. Others raised more fundamental objections:

Just teach us the rules we need to know for the exam.

This response (after the first of the three simulations) indicates that this student had not, at that stage understood that an understanding of ethics goes beyond the learning of a set of rules, or indeed that an effective approach to examining students in this area might equally go beyond the application of rules. It would be interesting to know whether the experiences of the subsequent simulations produced any shift in this student's view.

The profession of law course's close attention to the professional codes of conduct and its detailed practice context make it appropriate for a vocationally oriented course such as the American postgraduate law degree. A similar approach in England would not be appropriate for an undergraduate law degree, but would be valuable in a postgraduate course preparing students for practice. You may wonder why, in a book arguing for the use of clinical methods in the UK context, an example from the USA has been chosen, rather than one from the UK. The reason is simply that, to the best of our knowledge, there is no such course. The major challenge to the legal profession in the USA represented by the Watergate affair never happened in the UK and there has not been the same pressure to address legal ethics in such a formal way. For the reasons explained at the beginning of this chapter, however, there are pressures now for such a development.[21]

This approach to learning ethics has the twin value of requiring students to grapple with the theoretical underpinning of the ethical debate and then to experience the problems of applying it in practice. Both are essential elements of real understanding. The practice element may help many to understand the theory, which might otherwise be obscure. For those who understood the theoretical debate without experiencing the practice of ethical behaviour in difficult situations, their understanding risks being narrow, sterile, and, we would argue, fundamentally flawed. The lessons learned from being placed in such a situation are also likely to be much more thoroughly

---

[21] There appears to be a real need. The *Gazette* contains information every month about solicitors being struck off for breaches of professional conduct.

learned than those gained by reading and discussion alone. For these reasons I would argue that the use of clinical methods should play a part in an ethical legal education. It is a powerful tool to help legal educators to produce ethically mature graduates, part of their liberal educational objectives. It will also help them to accept the responsibility which is being placed upon them to produce lawyers who take the ethical element of their profession seriously.

Conclusion

In this chapter I have sought to present some of the ways in which clinical methods can help to develop an ethical perspective on the study of law. The limited development of ethical study in UK law degrees has led us to look in some detail at US courses. We would not suggest that this experience can be translated directly to the UK context. The fact that UK law degrees are first degrees, not postgraduate as in the USA, and that their objectives are not so clearly vocational are substantial differences that must be addressed in the design of courses for the UK.

Some clear principles, however, emerge to inform this process. The learning of the professional codes per se is best left to the vocational stage of legal education. If there is to be a critical study of the codes (and I would strongly urge that there should be), the best place for this is the law degree itself. The best place for exploring individual preferences and prejudices is throughout legal education.

If a clinical course were to attempt to introduce a study of ethics where the subject had not been discussed elsewhere in the degree, there would be a serious risk that the study would be shallow (as most clinic courses have many other competing objectives) and that the ethical element would appear unrelated to mainstream study of law. You may recall Julie Macfarlane's research findings mentioned on page 216, which found students' clinical experience leaving them sceptical about the values of the legal system. This raises the question of what we hope to achieve by introducing an ethical element into legal education. The desire, I would suggest, is not to achieve a uniformity of approach to ethical problems, but to develop in students an awareness of the ethical element to legal decision-making and to encourage ethical behaviour (even if we might disagree on specific conclusions that individuals might come to). Some of our students might adopt a particular position (for example, maximising client autonomy) which will inform all their decisions. Others might adopt a more pragmatic approach, recognising a variety of principles as potentially relevant and taking the view that the balance between them should be a function of the particular facts and circumstances of the case. I would not wish to impose one view over another, but I would be concerned to challenge the view that regards ethical perspectives as irrelevant. If there is to be cynicism, an effective ethics course should direct that cynicism to the failings of the current legal system rather than the application of principle itself.

This all suggests that some degree of integration is desirable. This could be achieved partly by encouraging the incorporation of an ethical element into the delivery of substantive subjects, and partly by designing preliminary courses (not necessarily clinically taught) which will introduce the appropriate concepts. Julian Webb argues for a three-stage development.[22] He proposes a first-year foundation course (such as legal system) which explores as part of its remit the ethics of the English legal system. This would be followed by a second-year legal profession and ethics course which would combine discussion of professional ethics with a study of the major ethical traditions. This is the place for significant simulated elements. The third stage would be a real client clinical course through which supervisors would facilitate students' application of their ideas and understanding of ethical issues to the discussions of how to conduct real cases.

This degree of structure is probably necessary, as it is an effective way of entrenching ethics in the body of the law degree curriculum. The alternative, incorporation into substantive subjects, seems unlikely to develop of its own accord. It has not done so to date, and every substantive area is replete with issues to occupy both teacher and students.

Indeed, in proposing a structured programme such as that described above, we have another agenda. Students undergoing such a course will be exposed to the ethical issues arising from legal systems, law itself and its practice. They will be encouraged to reflect on the material they are working with elsewhere upon their degree from an ethics perspective. This should, over time, begin to press the ethics agenda on those who currently ignore this perspective, and work towards a real shift in the approach towards ethics in the undergraduate law degree. This will contribute towards the development of the type of approach which the ACLEC report argues for. It will have sound educational value in its own right and it will give those students who go on to practise law a ready critical perspective for when they have to interpret and apply the codes which will bind them.

---

[22] J. Webb, 'Inventing the good: a prospectus for clinical education and the teaching of legal ethics in England' (1996) 30 Law Teach 270.

Finally, a simpler point about the use of clinical methods and ethics. Elsewhere in this book we have argued that experiencing real and realistic situations is the best way for students to deepen their understanding of the law and to acquire competence in its practice. Competence is an ethical duty.[23] It is pointless to have sound ethical standards if you are incapable of achieving the goals they suggest to you. Clinical methods contribute both to your critical understanding of ethical issues, and your ability to put that understanding into effect in an ethical and effective practice.

---

[23] Law Society, *Guide to the Professional Conduct of Solicitors*, 7th ed., principle 12.02. See also the illustrations in S. Nathanson, *What Lawyers Do* (London: Sweet & Maxwell, 1997), pp. 143–4.

7

The United States experience

Our focus in this book has been on the experience of clinical legal education in the United Kingdom. However, on a number of occasions we have referred, sometimes extensively, to that in the United States, where, for a variety of reasons, clinical methods are more widespread and better-established. A developing clinical movement in the UK would be wise to consider the issues which have faced clinicians in the US, both to understand better what they are doing through analysis of differences and similarities in the contexts, and to avoid pitfalls experienced by others.

Introduction

Scene 1: The student and the professor sit in the professor's law-school office planning for the upcoming negotiation with the husband in a divorce case. The student has researched and prepared a list of the issues in the case which must be settled, and she has had lengthy discussions with her client regarding how the client would like the case resolved. The student's first question to the professor is, 'I know that you taught us in our course on professional responsibility that I can negotiate with the husband directly since he is not represented by counsel, but what am I going to say to him to encourage him to cooperate when I must make clear that I can only represent the wife's interests during our discussion?'

Scene 2: A team of three students from the Clinic stand before the members of a community organisation and explain the advantages and disadvantages of becoming a non-profit corporation. All goes well, and the organisation votes to retain the Clinic to represent it to become a non-profit corporation so that it can help develop low-income housing in the neighbourhood.

Scene 3: After the trial and the judge's ruling in favour of the Clinic's client, the field supervisor and student sit in the courthouse conference room to discuss the student's performance. The supervisor sat next to the student through the whole trial, which the student conducted on his own. Periodically, the supervisor had nudged the student to remind him to object to an inappropriate cross-examination question and the student had chosen not to make the objection. Now the supervisor wants to know why the student made the strategic decision to let the question go unchallenged. The student responds that he did not want to be too hard on the opposing counsel who had been so patient with him during his direct examination.

These scenes capture much of the essence of clinical education in the United States and illustrate the similarities and differences in the experiences of the US and England. The pedagogy in the two countries is essentially the same as illustrated by the preparation and planning in scene 1, execution of an exercise in scene 2, and reflection and feedback in scene 3. The students are taking significant responsibility for their own learning, and under the supervision of the teacher, the students are exercising independent judgment. The settings include the law school, the community, and the courts. Scene 1 appears to be taking place in an in-house clinic where the supervisor is a law professor, scene 2 could be a simulated role-play or a case in a transaction clinic, and scene 3 has a field supervisor which implies it is an 'externship' or out-of-the-law school placement. The details and nuances of clinical legal education in the US are described in more depth in the rest of this chapter and then compared to the English experience.

Although the programmes in the two countries share many common goals, there are differences which are primarily attributable to context and history. An obvious distinction is that in the US 'lawyers' or 'attorneys', two terms used interchangeably, may engage in all aspects of the practice of law because there is no solicitor–barrister distinction. The students in the examples are working at all stages of client representation, engaged in transactions, and participating in litigation. In most states in the US students who have completed certain minimal educational requirements may receive a 'student practice licence' which allows them, so long as they are adequately supervised by a practising attorney, to do all work usually reserved to lawyers admitted to the Bar including appearing in court.[1]

Another difference between the two countries is that the students in the United States have all completed an undergraduate course of study and are now enrolled in a distinct 'professional school', which is parallel to graduate school.[2] Most students intend to use their law degree to practise law in some setting such as private practice, a corporation, or the government. A smaller percentage expect to use their law degree in business or politics and an even smaller group intend to teach.

Upon completion of law school, a student who wants to engage in any area of the practice of law must become licensed in the State in which they want to practise. The admissions process is a 'Bar exam' which is a two to three-day multiple choice and essay exam[3] which has no skills component in most States.[4] Students often take an optional Bar review which is a cram course on black-letter law. These courses are offered by private companies that have no association with the law schools and are usually taught for a few weeks before the Bar exam is offered in each State. Completion of an accredited law-school curriculum and successful passage of the Bar exams is all that is necessary for a person to be licensed. There is no articling or period of apprenticeship before the newly admitted lawyer is allowed to practise law independently.

The number of law schools in the United States distinguishes the two countries because there are over 170 accredited law schools in the US. Most schools have some live-client skills program, but there is much variation in the detail.

Most of these law schools are accredited by the American Bar Association (ABA) which is the organisation designated by the United States Department

---

[1] See Frank G. Avellone, 'The state of State student practice: proposals for reforming Ohio's legal internship rule (1990) 17 Ohio NUL Rev 13 (providing more discussion on student practice rules).

[2] See 'Report of the committee on the future of the in-house clinic' (1992) 42 J Legal Educ 508 for a discussion on the variations.

[3] There is a separate Bar exam on professional responsibility which is made up of essays and multiple-choice questions, which all students must pass. They may take the professional responsibility component while they are still in law school.

[4] At this time, only California has a 'skills component' to its Bar examination and it still resembles an academic question rather than any 'performance'-type assessment. Other jurisdictions are beginning to consider adding a skills component and are watching the California experience.

of Education to accredit law schools. Almost all institutions also are voluntary members of the Association of American Law Schools which was originally conceived as an exclusive 'learned society' but has become a general membership organisation of law schools that meet basic requirements. Most States require that a student graduate from an ABA-accredited law school before he or she may take the Bar examination to be admitted to practice. In order to be accredited by the ABA, the law school must comply with the standards and interpretations promulgated and amended over the years by the organisation. The standards address a wide range of issues designed to assure minimal quality and to protect consumers while still allowing autonomy for individual schools. The availability and quality of 'skills training' and clinical education have been areas that the ABA has taken a special interest in, partly because of the concern of practitioners who make up the membership of the ABA that schools are not adequately addressing these issues, and partly because clinic and skills teachers have seen the ABA as an ally in encouraging schools to provide programs which address issues of ethics and quality. The MacCrate Report referred to in chapters 1 and 2 was a product of an ABA committee's attempt to examine seriously what lawyers need to learn and where they should learn it.[5] The ABA has begun to implement the report through modification of its standards and interpretations. For example, one provision of particular significance for clinical approaches is standard 302(d):

A law school shall offer live-client or other real-life practice experiences. This might be accomplished through clinics or externships. A law school need not offer this experience to all students.

So, unlike the British experience where CLEO has begun to establish standards of good practice for clinical programs,[6] in the US there has been a reliance on the ABA. Only recently, has the Clinical Legal Education Association, the CLEO parallel in the States, begun to consider developing independent standards of good practice. Throughout this chapter, references will be made to the ABA standards.[7]

---

[5] Its recommendations can be found in the appendix to this chapter.
[6] See pages 120–135.
[7] When a school is initially accredited and every seven years thereafter, the school is inspected to ensure that it is meeting these standards. In addition, each year, every school must submit written information for review. The seven-yearly 'sabbatical site inspections' are conducted by a team made up of law-school faculty, members of the Bar, and lay members of the public. In recent years, the ABA has made an attempt to ensure that a law-school faculty member with experience in skills training is included in the team.

Genesis of clinical education

Aside from contextual distinctions, there is a distinction between England
and the United States in the genesis of clinical education. Each of the scenes
presented at the start of this chapter presents professional responsibility or
ethical issues illustrating one of the threshold rationales for allowing clinical
education into the academy. As is described in chapter 6 the 1970s saw a
recognition of the need for law schools to focus on ethics. The Ford
Foundation responded by making available grants with emphasis on teaching
professional responsibility. The assumption of these grants was that students
could best understand the complexity of ethical issues if they are faced with
real problems. Scene 1 at the beginning of this chapter illustrates this. The
student has had the mandatory classroom course of ethics, but only when she
is confronted with the implementation of the rules with a real person does
she understand the ethical dilemma.[8] The professional responsibility impetus
has continued to motivate clinical training.

However, many would argue that the real heart of clinical legal education in the
United States is the public-service/poverty-law mission. Although the clinical
movement in England has resulted in programmes which provide services to
low-income clients in either law-school or agency settings, the poverty mission
has not been as dominant a motivating force as it has been in the United States.
The historical roots of providing service to the poor has left a permanent mark
on clinical education in the United States with far-reaching implications that are
both good and bad. Although few law schools had clinics before the 1960s, a
major stimulus for the wave of programmes which developed during the 1960s
and early 1970s was the recognition of the need to serve the unrepresented, to
sensitise students to their ethical and moral responsibilities to do pro bono
work, to train students in poverty so that they could go into public-interest
work, and to give law schools a role in providing service to their communities.

For some clinicians in the United States, clinical education is not simply a
pedagogical method, it is a philosophy about the role of lawyers in our
society. For these people, the very foundations of clinical education are in
radical, or at least liberal, reform which means that their programmes have

---

[8] Chapter 6 advocates a similar focus on ethics in the English legal education system.
Professional Responsibility is one of the few mandatory courses in the US law-school
curriculum. See ABA standard 302(b): 'A law school shall require of all students in the JD
degree program instruction in the history, goals, structure, duties, values, and responsibilities of
the legal profession and its members, including instruction in the Model Rules of Professional
Conduct of the American Bar Association. A law school should involve members of the Bench
and Bar in this instruction.'

a political agenda grounded in liberalism that remains committed to using the legal system as a vehicle for change.

This philosophy implies a faith in the legal system as a means of reform, which can be contrasted with academic theoreticians, such as scholars in critical legal studies, who call for a re-examination of the whole legal system as a system for remedying the rights of the disempowered. The presence of clinic programmes, which provide a context for testing theories, is an example of how the clinical movement contributes to the scholarly mission associated with most law schools in the United States.

Types of cases

A commitment to a poverty-rights agenda can affect the types of cases accepted in some clinics. There are those who see 'poverty law' as a specific area of the law, and their programmes will only accept cases associated with providing basic services to low-income clients. A different approach to the same goal is to represent only low-income clients regardless of the nature of the case. The State student practice rules sometimes limit student representation to either settings or cases where poor people are served.[9]

Assuming a clinic is oriented towards poverty law, the question becomes whether the clinic should concentrate on small individual cases or on complex litigation. One position is that lawyers are most effective if they focus on complex, impact cases, such as class actions. Another position is that individual representation in small cases is of more value to clients because it has a positive impact on the individuals. Outside the academy, within the poverty-law community, comprised of legal-services lawyers in the civil arena and public defenders in the criminal arena, there is debate about how poverty-law attorneys can be most effective in meeting the needs of their clients and addressing fundamental questions of injustice in our society.[10] Clinical legal educators are in a unique position to contribute

---

[9] Some clinicians base their selection of cases on the student practice rule in their state, which may limit the work students are permitted to perform. For example, in Kansas, the Supreme Court rule allowing students to practise limits the client base to 'indigent' persons. Consequently, the clinical students can represent only poor people. In contrast, the Illinois student practice rule has no such limitation and there is more variation in the types of cases accepted by the numerous clinics in that State.

[10] What is beyond the scope of this book but a phenomenon that has a significant impact is the current shift in political philosophy in the United States regarding the responsibility of the government to provide services and support for poor people. The growing trend is towards an assumption that government is no longer responsible, and the federal government is trying to extract itself from providing any services. Consequently, the federal legal services program has been eviscerated and what is left is so highly regulated that it has lost all autonomy. We will not know the implications for clinical education of these paradigm shifts for some time.

answers to these dilemmas and they do so in three ways: by continuing to represent individuals in small cases to make systemic changes; by taking on complex, impact cases which change the law; and by producing scholarship tested by reality.

In addition to the broader goal of changing inequities in society, clinical programs must take into account what types of cases are the best learning vehicles for their students. This question is shared by the British and US programs and is impacted by the contextual differences described above. Some US clinicians argue that simple cases for individual clients, which students can see from initial interview to resolution, are the best learning tools. This group would suggest it is best if a student can have complete responsibility because they focus on the value of students developing independent judgment as described in the Introduction of this book.[11] Others argue that complex litigation, with opportunities for discovery[12] and pre-trial motions,[13] makes a better learning vehicle. They contend that the complex cases are more valuable because the student can learn the larger context even if his or her personal role is limited, if only because more complex cases raise a greater variety of substantive and procedural issues. This approach focuses more on the student learning law and processes, which is another benefit of clinical education identified in the Introduction. This is obviously a spectrum and various programs find ways to facilitate students having a variety of opportunities. The choice that faculties in both countries ultimately make are affected, amongst other factors, by the training the students bring to the clinic, the number of credits they commit to the program, and the number of semesters for which they enrol.

Programs may also be influenced to choose cases based on where they anticipate the students will go after graduation. In the States, a less prestigious, regional law school whose graduates enter small firms and local government is more likely to have a clinic that focuses on a general practice. In contrast, a school which sees most of its graduates enter large firms doing complex federal litigation or multi-party transactions may choose cases that provide opportunities to develop skills or knowledge applicable to this work. The rationale underlying a clinical programme as part of a law degree in the British system, where students are focusing more on learning law than on

---

[11] Page xiv.

[12] The process whereby one party can require the other to provide relevant documents in order to help with the preparation of a case.

[13] Interlocutory arguments in court, used tactically in the USA to a greater extent than in the UK.

preparing themselves to move right into the job market, would imply that career tracks may have less of an influence on case choices in England than in the US.

One controversial issue shared in both countries is the practice of using poor people as 'guinea pigs' for law students. The 'underprivileged' are expected to be appreciative of free legal services that they probably could not receive elsewhere. Most law-school clinics rightfully pride themselves on the quality of service they deliver to their clients, which is frequently equal or superior to private practitioners' service to their clients. Nevertheless, the underlying liberal assumptions that serve as the rationale for clinical work should be examined. Whose interests do they really serve: the clients', the students', the supervisors', or the law schools'?[14]

Replicating private practice

Although an important element of clinical education is experiential learning grounded in reality, most clinics cannot claim to replicate all aspects of private practice. For example, students may be asked to keep track of their billable hours, and clients may be asked to pay costs or some nominal fees for representation, but only a handful of clinics have students making decisions about cases based on the economics of private law practice. There are a few fee-generating clinics where the programs and faculty receive their financial support from attorney's fees collected in cases.[15] However, the fee-generating clinics do not replicate private practice completely because the students are not preoccupied with developing a practice by finding clients, fostering long-term client relationships, or other 'rain-making' activities as they would be in a law firm. Although the fee-generating clinics may seem appealing as a source of revenue, many in the US clinical movement see them as tainting the teaching and service mission of the clinics.[16]

---

[14] In externships, or 'agency' placements outside the law school, there is even greater potential for abuse. Offices that are strapped for staff may find the prospect of free student workers to be a potential gold mine. This situation invites exploitation of the students and potential for neglect of cases. This is discussed further later in the chapter.

[15] In the UK the Law Society rules prevent a free legal service from collecting fees. This makes it difficult to recover costs from a losing opponent.

[16] See, e.g., the exchange regarding the fee-generating clinic at IIT Kent Law School which begins with the articles Richard A. Matasar, 'The MacCrate Report from the Dean's perspective' (1994) 1 Clinical L Rev 457 at pp. 488–91 and Laser, 'Significant curricular developments: the MacCrate Report and beyond' (1994) 1 Clinical L Rev 425 at pp. 437–42 and the response in Martin Guggenheim, 'Fee-generating clinics: Can we bear the costs?' (1995) 1 Clinical L Rev 677 and Lisa G. Lerman, 'Fee-for-service clinical teaching: slipping toward commercialism' (1995) 1 Clinical L Rev 685.

The opposition arguments are that if a client is paying for the services, it is harder to allow the student to take complete responsibility, so the teaching method shifts to a modelling or mentoring method where the student watches the teacher. The students begin to take on the role of a law clerk or assistant rather than the lawyer. The teacher must make pedagogical decisions based on generating income rather than on teaching the students. Finally, cases are chosen because they will result in fees rather than because they are good learning vehicles or provide public service.

There are discrepancies other than economics between most US law-school clinics and real practice. Students generally have small caseloads, engage in team representation of simple cases, do extensive preparation of small files, and may transfer cases among each other. The focus on the students' learning rather than getting cases handled in an efficient manner runs counter to real practice. Members of the Bar sometimes critique clinics for creating a deceptively safe environment which is too far removed from reality. However, there has not been a great movement to respond to these criticisms.

It appears that the British attitude on this issue is similar to the United States. In fact, there is less incentive to replicate completely a private practice in the British system because of the emphasis on learning law rather than preparing students to enter practice immediately.

Skills training

Clinical education has been driven by skills training as well as the motivation to teach ethics or to provide public service. 'Skills training' could be defined as learning techniques which can be transferred to other settings. Some clinics want to de-emphasise the political agenda of their programmes to make them more palatable to various constituents, such as law-school faculties and administrations, conservative students, local Bars, funding sources, and alumni. By focusing on 'skills' instead of on poverty law and justice, the programmes seem less objectionable.

For example, a litigation clinic would have as one of its goals learning the skill of direct examination.[17] A transactional clinic may emphasis the skill of negotiating. The American Bar Association MacCrate Report provided a useful checklist for organising the skills which could be included in a particular curriculum. These are set out in the appendix to this chapter.

---

[17] This concept covers the examination-in-chief of, in particular, the lawyer's own client.

Moreover, the American Bar Association has now included a standard that a law school should provide training in professional skills. The ABA interpretations incorporate terms identified by the MacCrate Report, but also add the caveat that not every student need be accommodated.

As in England, there is a question about the intersection of simulation, or role-playing, and live-client clinical education either within the school or in an external placement. Students may be expected to take a simulation course as a prerequisite to a live-client experience. Teachers may also use simulation to teach skills within their programs, and many US clinicians have become the major theoreticians, scholars and teachers of simulation courses within their schools. Clinicians have also assisted in integrating simulation methods into the rest of the law-school curriculum.

However, most US clinicians would agree that simulations have limited value and do not teach a fraction of what is taught in a real-client clinic. Simulations do not have the complexity upon which students can draw to learn and develop their skills. Real cases create the challenge of interviewing a person who is both similar and different from the student, the frustration of developing a legal strategy that takes into account the strengths and weaknesses of real facts, the patience of counselling someone whose life is messy and uncertain, the insight required to negotiate with attorneys, the shock of experiencing the gaps between the theories of procedure and the realities of actual courtrooms, and the intimidation of looking in the eyes of a person wearing a robe who has the power of a judge. Experiencing all of these feelings, organising the testimony, and asking the individual who has real losses at stake a non-leading question is very different from role-playing a direct examination. This is illustrated by scene 3 described at the beginning of this chapter, which comes from a real case. The student had his client testify and the opposing counsel had been very tolerant of his performance. During the cross-examination of the client, the opposing lawyer had gotten into some irrelevant and dangerous areas, yet the student had not objected. The student did not want to irritate the opposing lawyer but felt a loyalty to his client. These complex feelings are not experienced during a simulation because not enough is at stake.

Despite the richness of the live-client opportunity and the service it provides, some schools have failed to develop real-client clinics because preplanned simulation programs can deliver skills training more efficiently to a larger number of students. Economics dictates a preference for the less complex.

Economics of clinical education

What some perceive as the relatively high cost of clinical legal education is a reality on both sides of the Atlantic, and it has been a barrier to some schools' willingness to develop programs.[18] The Langdellian model of legal education described in chapter 2 assumes a large lecture hall, full of students and a single professor.[19] This model facilitates the 'education' of a large number of law students with few faculty teaching hours. In the 1960s, law faculties and administrations acculturated to the Langdellian model began discussing the implications of clinical education. It was not clear to them whether the pedagogical goals of clinics were worth the expense, and whether clinics would undermine the law school's image as an academic institution as opposed to a vocational school.

For this reason, some schools interested in starting law clinics sought money from outside sources and, until recently, outside funding or 'soft money' played an integral part in US clinical education.[20] The first major grants for clinics were provided through the Ford Foundation CLEPR program.[21] This program 'was born in part from the idea of the multiversity of the 1960s; it was at its core a bottom-up legal service delivery reform. . . . [It] introduced broader experiential education models into legal education but taught professional responsibility almost exclusively through exposing students to service to the poor.'[22] After the CLEPR grants were discontinued, the federal government, through the Department of Education, provided grant money to

---

[18] The cost of clinical education stems in part from the marginalisation of the faculty which is discussed in more detail below. If the clinic faculty are precluded from teaching large lecture classes, they are expensive because they only teach a small number of students. In schools where the clinical faculty are integrated into the non-clinical faculty, they are more likely to teach some of the large non-clinical courses, which results in more tuition dollars.

[19] See David R. Barnhizer, 'The university ideal and clinical legal education' (1990) 35 NYL Sch L Rev 87; Mark Spiegel, 'Theory and practice in legal education: an essay on clinical education' (1987) 34 UCLA L Rev 577; Norman Redlich, 'Clinical education: stranger in an elitist club' (1981) 31 J Legal Educ 201; William Pincus, 'The clinical component in university professional education' (1971) 32 Ohio St LJ 283; see also Roger S. Haydock, 'Clinical legal education: the history and development of a law clinic' (1984) 9 Wm Mitchell L Rev 101.

[20] Funding for legal education in the United States is somewhat dependent on whether a school is public or private. Both rely on tuition dollars and private donations or endowments. Public schools rely more heavily on State funds.

[21] See William Pincus, 'Clinical practice innovations in law schools' (1969) 28 Legal Aid Briefcase 47. Mr Pincus was the president of CLEPR and strongly advocated the development of clinical education.

[22] James E. Moliterno, 'Legal education, experiential education and professional responsibility' (1996) 38 Wm & Mary L Rev 71 at pp. 92–3. For more detailed information see Michael Meltsner and Philip G. Schrag, 'Report from a CLEPR colony' (1976) 76 Colum L Rev 581, and 'Scenes from a clinic' (1978) 127 U Pa L Rev 1.

law schools for the expansion, development, and continuation of clinical programs. The program was commonly referred to as the Title IX Program.[23] The parameters of the program were: the money was to be used to provide service to low-income people; priority was given to programs that served people who traditionally did not have access to legal services;[24] law schools were required to provide a minimum financial match to the federal funds, and the greater the law-school contribution, the more likely the project would be funded. Historically, money was provided only for programs where disputes were resolved in the courtroom or at administrative hearings. Changes in Title IX, however, made it possible to obtain funding for alternative dispute resolution programs.

Another source for grant money for clinical education in the United States was the Federal Legal Services Corporation which was designed to fund full-service law offices for low-income people. Policy makers were influenced to use a portion of this money for law-school clinics so long as they could show a significant number of clients were served. The emphasis in this program was on delivery of service rather than education, and far fewer schools relied on it for funding. In the 1990s, the federal government in the United States has been withdrawing from providing assistance to low-income people in many forums. As part of this retrenchment, the Title IX program was dismantled and the Legal Services Corporation's resources were so severely cut that the law-school initiatives disappeared.

The other common source of grant money was the Interest on Lawyers' Trust Accounts or State IOLTA programs. In the United States, lawyers must put clients' funds into a separate, interest-bearing account. Some States chose to use the interest on these accounts to fund public-service projects such as law-school clinics. As interest rates have dropped and priorities have shifted, these funds have generally dried up as well.

The consequence of the loss of 'soft money' has forced law schools to decide whether to fund clinical education in a similar fashion to all law-school education or to let their programs wither. There are people in the clinical legal education community who mourn the loss of the soft money because it allowed for experimentation and growth of clinical programs. Others argue that it was a foundation made of clay because law schools relied too heavily on the availability of grants and did not incorporate the expenses of the clinics into the 'real budget'. This perpetuated the marginalisation of the

---

[23] Higher Education Act, 20 USC s. 1134(u) (1988); 34 CFR ss. 74, 75, 77 (1965).
[24] Ibid.; see also 34 CFR ss. 639.11(a), 639.31(a)(2)(v) (1992).

clinics. Clinical staff could not be given the same status as the rest of the faculty because it was never clear if they would continue to be employed if their funding disappeared. Deans and development officers made no attempt to search for recurring, sustainable funds because the grants were easier to access. Consequently, programs stumbled along uncertain whether they would be funded but without hope for institutional support. Programs were so tenuous that offices could not assure clients or other service providers that they would be around in the following year to continue representation.

The irony of the timing of the loss of soft money is that it came at the same time as the MacCrate Report which lauded the importance of clinical legal education and the changes in the American Bar Association accreditation standards encouraging the availability of professional skills training.[25]

The loss of soft money has resulted in the demise of some programs and unemployment for some clinic teachers. However, the fallout is still unclear and in the final analysis, forcing the faculty to support clinic programs out of resources available for traditional legal education may ultimately strengthen clinical legal education.

Externships

For a number of reasons, including avoiding the difficult issues surrounding the expense and politics of in-school clinics, some schools have turned to 'externship' programs. Like the agency placements described in chapter 4, externship programs involve students receiving law-school credit for working in legal settings outside the school. In the United States, students may not receive financial compensation for work which warrants educational credit. Externships have many advantages, such as lower cost, variety in opportunities, work experience, service to the community, and flexibility.[26] The main disadvantage is the potential for a lack of control over the quality of the educational experience.

During the early history of the clinical movement, there was tension between people involved in externships and in-house clinics. Historically, some

---

[25] See discussion on pages 9 and 10 and ABA standard 302 in note 8.
[26] See, e.g., Robert F. Seibel and Linda H. Morton, 'Field placement programs: practices, problems and possibilities' (1996) 2 Clinical L Rev 413; Janet Motley, 'Self-directed learning and the out-of-house placement' (1989) 19 NM L Rev 211; Henry Rose, 'Legal externships: Can they be valuable clinical experiences for law students?' (1987) 12 Nova L Rev 15; and Linda Morton, 'Creating a classroom component for field placement programs: enhancing clinical goals with feminist pedagogy' (1993) 45 Me L Rev 19. For an argument that there does not need to be input from professional educators, see Daniel J. Givelber, et al., 'Learning through work: an empirical study of legal internships' (1995) 45 J Legal Educ 1.

clinicians who taught in programs located within their schools, commonly referred to as 'in-house clinics', were suspicious and sometimes even hostile to externship programs. This was partially based on a fear that the less expensive externship would undermine the in-house program. In addition, at some schools, in-house clinicians did not want their programs to be associated with externships because the externships were poorly planned and poorly supervised.

This tension has subsided as the clinical movement has become more receptive to a wider variety of structures. The in-house clinical movement has matured and become more sophisticated. There is greater self-confidence in the value of clinicians' work. Externships have improved and become pedagogically more sound because of the use of classroom components, learning contracts, field site visits, evaluation processes, and grading criteria. The American Bar Association recently amended its accreditation standards to pressure schools to provide more academic rigour to their externship programs and only time will tell whether these standards are implemented. As the parallels rather than the differences have become apparent, the two movements have grown together. It appears the tension between in-school programs and externships has not developed in the UK. The approach described in this text which assumes these environments are different, but complementary, is probably the best approach.

Marginalisation

Even in schools that have resolved these difficult issues, clinical programs continue to struggle with multiple problems of marginalisation. As the British programs develop further, there is the potential for the same marginalisation. However, some of it can be avoided because it can be anticipated.

Marginalisation from the students' perspective

Students' perceptions of a program's significance are influenced by the respect and resources committed to it. Symbolically, some clinics are given terrible physical plants, and so many were placed in the cellar that one author used this as the title of her article.[27] The programs are so far removed from the curriculum in some schools, that the clinic is little more than extracurricular volunteer work.

---

[27] See Marjorie McDiarmid, 'What's going on down there in the basement: in-house clinics expand their beachhead' (1990) 35 NYL Sch L Rev 239.

As in England, in the US, most students enrol for a certain number of course credits for either in-house programs or externships. Most traditional courses in the American law schools are graded but clinical education courses whether internal or external are sometimes pass/fail.[28] When the program is pass/fail or ungraded and the work does not affect the student's overall grade point average, students see the program as having less value. The decision whether to grade is complex and continues to be debated in the US. Some would argue that students' hard work and commitment in their clinics should get the same recognition and reward as in other courses: within the academic world, that means grades. A grade sends the message that the clinic is as worthwhile as the rest of the curriculum. Others fear that grading taints the relationship between the supervisor and the students. It interferes with the student's natural inclination to come to the professor with questions or to reveal his or her weaknesses. The response to this argument is that, regardless of the existence of grading, students realise that professors and supervisors are in a position of power and authority. Therefore, it is hypocritical to pretend that no hierarchy exists. How to assign a grade is difficult but the debate in Britain described elsewhere in this book seems very similar to that in the US.

Despite some students' perceptions that a clinic is on the fringe of the academy, students want to participate. This text is peppered with comments from students who have participated in British law school programmes, and their reports could easily have come from their US counterparts. The most common reasons students participate is their desire to see if they will like being a lawyer, the hope of gaining practical experience, and a commitment to the social causes that the clinic represents.

Students are selected to participate by a variety of means. Most programs have basic prerequisites such as completion of a certain number of credits, good academic standing, or specific substantive or simulation courses. For externships, the two issues are who selects the students who may participate, and who matches the students with the placements. Some schools allow the field placements to select the students according to the placement criteria, while other law schools preselect and match the students. There are schools which allow the students to find or develop any placement so long as it comports with particular criteria. At other law schools, the students may work at only limited sites which are pre-approved by the institution.

---

[28] ABA 305, interpretation 305-2(e)(3). ABA standards require that for externships a law-school faculty member, rather than a field supervisor, must have the ultimate decision over what grade a student will receive.

In-house clinics use various selection procedures for choosing which students will be allowed to participate. Some use a random selection process similar to any law-school class — first to be enrolled in the limited slots are allowed to participate. Other programs have complex application processes, which may even include an interview by the clinic staff. Such a process requires resolving difficult questions, such as whether it is the students with particular political bent, students who have the highest grades, students who the faculty think will be easy to supervise, or students who contribute diversity to the program.

Marginalisation of the faculty

The status of in-house clinical faculty has been a perpetual struggle within United States law schools. Law-school professors tend to be very privileged within the university hierarchy in the United States. Since they teach in a professional school and there is a perception that they could earn large salaries outside of the academy, the law faculty are paid higher salaries than some other departments where the faculty are not perceived to have the same lucrative opportunities. The facilities in law schools tend to be more plush than the rest of the academy. Law professors usually have fewer classroom contact hours with students than their colleagues in other departments, and they are not responsible for mentoring or shepherding graduate students. Law professors generally are not expected to raise grants for their research like scientists, and they are given law-school funds to hire student research assistants. Similarly, they are provided with school resources to attend professional development conferences.

The ultimate plum that law professors share with their counterparts in other parts of the academy is tenure. At most law schools in the United States, everyone who teaches is either tenured or tenure track, except for the clinical teachers who have lost the struggle to achieve that status, and the research and writing professors.[29] Tenure means lifetime job security unless the professor engages in egregious activities or the institution closes. It also includes the right to participate in faculty governance on all issues not reserved for administration. Few workers in the United States share such job security.

Obviously, it is a much coveted reward. Law professors must go through a retention, promotion and tenuring process in which their teaching, scholarship and public service are scrutinised by the law school and the university.

---

[29] Clinicians and research and writing teachers are now making a more concerted effort to combine their efforts to raise the status of the research and writing faculty. They have been the only group more marginalised than the clinic faculty. For example, in the summer of 1996, the two groups worked together to amend the ABA standards for research and writing programs.

The rigour of these processes vary from institution to institution, but it often takes years to reach the status of full, tenured professor.

At some institutions, the faculty who teach in the clinic are on the same tenure track as all other law faculty. Their work is scrutinised and valued to the same extent as all others and they are given the same benefits. They become skilled teachers and theoreticians. These professors have had the longevity to develop sophisticated, dynamic programs which make a meaningful contribution to their institutions, clinics and communities. They are likely to have generated scholarship in both clinical legal education and substantive law. They often teach large lecture classes so they are less costly additions to the law school. They develop lasting relationships with faculty in the rest of the university which facilitates interdisciplinary work. Finally, they have time to be active in the local, state and national bar associations.

Other institutions, however, have clinical instructors who are at the other end of the spectrum. These instructors may have uncertain one-year contracts, no meaningful relationship to, participation in, or responsibilities within the institution, and receive salaries and benefits substantially lower than the rest of the faculty. Their positions create numerous personal and institutional risks. For example, the uncertainty of the position can make it difficult to recruit highly qualified faculty members. The one-year contract complicates planning and commitment within the clinic program, the institution, the community and the Bar. Consequently, the short-term instructor may never understand his or her role as a teacher or be a part of the faculty.

The distinctions between clinical education and traditional law-school teaching are evident in the debates regarding the qualifications of a good clinical director or instructor, his or her role on the faculty, and his or her expectations for tenure. The ambivalence concerning the law clinics' status within law schools and the numerous prejudices and stereotypes regarding clinical education fuel the debate. For example, in choosing a clinical professor the following questions arise: (a) Should a familiarity with the local court system and Bar take precedence over prestigious academic credentials? (b) Should clinicians simply be required to have experience with poverty law, or should they also have experience supervising, managing and training people? (c) Should warmth, patience, and compassion with students and clients be a requirement, or should students be exposed to the competitive real world by working with an instructor who, on balance, has aggressive litigation skills? (d) Should credentials that are 'different' from the non-clinic instructor's be accepted? (e) What are the implications for the clinical instructor if they are 'different'?

Clinic instructors, whether or not they teach in the classroom, are immersed in all of the intellectual challenges the law presents: developing case strategies, learning and applying the law, testing where the law can be changed, and studying ethics, justice, and legal morality at work. Clinic instructors have the opportunity to experiment with a wider range of teaching techniques than do traditional classroom teachers. They write on a wider variety of legal issues and have the option of substantially changing their work within the clinic without having to change jobs. Clinic teachers have the pleasure of working individually with students and getting to know them in a way traditional classroom teachers rarely do. Moreover, clinic instructors have the satisfaction of making a contribution to their individual clients' lives. The result of this is that outstanding people have committed their careers to this work despite institutional marginalisation.[30] In the United States, most law reviews are sponsored by an individual law school and the articles are selected and edited by law students. A few peer-review journals have emerged, but they are the exception. The AALS has published the *Journal of Legal Education* for many years, but a number of factors made it difficult to publish clinical education articles very frequently in that journal.[31]

---

[30] Various other issues arise when one examines the makeup of clinicians. Age, class, and geographic location all affect the culture of clinical education. Clinicians have developed a very strong sense of community with one another. There are national and regional networks unparalleled in legal education. This phenomenon can be attributed partly to clinicians' sense of isolation within their own institutions, and their need to find support from others similarly situated. It may also be attributed to the types of people drawn to clinical work.

Two organisations have provided national networks for clinicians — the Association of American Law Schools (AALS) Section on Clinical Legal Education and the Clinical Legal Education Association (CLEA). The AALS is the umbrella organisation for all law schools whereas CLEA is an independent organisation of people primarily interested in clinical education. The British counterpart is CLEO. Unlike the AALS, which must be responsive to the competing interests in legal education, CLEA is able to engage in activities focused just on clinical education. So, for example, when the Federal government was eliminating the funding for clinical education, CLEA could exert some influence to fend off the attacks.

Clinical teachers have had a history of gathering at regularly scheduled conferences and meetings. These meetings have provided a vehicle for support and the intellectual exchange of information, training and strategy. There are both national meetings and regional meetings which have been critically important to the development of clinical education in the United States. Similar traditions are brewing in Britain.

Although there has been a heavy reliance on oral communications, clinicians are also tremendously prolific. The CLEA now has a Web page which includes an annotated bibliography that barely captures all of the literature.

[31] In 1994, a broad-based coalition of people came together to create a peer review publication called the *Clinical Law Review*. This is jointly sponsored by the Clinical Legal Education Association, New York University Law School and the Association of American Law Schools. The clinical movement has grown in numbers which requires multiple means of communication, and the *Clinical Law Review* has proven to be a tremendous success at examining complex issues in a manner accessible to this larger community.

Clinical teachers' work

Most clinics are based on individual supervision of students representing clients in actual cases with a classroom component taught by the clinic faculty. This simple description masks the complexity of the goals and methods of clinical education and the difficulty of the clinic teacher's task. The scenarios at the beginning of the chapter illustrate these elements. A major component of clinical education is the relationship between the clinic student, the supervisor, and the client. The implications of this triangular relationship have been lost in much of the research about clinics because scholars tend to focus on the relationship of the lawyer and the client or the supervisor and the student. The clinical supervisor is constantly required to decide whether and how to intervene in the student's relationship with the client and the student's work on the case. The tension is caused by the sometimes competing goals of letting the student be responsible for the case and the need to ensure quality of service to the client. The challenge for the supervisor is determining if there truly is an inconsistency and whether the faculty intervention will help or hinder the situation. As the rest of this book describes, these tensions exist in the British programs as well.

The triangulation question is part of the larger debate about how controlling or non-directive a clinic supervisor should be.[32] Even more crucial is the issue of when and how to give the students feedback. What constitutes effective evaluation for learning purposes and who is responsible for the student's evaluation has been a major focus of discussion amongst clinicians. These questions are essential parts of clinical education, which relies heavily on individualised, experiential learning. The benefits of this model cannot be overstated and are shared on both sides of the Atlantic despite the different contexts.

---

[32] See discussion in chapters 2 and 3.

Appendix: recommendations of the MacCrate Commission

The report of the MacCrate Commission has been important in influencing
the development of legal education in the United States. We present the
recommendations in respect of fundamental lawyering skills and fundamental
values of the profession as indicative of what is informing both clinical and
non-clinical teaching there, but would add one caveat. These objectives are
professionally and vocationally oriented. They do not, therefore, reflect what
we would advocate as the skills which must be addressed at the undergraduate
stage of legal education, where the educational values we have expressed
elsewhere in this book should predominate. Nonetheless, the skills and values
are highly relevant to undergraduate education as means by which law can be
more effectively studied and understood. For vocationally-oriented courses
the relevance of the MacCrate skills and values is self-evident.

Fundamental lawyering skills

Skill 1: Problem solving   In order to develop and evaluate strategies for
solving a problem or accomplishing an objective, a lawyer should be familiar
with the skills and concepts involved in:

1.1   identifying and diagnosing the problem;
1.2   generating alternative solutions and strategies;
1.3   developing a plan of action;
1.4   implementing the plan;
1.5   keeping the planning process open to new information and new ideas.

Skill 2: Legal analysis and reasoning   In order to analyse and apply legal
rules and principles, a lawyer should be familiar with the skills and concepts
involved in:

2.1   identifying and formulating legal issues;
2.2   formulating relevant legal theories;
2.3   elaborating legal theory;
2.4   evaluating legal theory;
2.5   criticising and synthesising legal argumentation.

Skill 3: Legal research   In order to identify legal issues and to research
them thoroughly and efficiently, a lawyer should have:

3.1   knowledge of the nature of legal rules and institutions;

3.2 knowledge of and ability to use the most fundamental tools of legal research;

3.3 understanding of the process of devising and implementing a coherent and effective research design.

Skill 4: Factual investigation In order to plan, direct, and (where applicable) participate in factual investigation, a lawyer should be familiar with the skills and concepts involved in:

4.1 determining the need for factual investigation;

4.2 planning a factual investigation;

4.3 implementing the investigative strategy;

4.4 memorialising and organising information in an accessible form;

4.5 deciding whether to conclude the process of fact-gathering;

4.6 evaluating the information that has been gathered.

Skill 5: Communication In order to communicate effectively, whether orally or in writing, a lawyer should be familiar with the skills and concepts involved in:

5.1 assessing the perspective of the recipient of the communication;

5.2 using effective methods of communication.

Skill 6: Counselling In order to counsel clients about decisions or courses of action, a lawyer should be familiar with the skills and concepts involved in:

6.1 establishing a counselling relationship that respects the nature and bounds of a lawyer's role;

6.2 gathering information relevant to the decision to be made;

6.3 analysing the decision to be made;

6.4 counselling the client about the decision to be made;

6.5 ascertaining and implementing the client's decision.

Skill 7: Negotiation In order to negotiate in either a dispute-resolution or transactional context, a lawyer should be familiar with the skills and concepts involved in:

7.1 preparing for negotiation;

7.2 conducting a negotiation session;

7.3 counselling the client about the terms obtained from the other side in the negotiation and implementing the client's decision.

Skill 8:   Litigation and alternative dispute resolution procedures   In order
to employ, or to advise a client about, the options of litigation and alternative
dispute resolution, a lawyer should understand the potential functions and
consequences of these processes and should have a working knowledge of
the fundamentals of:

8.1   litigation at the trial-court level;
8.2   litigation at the appellate level;
8.3   advocacy in administrative and executive forums;
8.4   proceedings in other dispute-resolution forums.

Skill 9:   Organisation and management of legal work   In order to practise
effectively, a lawyer should be familiar with the skills and concepts required
for efficient management, including:

9.1   formulating goals and principles for effective practice management;
9.2   developing systems and procedures to ensure that time, effort, and
      resources are allocated efficiently;
9.3   developing systems and procedures to ensure that work is performed
      and completed at the appropriate time;
9.4   developing systems and procedures for effectively working with other
      people;
9.5   developing systems and procedures for efficiently administering a law
      office.

Skill 10:   Recognising and resolving ethical dilemmas   In order to represent a client consistently with applicable ethical standards, a lawyer should
be familiar with:

10.1   the nature and sources of ethical standards;
10.2   the means by which ethical standards are enforced;
10.3   the processes for recognising and resolving ethical dilemmas.

Fundamental values of the profession

Value 1:   Provision of competent representation   As a member of a profession dedicated to the service of clients, a lawyer should be committed to the
values of:

1.1   attaining a level of competence in one's own field of practice;
1.2   maintaining a level of competence in one's own field of practice;

1.3   representing clients in a competent manner.

Value 2:   Striving to promote justice, fairness and morality   As a member of a profession that bears special responsibilities for the quality of justice, a lawyer should be committed to the values of:

2.1   promoting justice, fairness, and morality in one's own daily practice;
2.2   contributing to the profession's fulfillment of its responsibility to ensure that adequate legal services are provided to those who cannot afford to pay for them;
2.3   contributing to the profession's fulfilment of its responsibility to enhance the capacity of law and legal institutions to do justice.

Value 3:   Striving to improve the profession   As a member of a self-governing profession, a lawyer should be committed to the values of:

3.1   participating in activities designed to improve the profession;
3.2   assisting in the training and preparation of new lawyers;
3.3   striving to rid the profession of bias based on race, religion, ethnic origin, gender, sexual orientation, or disability, and to rectify the effects of these biases.

Value 4:   Professional self-development   As a member of a learned profession, a lawyer should be committed to the values of:

4.1   seeking out and taking advantage of opportunities to increase his or her knowledge and improve his or her skills;
4.2   selecting and maintaining employment that will allow the lawyer to develop as a professional and to pursue his or her professional and personal goals.

8

Conclusion

The conclusion takes three parts. First, Richard Grimes summarises the strengths of the clinical idea, what clinical legal education has achieved to date and where we go from here.

The second part is of a more personal nature. Hugh Brayne revisits, in the light of the contributions to this book, the key issue of how the clinical idea can move forward while we rigidly separate academic and vocational legal education.

The third part of the conclusion is an outsider insider view. Adrian Evans runs a clinical programme at Monash University in Australia, and has more experience than any of the authors. We invited him to take a critical look at what we had written from a safe distance. He disagrees with some of what we say, which is good for bringing debate to the fore. But overall we have corroboration for the claims we have made in this book on behalf of clinical legal education.

Richard Grimes: a perspective of optimism

In this book we have set out to describe what the clinic can offer as a teaching and learning methodology. We have tried to look at the clinic from the perspective of the student *and* the lecturer. If the clinic is about anything, in our experience, it is about a process of learning — a process that seemingly challenges some of the more traditional teaching methods. This does not mean that the two approaches are necessarily in conflict. One can, and we argue should, be used to complement the other. The value of clinic is not simply in its innovation and effectiveness but in the potential it offers as a teaching and learning tool within the law programme as a whole. It will be clear from the content of many of the preceding pages that we are enthusiasts for clinical legal education. Learning by doing is a powerful way of studying law and the practical and ethical issues surrounding it. It is, however, only a part (we believe a significant one) of the armoury to be used in the struggle to achieve effective and relevant legal education. We do not think that it should be free-standing. It is an integral component of a long-term strategy for education. As we hope has been made clear, that strategy is best founded on a theoretical framework which gives a clear view of the learning objectives involved and of criteria to be used to evaluate whether those outcomes have been achieved.

The learning implicit in the clinic is a two-way process. It is learning for both staff and students. Some of that learning is shared in the sense of increasing our knowledge and understanding of common issues. Effectively conducted research may bring new insights to both the student and the lecturer. Would any of us who are engaged in teaching be so bold as to suggest that we have a monopoly of such knowledge? Learning can also concentrate on particular aspects of comprehension. For students this is perhaps focused more on the substantive rules, or the lawyering skills. They still have to graduate or qualify. For teaching staff other issues become significant, including curriculum development and assessment.

In this concluding chapter we draw together some of the themes of the book with the aim of addressing the concerns of both the law teacher and the student. Indeed, your respective concerns are likely to be not so different. We expect that this will become clearer to you if or when you have experienced the collaborative approach which is encouraged by effective clinical work. At any rate it is useful for both teachers and students to have some idea of the others' concerns in the practical and theoretical setting occupied by the clinic.

The following section was initially conceived with the law teacher in mind. However, we hope that it will be of equal interest to students.

Learning and empowerment

We are of the view that the most valuable assets on the learning balance sheet are the students. This is not said in any flippant or patronising way. The students are the reason for running the clinic and are a major component in the learning methodology that goes on there. This is about a learning partnership that sees a sharing of ownership of how and what is learnt. We are long enough in the tooth in our respective teaching careers to realise that there is a power relationship between the lecturer and the student and that the balance of power is not evenly distributed, even in the user-friendly setting of the clinic. There is an 'us and them' situation. What the clinic enables both sides to do is to examine the relationship and where possible empower the student to take an active part in the learning process. This increase in activity brings with it opportunities to examine, in detail, the nuts and bolts of the education that is happening.

What do you (students) expect to learn? Is this what we (law teachers) have as our objectives? How do we (students and law teachers) know when these outcomes have been achieved? To what extent should the design of outcomes and objectives, and the assessment of progress towards them, be a process that is shared between law teacher and student? These are questions of fundamental importance to those engaged in experiential learning, as the clinic throws into focus, through its use of student-centred methods, the participation of both law teacher and student in the whole educational experience. To address these issues is to embark on a process of analysis, a central tenet of which is the empowerment of students.

Learning and integration

The clinic is a vehicle for the study of law. It provides a unique opportunity for students to *do* law and to think, critically and analytically, about that experience. In the clinic, whether simulated or real-client, the student encounters legal problems and issues that arise in the practice of law and the delivery of legal services. These may not neatly, or obviously, fall into the subject-specific pigeon-holes that we, as staff and students, are used to. A problem stemming from a road traffic accident may involve principles of negligence, insurance law, civil procedure, law relating to road traffic offences and a host of other considerations. The opportunity for the student to research and examine the relevant legal considerations is present but how does he or she relate this to the rest of the law programme? Where do the classes in tort, crime and legal systems fit in? What if optional units are offered in, say, the law of insurance or civil litigation? How do we ensure as educational providers that the most is made of the educational experience? The answer, as simple as it sounds, but as complex as it is, can be summed up in one word — integration. If, as law teachers, we are concerned with maximising learning and utilising available and pressured resources, it is essential that the clinic forms an integral part of the curriculum as one means by which law can be effectively studied.

How does integration take place? None of us has a ready-made solution nor the benefit of having worked in a fully integrated clinical learning environment. A starting point must be for the law school, as a whole, to have clearly articulated learning objectives coupled with assessment criteria that are capable of demonstrating whether those objectives have been met. The role of skills (both intellectual, transferable and legal, so far as they are different) has to be addressed as part of the framework for learning. The use of the clinical work in other aspects of the law-school programme has to be developed, making the most of the cases, simulated and real, that generate so much useful learning material. The close liaison and where appropriate involvement of colleagues in both regular classes and clinical sessions is necessary to ensure that neither is isolated and both work for common goals. We do not suggest for a moment that we have yet fully met these challenges in our own clinical practice nor within our own institutions, but we are conscious of the need for effective integration based on defined objectives and we are in our own ways moving slowly but steadily towards these ends.

Speaking from personal experience all three of us acknowledge that the integration aim is at the end of a steep uphill route with many obstacles on the way. The rewards in terms of improving academic results and building more cohesive teams are in our view well worth striving for.

Assessment

Assessment is central to the learning process. It is the way in which progress can be monitored, standards set and feedback given. It controls a major part of the law-school agenda, be it in terms of the time taken by students in going through the required hoops or in staff time expended in setting, overseeing and marking the devices used for assessment. We (law teachers and students) have all heard the student ask: is this topic going to be on the examination paper? We are all tempted perhaps to give the topic less than serious attention if the answer is in the negative. Assessment is seemingly as much or perhaps more of a burden than it is a benefit. A necessary evil?

Those involved in clinical work commonly view assessment in a very different light. With clearly stated learning outcomes, and with an ethos dedicated to learning by doing and on reflection on the doing, assessment takes on a more positive form. Couple this with greater student involvement in the process and opportunities open up. The assessment phase of any academically accredited course requires meaningful assessment but not simply to gauge progress. The learning potential of assessment has largely been ignored by the traditional law school beyond perhaps hastily and sometimes illegibly written comments on the bottom of a three-page essay. A range of assessment techniques, including group and peer assessment, learning contracts and portfolios of students' work, are made possible in a setting where learning rather than weighing learning is the driving force.

From our experience learning in the clinic is enjoyable. Students tend to do very well in terms of assessment. Perhaps clinicians are soft assessors? We think not (even if we are nice people!). Perhaps the better explanation is that students relate better to a regime in which they are more involved, in which they have some ownership in what is going on and where they volunteer to work long hours producing work that many qualified professionals would be proud of.

Resourcing the clinic

One of the problems faced by the clinic is that it can be resource intensive. This is often the case with high staff-to-student ratios and the additional requirements to equip (especially real-client) clinics. Any law teacher involved in a clinical programme, whether in the design or actual delivery stage will face the issue of resourcing. With more students cramming into lecture halls and less staff time to allocate to these numbers the climate can hardly be said to favour a sudden and rapid growth of clinical legal education. It is true that clinics can be resource intensive. But what resources are we talking about? When viewed in conventional 'so many students means so much staff time' frame the clinic looks a relatively unattractive option. We strongly believe that this is not the only, or even the most appropriate, measure of resource use. Does it really matter how much teaching is supplied? What matters is how much useful learning is being received.

If the clinic is the effective teaching medium that we suggest, then perhaps it is good value in terms of resources spent. The clinical effect can overspill into other subjects. Students improve as a result of the resources devoted to the clinic and this impacts on their other studies. Research currently being conducted at Sheffield Hallam University is beginning to produce significant evidence of this claim.[1] The materials generated in the clinic can be used (subject to the preservation, where appropriate, of confidentiality) in other courses. Students appear to relate the clinical experience back to other legal and related topics. Students do more work on their own in clinic than elsewhere in the degree course. Its value is both quantitative and qualitative.

Another aspect of resource use should also be mentioned. This links in with what has been said before about the students themselves. As a resource they can provide the means by which the traditional work of the lecturer can be partly (and under supervision) discharged. The use of teams or 'firms' is a device that operates usefully in the clinic. The students provide, in part, their own structure for learning. They are involved in assessment through personal, peer and group reviews. They can be organised in a such a way that the more experienced firm members assist the less experienced. None of this involves the abdication of staff responsibility. Rather, it is maximising the learning potential of all concerned and in doing so sees the effective use of resources.

The acquisition of skills in the clinical process is an additional benefit of this mode of study, a fact recognised amongst others by potential employers. We strongly argue, particularly in the so-called 'academic' stage, that skills acquisition is a useful spin-off of the clinical experience although not its principal aim. In the dedicated vocational courses the clinic serves the skills requirement in a more demonstrable way. In either case the clinic represents good value for money in terms of skills acquisition — skills both specific to law and transferable to other aspects of students' study and future careers.

Those committed to a more hands-on approach to learning will therefore argue for resourcing on the ground that the clinic is resource effective when appreciated in the context of the development of learning strategies, in improving the learning experience of the student and in making the course of study (whether 'academic' or 'vocational') more meaningful as a whole.

Staff development

The setting up and running of the clinic is, like all innovations that stimulate enthusiasm and powerful responses, as rewarding and enjoyable as it is exhausting and demanding. It is easy to fall back on the keenness of others in order to secure the necessary progress. If the clinic is to achieve its

---

[1] This research, currently unpublished, is being conducted by Richard Grimes, Sarah Cracknell and David Steyne, see chapter 1, note 31.

potential within the law-school curriculum, and if it is not to overburden the committed and trouble the rest, then a proper system of staff development is required. All of us need time and space to further our own understanding and skills. Nowhere is this more true than in clinical legal education. With innovations in teaching methods and assessment techniques many law teachers will feel the need for support. How do I do group teaching? What is peer assessment? How do I write a set of learning outcomes? These are questions that may be more familiar to some of us than others but that is no excuse for not providing the necessary staff development for all those who feel in need of it. Asking colleagues to review and in some cases justify their own practices is understandably threatening, and care must be taken to avoid alienating those who are a little uncomfortable with a close scrutiny of the hows and whys of their own programmes. In some ways the clinic is a victim of its own success, for staff and students become vocal in their praise of the methodology and this turns sometimes unwarranted attention on the ways in which other courses are structured and managed.

We return to the point of integration. If the clinic does form a properly reasoned part of the law-school curriculum, part of the struggle to develop complementary means for teaching and studying law and the legal process will have been won.

You know by now that we are self-confessed enthusiasts. We have been doing and have been associated with the clinic, in its various guises, for many years, and in different settings and jurisdictions. The clinical experience is enormously powerful. In our view, it not only assists those studying law but it inspires teaching staff. Read the cluttered electronic pages of the 'listserve' of the (dominantly) US clinical scene if you doubt us (for how to get access to this see further reading and information, page 275. But the clinic is more than just another teaching method. It begins to bridge the gap between the study and the practice of law. We may not be simply, or exclusively, producing intending practitioners but we are, through the clinic, attempting to instil the learning for life ideal, highlighted by ACLEC, that is increasingly recognised as one of the fundamental ingredients to a successful career, be that in the courts and law offices or somewhere completely different. As law teachers we commend the clinic to you.

Hugh Brayne: getting past the academic/vocational minefield

A lot of this book has been about the distinction between academic and vocational learning. Yet once upon a time not so long ago all law learning was vocational, and the academic stage had to be created, and the universities who began to develop degree courses had to justify its difference from vocational learning. Much of what we say in this book, looking back, could be seen as apologetic. We often find ourselves saying: 'We're sorry what we do is set in a vocational context and is of such obvious vocational relevance. But have you realised how good it is at doing the things the real academics are doing? At the time of writing we have just seen a change of government in the UK, but without a change of policy on core issues such as spending. To me, it is a strange sight to see a government trying to achieve socialist objectives through Conservative means. New Labour dresses up as Tories. Do clinicians have to sell themselves by pretending that they do not espouse skills and vocationally useful outcomes?

Are our objectives purely academic and is vocational relevance unimportant? Why separate the two things so artificially. The chapter on simulation by Roger Burridge provides an opportunity for the rest of us, who have more of a bias towards real-client work, to gain a more objective view on this issue. Roger's programme is constructed to achieve outcomes relevant to academic not vocational legal education. Assessment aims at excluding the purely lawyering skills.

I wonder if this is how the programmes appear to the student customers? When I review the student feedback — including, interestingly, that of the Warwick students, where the course is more explicitly non-vocational than the real-client programmes — I find what the students are actually reflecting on includes their skills at doing the things lawyers do, and that many of the reflections on which we place so much emphasis take second place to this aspect. Indeed much student reflection turns on how well the lawyering task has been performed. I also think it is hard to strip out of the objectives that of doing the task well. At Warwick the objectives in fact do include lawyering skills. And quite rightly: I take it as axiomatic that it is easier to comment on a subject (such as the lawyer in society, the relationship between powerful and weak consumers of legal services) if the commentator understands the issues through direct experience, which is facilitated by competence in the roles he or she plays. A person who has learned the rules of drafting pleadings and can do a reasonably good job at drafting is probably better able to comment on proposals to change these rules than someone who has only an academic (meaning superficial here) understanding of how and why it is done that way.

Perhaps the clinicians should be less defensive. Certainly student feedback after clinical experience does not dwell on the issue of academic respectability versus vocational training. If you want to develop vocational skills, and if clinic simultaneously can provide or enable you to get insights into the other things we want you to learn in the rest of the course, why not just go for it?

Which brings me to a very important issue for the first time in this book. One of the depressing things about legal practice is a common failure of practitioners to take a theoretical, ethical or research-orientated approach to the task of representing clients. I have been accused, during locum work, of taking a 'too academic approach' when I try to solve a client's problems according to legal principles. I have upset courts and opponents during clinical work by quoting laws that the courts or practitioners do not currently know about or apply. 'You are just doing this case as an academic exercise' is a not infrequent criticism from a rattled opponent. We should always reflect on whether such a criticism is justified, but so far I am happy that this approach served our clients' interests.

Perhaps practitioners should continue to be academics. Is it good enough that trainees are often told when they start their contracts: 'You can forget what you learnt at law school. Now we will show you how it is really done.' If the trainee obeys that advice, further personal development of skills in legal and doctrinal theory can be expected to languish.

I think this is a direct result of the academic-vocational split. Academics distance themselves from the practitioners and have only themselves to blame when the practitioners say that academic law is of little relevance to them. I think at law school we do have to address the real practical issues involved in being a lawyer, and show through careful supervision and careful development of your practice experience, that practice and theory are two sides of one coin. This means that some academics, and all students, have to be to some extent practitioners. We have to get you, before you are corrupted by the philistine influence you may encounter later, to recognise that theory and constant research and self-improvement matter throughout your legal career. Perhaps you don't want to be a lawyer? Fine — these are standards of competent behaviour in any field. This is what distinguishes mechanical competence in tasks, whether legal or any other, from reflective and excellent performance.

By integrating vocational and academic tasks at law school we are encouraging you to believe that you should think before you act, now and later. The Legal Practice Course is too packed with other requirements to develop this approach properly.[2] Skills work there is non-reflective and competence-based — and anyway the skills you develop there are little snapshot skills polished for the purpose of asssessment within compartments (interviewing, negoti- ation etc.) in a way that is wholly unrelated to the proper demands of good practice. Hardly anyone fails these skills exercises anyway. Taking a client's problem from initial consultation through to dispute resolution or dispute avoidance, and picking up for proper academic consideration all the ethical issues, the legal issues, the contextual issues, the personal management issues and so on as you go, and taking responsibility for the proper completion of the tasks you encounter, while receiving guidance from an experienced practitioner or academic mentor, may, I believe, help you to develop standards and aspirations of excellence.

I will not make the claim that only the traditional idea of a real-client clinic can achieve this. The sort of teaching described by Roger Burridge — turning *Donoghue* v *Stephenson* into a real-client case in the classroom — or by Nigel Duncan — turning a piece of draft legislation into a real-life lobbying opportunity — show that there are other opportunities for teachers and students to work together in fusing practice with theory without having to set up more resource intensive clinical programmes.

In fact many of the claims I would like to have made at the outset of writing this book I realise in the conclusion must be made with caution or not at all. The clinical movement seemed to be taking off at great speed in the early 90s, and the Clinical Legal Education Organisation caught the mood and took off remarkably well. But those who were ready to jump into the activity with enthusiasm, to make clinic work despite a shortage of resources by using their own free time or cutting down on their career progresssion by using their research time, are probably now already identified. For the activity to move into a higher gear a number of things perhaps need to happen:

(a)   We need to win the argument that doing things that lawyers do is good for students' intellectual development and for their other legal studies — for this we will need research evidence.
(b)   We need to reach the students who are not experiencing clinical methods and stimulate demand from them.
(c)   The frequent praise that clinical programmes receive from education- al and other visitors (e.g., the Higher Education Funding Council thought the

---

[2] This criticism may be less true of the Bar Vocational Course, because skills lie at the core of its design.

clinical programme at Northumbria was a vital element of the excellent rating they gave to the school's teaching; Sir Ron Dearing visited Sheffield Hallam's programme and declared it inspiring) must be promulgated and exploited; recruiters of our graduates must be informed and their feedback on students with clinical experience disseminated.

(d)   The debate touched on in chapter 2 about what legal education is for needs to be entered more visibly by the clinicians (with an open mind).

(e)   Recent graduates who took clinic during their degrees and who now have postgraduate educational and vocational experience need to re-enter the law schools and contribute their skills and ideas.

(f)   Clinicians need to develop an academically respectable journal where the method, and research involving the clinical method, can be accessed.

(g)   CLEO needs to be organising workshops and conferences, offering start-up help to law lecturers and law students.

And finally, this book needs to sell lots of copies and we need to get your feedback on what's good and what's bad, in the book, and in clinical legal education.

I take the opportunity to mention one other discrete issue that a rereading of this book has also thrown into perspective.

One of the points clearly made by Nina Tarr (see pages 239–244) is the risk of allowing the learning experience to be corrupted by economic considerations. She mentions this in the context of real-client clinics which derive part of their income from fees. This is a real risk for those who obtain funding, whether through legal aid or other sources, to provide a service, or fill a gap in the range of legal services. But I wish to see this problem in perspective. All higher-education decisions seem at present to be driven first by economics and secondly by academic objectives. The funding of UK universities is dire, money has to be raised by increasing numbers of fee-paying students and efficiency gains in teaching provision (that is, worsening the staff student–ratio). If, to make a clinical programme work, some sacrifices of principle have to be made to achieve funding, is the alternative of not running a programme better for our students?

In order to end this section on a high note, I have selected a few student feedback quotes taken mainly from Sheffield Hallam's annual report for 1996 (with thanks for permission to do so to Sarah Cracknell, who compiled it), together with the first quote, which is recycled from chapter 4 from a Queen's University of Belfast student. As well as indicating the very positive

attitude of students who have the privilege of participation, it often shows
how irrelevant to students the academic–vocational debate is.

> It was as if for three years you had been learning to swim from reading
> books alone, not from actually getting into the water.

> The Law Clinic is a great learning environment which demands you to
> think for yourself because there is no comfort of sitting in lectures
> absorbing information.

> It has helped me to understand the power we have over people's lives.

> My approach to statute and case law has changed substantially. They are
> no longer words on a page which you photocopy for a tutorial but forget
> to read, they are tremendously real and frighteningly relevant.

> Instead of my other studies suffering I became more committed generally,
> and I think my marks have improved because of it.

> The Law Clinic has been one long exercise in confidence building.

> The Law Clinic has helped me develop personal skills which will benefit
> me in whatever career I may follow.

> It is easy to forget when studying law that the cases learned involve real
> people with real problems.

> With my other studies there is not much scope for personal participation;
> it is mainly finding out what other people say about the law and then
> writing it down.

> In the Law Clinic research of legal issues and of facts is a constant
> process. . . . with real clients and problems there are no such things as hard
> facts as encountered in assessments in other subjects.

> The Law Clinic has been the most demanding work I have ever done, both
> in terms of stamina and intellectual activity.

Feedback of this sort shows, I believe, that the direct experience of law in
practice enhances the all-important legal and intellectual skills we are trying
to develop in undergraduates, and simultaneously achieves a deep level of
learning, integration and personal development.

Adrian Evans: an Australian perspective

Introduction

If the authors of this book are right, 'clinical' techniques are destined to assume a greater role in legal education in the United Kingdom. These methods are already well established in the United States and South Africa, and their acceptance is advancing rapidly in Australia and other countries also. 'Learning by doing' is effective because it's good fun in whatever field it's practised. The application of the methodology to legal education is a natural thing: in a sense it seems trite to say any more than that.

The fact that this book is being written now, however, does say much more. Clinical techniques — the 'doing' that can lead to reflection, insight and then 'deep' learning — will probably entrench themselves in all sorts of law courses. They reflect and respond to many trends in Western professionalism — quality assurance, the rationalist 'efficiency' agenda and not least, the sheer boredom of law students. Be they practical exercises, group discussions or simulations, they are all claiming space in traditional law curricula.

What is not happening in a big way outside the Unites States or South Africa, but which the authors would like to encourage, is the 'real-client' version of clinical legal education. That is what this book is really about: it is a zealot's exhortation to all who would see the light in legal education. In that mission I am a happy collaborator.

Balanced legal education

In Australia, just as in the United Kingdom, the first 'real-client' clinic (at Springvale in Victoria)[3] has encouraged others, albeit over a long period of time.[4] It has taken a long time because a few graduates of the Monash course understandably took some time to get into positions within other universities where they could commence their own versions of the 'real-client' method. However, there is still no critical mass of real-client clinical approaches in Australia sufficient to ensure huge growth: and this has to do with the conflict between the ideals of a balanced legal education and perceived costs.

---

[3] This clinic commenced as a joint venture between Springvale Legal Service (SLS) and Monash University Law School in 1975.

[4] SLS was followed by Monash-Oakleigh (another Monash Clinic, but on the campus of the University) and La Trobe University in 1978, by Kingsford (University of New South Wales) in 1981, Newcastle (Newcastle University, New South Wales) in 1995, and most recently at Southern Communities Advocacy and Legal Education Service (Murdoch University, Perth, Western Australia) in early 1997.

The authors of this book assert correctly that undergraduate 'real-client' clinical programmes address many professional and social objectives of legal education. The consciousness of students of the effects of the justice system on real people (and their responses to that), the reality of ethical conflicts, the marriage of 'black-letter' law with technical competencies and especially the self-confidence to tackle other subjects within the legal curriculum, are all benefits for students of serious real-client method. The clinical package contains other goodies such as enhanced critical reflection, the value of collaborative learning and the higher productivity of team problem solving. It is deliverable to the ailing law school in the same way as meditation and Reiki are able to revive the willing cancer patient.

In more prosaic language, there can be no question that traditional Western law schools, operating without significant experiential methodology of some sort, are lacking balance in their teaching mission. As the authors assert, 'law studied out of the context of practice is an artificial concept'.[5] Real-client clinical process is simply the best of the clinical methods and the 'best' law schools cannot claim that title without it.

Regrettably, the focus of some of those elite schools, and there are examples of them in Australia as elsewhere, is upon the short term. Their perception is that the considerable cost of real-client teaching, because of the intensive staff-student ratio, is high. Moliterno thinks real-client clinics will eventually die off because of the high cost 'problems', but that clinical *methods* will survive and expand.[6] They appear to think that the existing self-perpetuating linkages between conventional, jurisprudence-based courses and the alumni system will entrench predominance of their own 'city and gown' connection indefinitely. In consequence, issues of long-term quality and innovation in teaching tend not to receive enough scrutiny from deans in those schools.

Costs of real-client teaching are higher than those associated with the traditionally low funding formulas associated with law schools. However, clinic costs are not high in comparison to the activities of many other faculties, and are a moderate investment when matched against the long-term gains to the credibility of the law school, particularly in the eyes of the practising profession.

Many law schools in Australia also have still to embrace this reality. My conclusion is therefore that real-client clinics in law schools are likely to proliferate to the extent of the courage of deans in the context of an enhanced

---

[5] See page 10.
[6] J. Moliterno, 'On the future of integration between skills and ethics teaching: clinical legal education in the year 2010' (1996) 46 J Legal Educ 67.

understanding of a balanced undergraduate legal education. I agree with the authors that clinical *approaches* to legal education will expand, but the growth of real-client options is not inevitable and will require vision and persistence. There is no basis for complacency, and in the United Kingdom no particular reason to think that the authors' central argument for real-client clinics will be accepted by the majority of legal educators.

Student and client empowerment

In this book the educational wholeness of the authors' vision is reflected in their commitment to collaboration with their students both in the design of clinical process and in the learning adventure. Throughout it is clear that they aim to develop students' *confidence*, over the length of a clinical placement, via the entry of those students into partnership with their supervisor in many educational quests.

This is definitely not a soft and frothy process — when it works it results in a mutual respect between teacher and student within a clear socio-legal awareness of the whole justice agenda. However, I do not believe that students are 'changed' in their political orientation. Their views are well-established, even if unarticulated, by the time they get to a clinic. 'Left' leaners and 'right' wingers are on the whole confirmed in their perceptions by clinical exposure. What changes for the better is that both perspectives are tempered by human contact with human problems, and then by the opportunity — provided by superiors and intensive peer discussion — to reflect on that exposure.

Three Australian examples of this process may expand the frame somewhat, and provide a basis for some criticism of the context in which law schools still place clinical programmes. At La Trobe University in Melbourne a unique clinical placement exists to provide an 'ethical audit' of a local government legal aid office. Adjacent to the university, the legal aid office handles a range of common legal problems on an in-house basis. Individual students from the La Trobe programme are attached to individual solicitors to 'audit' the performance of the latter from an ethical perspective.[7] Debate and discussion around particular actions are the nutrients for the growth of both student and solicitor. At Monash University in Melbourne, students are placed at either of two real-client local community services.[8] At Springvale Legal Service, about six kilometres from the law school campus, students are

---

[7] See J. Dickson and M.A. Noone, 'The challenge of teaching professional ethics' in Australian Professional Legal Education Council, *International Conference, Sydney 1996, Conference Papers*, vol. 2, pp. 846–859.
[8] Springvale Legal Service is the largest Victorian CLC and hosts the largest of the Australian real-client clinical programmes. Monash-Oakleigh (MOLS) is smaller but operates on a similar basis.

encouraged to see that their own education and the empowerment of their clients are mutually dependent. The ethos here is that clients who acquire legal power[9] from interactions with students legitimise the learning process for those students. The element of potential exploitation by students of their clients in the interests of the future income-earning potential of the students is to this extent diminished or eliminated. This seems to me to be a healthier orientation than that of the clinics at Sheffield Hallam or Northumbria, which (at least in the manner expressed in this book) appears to place the education of students on a higher priority plane than overall client interests.

In carrying this concept further, Springvale allocates each student within each semester to a task group of four to five students. Together they tackle an issue identified by the caseload as important to a number of clients, and implement strategies aimed at community legal education, research and law reform in relation to the issue (e.g., complaints against the legal profession). In addition, each of these task groups attempts to facilitate the establishment or growth of a *group* of clients who feel strongly and are affected by the task-group issue. As the client group develops, much of the initiative for law reform and community legal education can pass from the students and the clinic to the client group. Essentially, this involves a transfer of power at the political level; something which lawyers as a class have never been very keen about. The process is not new[10] but it is not common within traditional law curricula or clinical programmes.

I argue that client group development ought to be a normal part of the clinical process at least. The authors do not espouse it for the UK environment and this is, I think, a deficiency. Western legal education, even at the innovative and progressive end represented in this book, remains too closely identified with narrow vocational objectives or the commercial constitutional preoccupation of the Oxbridge and Ivy League tradition. The notion that lawyers ought to have at least as much of an opportunity (while still students) to systemically explore access to justice for ordinary citizens, is barely on the agenda.[11] In a sense, the authors have missed an opportunity to set their essential discussions in the context of an international revival of interest in society's expectations of lawyers. Competence and ethics in all their permutations are addressed here in abundance, but not I think the *purposes* to be served by the whole process.

[9] 'Power' is here understood to mean the confidence of clients to pursue their own legal problems with or without the assistance of the student.
[10] See, e.g., Paolo Freire, *Pedagogy of the Oppressed*, translated by Myra Ramos (Harmondsworth: Penguin, 1972).
[11] The fledgling 'Global Alliance for Justice Education'(GAJE), which arises out of the clinical legal education movement, has begun to form only this year.

In contrast to Springvale, Newcastle Legal Service, which operates from a central New South Wales steel city in a very similar environment to Newcastle upon Tyne, focuses on student learning as the major priority. Its similarity to Northumbria is striking in another way also. The law school at the University of Newcastle (New South Wales) offers the only Australian integrated law degree. Clinical processes are used in a sophisticated way[12] at every level and students graduate with an immediate right to practise. This law school is unquestionably at the vocational forefront of legal education in Australia, but like Northumbia, its inevitable tendency is to use clients for the educational process rather than to value client empowerment as an equal goal of the venture.

Elsewhere in Australia, as the next section shows, the needs of clients have not generally played a significant role in the structure and organisation of real-client clinics.

The essential issue of clinic control

Although few Australian real-client clinics are genuinely 'in-house' in the geographical sense,[13] all except Springvale are legally controlled by the relevant law school. The description 'in-house' or 'placement' is therefore confusing in terms of the nature of the educational process at each real-client site. The key issue is control of service delivery. It seems that where, in historical terms, initiatives for a real-client clinic have come only from the law school then that law school has controlled the method of delivery and hence the value base of the process. I suggest this has not been beneficial for the ultimate integrity of each clinic in Australia. I doubt also whether it will change. The most recent clinic, which opened in Perth, Western Australia in April 1997 (SCALES, Murdoch University) includes stakeholders who are *representatives* of the local community only in the sense that they are local practitioners or councillors approached *by the law school* to sit on the management committee.

Grass-roots user groups or client groups rarely seem to attract community legal services *from* law-school environments and the resulting programmes

---

[12] Roger Burridge clearly describes (pages 185–208) the simulation methodologies practised at a high level at the University of Warwick and, in Australia, at the Universities of Newcastle and Wodonga. Burridge captures the essence of the simulation/real-client relationship: they are ideally *sequential* clinical methodologies: Newcastle uses both techniques in a sequential manner.

[13] MOLS serves a local community but operates from the main Monash law school campus in Melbourne. Kingsford (University of New South Wales), SCALES (Murdoch University) and Newcastle (University of Newcastle) are all located in 'poorer' urban areas between 5 and 40 kilometres from the relevant law schools.

often have serious deficiencies from the client point of view. Thus the authors advocate a staff–student ratio of 1 : 12 as feasible for adequate legal supervision of students' files, and would generally support a relatively low number of files per student — say up to six each. These ratios are achieved within semesters that start and finish only according to university timetables and do not, e.g., require students to attend to clients during vacation periods. The tendency is to run down a case so that not much is likely to happen during the vacation.

If, however, the emphasis were shifted slightly to a community conscious-ness, better educational *and* client service objectives are achievable. The combination, e.g., of a staff–student ratio of a maximum 1 : 8 (normal in the United States and Australia), of a student-to-client ratio of 1 : 10–15 and of continuous service (zero vacation absences) can assist all of the following:

   (a)   tighter supervision because of greater opportunities for teacher–student interaction;
   (b)   greater variety of clients and problems;
   (c)   greater professionalism by avoiding vacation transfer of file from student to supervisor.

I do not agree with the authors that two students should be allocated to each client or case. In a busy clinic, this is highly likely to lead to dangerous communication mishaps.[14] It is, I think, also unrealistic if a reasonable number of files per student is to be achieved.

When the community and the law school genuinely share control of service delivery the result is likely to be a trade-off that reduces client 'guinea pig' potential. In my experience, this also helps the law school to remain collaborative, accountable and even politically protected. It certainly in-creases the legitimacy of law-school requests for block government grants to assist clinic running costs.

Ethics in the clinical chain

The authors are, I think, very clear about the central importance of an awareness of ethics amongst students in clinical programmes. They discuss

---

[14] It is said that having two students to each client gives continuity and student protection. Neither are achieved when the inevitable communication problems emerge. However, the tangible benefits of more than 'one head' on a case are achievable by peer-group case-review sessions, conducted weekly along the lines, e.g., of the Juss-Buss clinic of the University of Oslo in Norway.

the distinction between, on the one hand, the rote learning of codes of ethics in professional conduct courses and, on the other hand, the critical study of ethical principles, concluding as I do that the former has a bit to do with an undergraduate law degree, but also that the latter ought to have everything to do with it. Ideally, the authors and I would like to see the exploration of ethics proceed within an experiential framework in law schools, but we part company on the details.

Julian Webb's proposal for a three-stage ethics programme[15] comprising a first-year foundation programme, a second year legal profession and ethics course and then a final-year live-client clinic is more or less adopted by the authors as the best idea around. It is a coherent and structured approach but I seriously doubt if it will work if it leaves out the harder task of the integration of experiential method — including ethics — into mainstream subjects. Students have a finely tuned ear for the relative importance of different law-school subjects to the wider culture. They 'know' that, e.g., tax, corporations and securities are or will be their bread and butter and, where ethics remains a separate course entirely, they 'know' that the 'scruples department' is designed to inhibit their future income-earning potential. The sheer weight of substantive law subjects, if devoid of good simulations which include ethical scenarios, is quite sufficient to encourage the myth of a value-neutral legal system, regardless of the staged process advocated above.

I agree totally with the authors that the incorporation of experiential methods (with ethical dimensions) into major subject areas is unlikely to occur by natural processes: but there is no wonder in that. Mainstream subject teachers remain besieged by the culture of the city despite themselves and can identify no market force that says 'put ethics first'. It is and will remain the job of clinical teachers and students with vision and perseverance to inform, encourage and assist their colleagues (in mainstream subjects) to redesign their courses progessively. It does take years but that is no surprise either because the only effective method of conversion is persuasion, not coercion, and certainly not some directive from a dean who may not have the respect of all the staff.

There is a sequential approach to teaching ethics in the undergraduate degree. It properly covers first the broad concepts in the context of a systemic overview, secondly the contemporaneous interaction of ethical conflicts into mainstream simulations, *alongside* a separate and critical course on ethics,

---

[15] See chapter 6, note 22.

and thirdly it requires the reality-testing and tempering process of a real-client clinic.

Regardless of the process followed within a particular law school, clinical teaching and the ethical discovery process are properly inseparable. On this point, as on most, I agree with the authors completely.

Endnote

Which gives the three primary authors considerable food for thought on the future of clinical education and the development of our own courses. We hope that if our proposals lead you to agreement or disagreement, you will contact us with your own ideas and experience, or contact CLEO as a forum for taking the debate further.[16]

---

[16] CLEO can be contacted through Sarah Cracknell, Sheffield Hallam University Student Law Clinic, Dyson House, Pond Street, Sheffield;
tel 0114 2533703; e-mail < s.a.cracknell@shu.ac.uk > .

Further reading and information

This list is not intended to be a definitive bibliography on clinical legal education. Rather it is a collection of writings and contacts on clinic which we have found useful in formulating our ideas, conducting discussions and furthering our own clinical practice.

We welcome other recommendations from readers.

Clinical Legal Education Association: CLEA (USA)

Secretary-Treasurer
Mark J. Heyrman
University of Chicago Law School
6020 South University Avenue, Chicago
Illinois 60637

Telephone: 1-312-702-9611
E-mail: < Mark _ Heyrman@law.uchicago.edu >
Directory of clinical legal education: < http://www2.wc1.american.edu/clinic >
Listserv (email list):   < Lawclinic@lawlib.wuacc.edu >

Clinical Legal Education Organisation: CLEO (UK)

c/o Administrator
Law Clinic
Sheffield Hallam University
Room 815, Dyson House
City Campus, Pond Street
Sheffield S1 1WB

Telephone: 0114-253 3703
E-mail: <Law-clinic@shu.ac.uk>

National Centre for Legal Education

University of Warwick
Coventry
CV4 7AL

Telephone: 01203-523117
E-Mail: <ncle@warwick.ac.uk>
Website: <http://www.law.warwick.ac.uk/ncle>

Clinical Legal Education (Australia)

Kingsford Legal Centre
11 Rainbow Street
Kingsford, Sydney
New South Wales 2032
Australia

Telephone: 61-2-9398 6366
E-mail: <legal@unsw.edu.au>

Centre for Legal Education

Level 14
130 Pitt Street
Sydney
New South Wales 2001
Australia

Telephone: 61-2-9221-3699
E-mail: <cle.@fl.asn.au>
Website: <http://www.fl.asn.au/cle>

Nina W. Tarr and Kathy Kirk

Clinical Skills and Education Bibliography

Washburn Law School
Washburn University of Topeka
Topeka
Kansas 66621
USA 1993

(An excellent if now rather dated collection of articles and books on skills and on clinic.)

M. Le Brun and R. Johnstone

The Quiet (R)evolution — improving student learning in law
Law Book Co. (Sydney, 1994)

(A valuable account of learning and teaching in law schools.)

Simon Rice (with Graeme Coss)

A guide to implementing clinical teaching method in the law school curriculum
Centre for Legal Education (Sydney, 1996)

A. Hurder, F. Bloch, S. Brooks and S. Kay

Clinical Anthology: Readings for Live-Client Clinics
Anderson Publishing (Cincinnati, 1997)

The Law Teacher

General Editor
Nigel Duncan
Inns of Court School of Law
4 Gray's Inn Place
London WC1R 4AJ

E-mail: N.J.Duncan@icsl.ac.uk

(Thrice-yearly journal by Sweet and Maxwell of law teaching — often features articles on clinical education.)

Clinical Law Review

Editor in Chief
Isabelle Gunning
Southwestern University
School of Law
675 South Westmoreland Avenue
Los Angeles
CA 90005
USA

(Semi-annual journal devoted exclusively to clinical education but almost entirely US focused.)

Journal of Legal Education

Cape Western Reserve University
School of Law
11075 East Boulevard
Cleveland
OH 44106-7148
USA

(Quarterly journal by the Association of American Law Schools which regularly features articles on clinical and related issues.)

Journal of Professional Legal Education

Australasian Professional Legal Education Council
The College of Law
PO Box 2
St Leonards NSW 2065
Australia

E-mail: colllaw@enternet.com.au

(A bi-annual journal concerned with all aspects of continuing and practical legal education.)